Thinking Thinking: About My Life

By

Yu Nien Tze Chang

(Yu Hsiang Hsiang, "Thinking Thinking")

Commentary by

Eva Chang

Eva Chang, Inc., Publisher

Printed in the United States of America

ISBN-13: 978-1981530076

ISBN-10: 198153007X

December 7, 1948

Contents

Organizations

Charts

Preface

*I*n today's world, where the path of the American middle class follows an orderly progression from school to career to a home in the suburbs, I marvel at how my immigrant family somehow found success and achieved the American dream in a totally unorthodox manner. My parents left a country where they were clearly in the upper echelons of society, to start over at the bottom of the societal ladder in their new country. Yet they survived and prospered, finding refuge and success in a strange new land.

I cannot conceive how I would fare if I had to flee to a new country where I barely spoke the language, did not know the culture, looked different, and lacked academic credentials.

When you are young, you only know the world that surrounds you, and you have no sense of scale, of how your life fits into the world beyond your walls. Your frame of reference is formed by your parents and your family. No matter how unusual your family life, it is not until you are much older that you may realize that your upbringing was somewhat unusual. Now that I have that perspective, I appreciate that my family history has some unique twists and turns that are worth sharing.

I have asked my mother to record her story to be able to share it with her grandchildren and with anyone else who may have an interest. Our family history is unique, not only for the story arc of immigration and assimilation, but also because my mother and father had such unique backgrounds. My mother's father was and is a famous respected historical figure in the tumultuous days of the Chinese Revolution and ensuing political upheavals. My mother was privileged to have encountered many distinguished political figures in her younger years. She traveled, went to college, and was exposed to Western culture at a time when most Chinese women lived in poverty in rural settings.

And you could say that my father was essentially a high school dropout who left home to join a monastery in Tibet in order to study Buddhism. Yet he became an acknowledged expert in Buddhist studies, publishing many books which have been translated into multiple languages and eventually attaining a tenured professorship in a well-known university in the US.

I am at a loss for words to describe how proud I am of my parents and what they have achieved in one generation. I hope that this story will help to share the source of pride and achievement for all who may read it.

My mother wrote the manuscript, and I have edited it with a very light hand. I know that there are many places where the wording is slightly awkward, but I wanted to preserve the nuances of her writing, so that no reader will forget that the story is one written by someone whose first language is not English. What charm would the story have if it sounded as if I wrote it for English Composition class?

I also apologize for any confusion which may arise due to the various systems of Romanizations which are used in this story. Over the last century, there have been various systems used for transliterations of Chinese words. There are the older Wade-Giles system, the Yale system, and the current Pinyin system, as well as variants used during the immigration process and so on. I have tried to use the current Pinyin system for place names such as Chongqing (previously Chungching or Chungking), but I have retained the names of people and institutions that still use their Wade-Giles spellings. I have added their Pinyin spellings for reference.

Preface

Throughout the text, comments that I have added are italicized.

The last section consists of reference materials, mostly from internet sources, which provide additional details and insights into some of the more colorful characters that my parents encountered during their journey to assimilation. The interested reader should delve into some of these materials for him/herself.

I recommend that the reader start by learning about my grandfather on page 270 and about my father on page 276 before beginning my mother's story.

I hope this story will inspire our next generation to follow their dreams and to keep striving in spite of what seem like insurmountable hurdles.

Eva Chang, May 2017

Map of China

Map of China

Apologies for the blurry map, but it was difficult to find a simple map with just major cities and province names on it.

PART I

Recollections from Two Worlds

Introduction

The great educator, Confucius said, "When one's parents are living, one does not roam afar." Therefore, for thousands of years, we Chinese would not leave our home towns and travel to distant places except in desperation or extreme necessity. Needless to say, traveling to foreign countries would never even be under consideration.

But things gradually changed. Around the Tang dynasty (618-907), the Silk Route was already a popular trading route between China and the mid-East area. The trading even reached the European countries. By the 14th or 15th century, some Chinese emperors had even dispatched large fleets abroad, which started the trend of doing business by sea routes. The Arabs, Indians, and countries in the South Sea area were all trading with Chinese merchants. Unfortunately, the last empire, the Qing dynasty (1644-1911), was so ignorant, corrupt, and conceited that it eventually resulted in the defeats of the Opium War and the Boxer Rebellion. As more foreigners and foreign countries took advantage of China, it became a very weak and poor country. Later, when the United States was developing its western territory, large numbers of poor and uneducated people, mostly from the Chinese coastal provinces, were forcefully "Shanghaied" to the US as cheap laborers. These people did not know any European language. Without education, and without knowing about their rights to protect themselves, they worked and lived almost like the captive black slaves in the US.

Eventually, the Qing dynasty court officials found out that the Western culture could produce more advanced weapons. In order to strengthen their national defense, they started to send young students abroad to learn the Western ways.

The Chinese people who came to the US from the 1800s through the twentieth century suffered many years of discrimination and were treated with condescension in American society until WWII,

2

when China was considered an ally. Gradually, they began to be treated slightly better during and after this war.

After the Qing dynasty was overthrown and the Republic of China was established in 1911, more Chinese students came to study for their doctorate degrees in the US. Usually, these students would stay for three or four years. Soon after graduating, they would return to China to start their careers. When WWII broke out, first between China and Japan, and later between Japan and the US, the situation quickly changed. During the 1940s, because of the war, large numbers of Chinese students could not return home. These highly educated young people had to stay in the US. However, it was a difficult time for them, due to their student visa status, their language skills, their exhausted financial support, and their skin color. Ideal positions were usually beyond their reach. Then in 1948, the Communist Chinese government took over all of mainland China, and established the People's Republic of China. The US government allowed the non-Communist Chinese people in the US to stay and to apply for more decent jobs. Later, students from Communist China on the mainland stopped coming to the US, but more and more young students from Taiwan would come, and they also remained after their graduation. Among these, there were outstanding scholars, even a few Nobel Prize winners. The majority of these well-educated people stayed, married, and became naturalized citizens. Their hard work and achievements in various fields slowly changed the way the Chinese people are perceived in American society.

My husband and I did not want to live under Communist rule. We fled to the US when the Communists took over the mainland. When we first arrived in this country, we never thought we would be staying in this country for this long. We thought, maybe after three to five years, we would be returning to China. Then, we both became permanent residents, and eventually, we became naturalized citizens!

Just like in so many other immigrant families, the younger generations are seeking their roots. It is at my daughter's request that I decided to relate a brief history of both the Chang and Yu families.

After all, both my husband and my "roots" were dug up from an old and faraway land and transplanted into this New World. I know that all the memories could not always present themselves as sharp pictures, but maybe, just maybe, with this long narration, I can still offer a little of the fading history.

See page 313 for a history of Chinese-American Assimilation from the Hoover Library.

The first passport, 1946

No one has truly told me about my birth. I was never sure about the true story. All I know about my arrival in this world seemed to be accumulated by hearsay. Somehow, certain facts were confirmed through people's repeated conversations. I was born in Beijing in 1926, and I know that my mother was so weak and so sick she almost died. Then we moved to Shanghai *(over six hundred miles south)*. I only remember when I was about five years old, there was a heavy snow. When I was six, we moved to a large house, and there, I started school. In that large house, my mother, my older brother Peng, and I lived on the second floor.

Back in that era, it was a very common practice for a husband to have more than one wife. My father's first wife, whom I referred to as my Number One mother, lived in Nanjing *(185 miles northwest of Shanghai)*, where the capital was. The Number Two Wife had died before I was born. The Number Three Wife lived above us on the third floor. I remember she loved me very much because she did not have any children of her own.

I guess my mother was Number Four. My father lived between the two houses. A Number Five wife never lived with us. All together, there were seven children from the different mothers.

The first child was my oldest sister from my Number One mother. The Number Two mother had my eldest brother, Wang De. My mother had four of us: my brother Peng, me, and my two younger sisters. The youngest brother was from the Number Five wife.

Refer to the Yu Family Tree on page 318 if some of the above is confusing. Page 270 has a historical profile of my grandfather.

Among the children, we never referred to each other as half-brothers or half-sisters. My oldest sister was twenty-four years older than me. The second child, my oldest brother Wang De, got married when I was only five. My brother Peng is ten years my senior. We all got along very well. Also, both of my older brothers went abroad to study while I was just a young girl, so I guess there was no occasion for us to be unhappy with each other. I must have done all right in school, because I often brought awards home. My mother was looking after me, but my two younger sisters each had their own nannies. When I turned nine years old, my mother's health took a downturn, so she made a decision and sent me to Suzhou *(about sixty miles west of Shanghai)* to live with my godparents. Suzhou being only two hours' train ride from Shanghai, I was always home for weekends. But that summer, my mother had to be moved to a German hospital. Therefore, after the summer vacation, I remained home. Both my brother Peng and I had to stay in a room in the hospital so as to be near my mother. I knew something awful was happening, but no one would explain to me about the truth. Indeed, in the month of September, my mother left us.

After the funeral, my brother and I watched the train that took my mother's coffin back to my father's native home town to be buried, and I went back to Suzhou to be with my godparents again.

My mom was born on the eleventh day of the Chinese Lunar New Year, in the year of the Tiger, 4624 (1926). She uses January 11 as her birthdate, for convenience. However, the date on the Gregorian calendar was February 23, 1926. But ever since I can remember, we have always observed her birthday on the eleventh day of each Chinese Lunar Year. Therefore, her birthday falls on a different Gregorian day every year. To complicate matters further,

her passport shows her year of birth as 1925, so all of her official records show that year as her year of birth. I like to say that she has three birthdays, but we never know when her next one is.

My godparents, the Lin family, used to live in Shanghai too. Our families and a few other families were often together for various occasions because they were all my father's close friends, especially my godfather, who was a comrade during the early revolutionary movement, and a faithful follower of Dr. Sun Yat-sen as well. They later bought a house in Suzhou and moved there. They had three children. The eldest son, Chi Fang *(Ji Fang)*, was even older than my brother Peng. The middle girl, Chi Chou *(Ji Zhou)*, was three years older than the youngest boy, Chi Sun *(Ji Sun)*, who was three years older than me. Together, we made very good playmates. The first year I went to Suzhou, I was sent to a famous private elementary school. I was enrolled in the fourth grade. Chi Chou was in the same school as I was, but in the high school. Chi Sun was in a boys' school. We all left for school at the same time, had our lunch in school, then went home when the school dismissed us at five o'clock in the afternoon.

When we were all home, my godmother would always have some delicious snack waiting for us—it might be wontons or some Chinese cake or some other delicacy. On Saturdays, we only had to go to school for half of the day, so in the afternoon, we were often taken to see a movie, or exchange visits with other friends of the family. Of course, when my father was in Shanghai, he would still send for me to go back to my own house, and sometimes, even the whole Lin family would go to Shanghai for a fun weekend too.

Those were the most memorable three years of my childhood. My godmother taught me how to behave with better manners and provided my life with an orderly daily routine. If I have formed any good habits, I learned them during those years. My godfather did not always stay for long at home. He stayed somewhere out of town. He tried to encourage us to have good handwriting by awarding us money when we sent him letters that were well composed and had neatly written characters. But he was more strict with the boys than with my sister Chi Chou and me. When the oldest brother Chi Fang went to Japan to study, Chi Sun became the only boy with us. However, that did not last for long. One day, a letter came from the remote Ji Lin province. A distantly related uncle of my godfather had died. He left a widow with two young children. She was asking for help. My godparents welcomed them. Soon, they arrived to join us. That, for us children, was a nice addition. Even though the children were about my age, since they were one generation older, we addressed the girl as "Little Aunt" and the boy as "Little Uncle." Life was uneventful and happy. I did not even miss my mother.

When I was in Shanghai during long school vacations, my father would teach me to start writing in the cursive style of calligraphy with brushes. I knew he was famous for his calligraphy because there were people constantly coming to our house, asking for his writings, for as long as I could remember. Every day, whenever he had time, his attendant would have the ink, brushes, paper, and his personal seal ready for him to use. Someone was usually standing across the desk from my father, and moved the finished work to spread on the floor for the ink to dry. When I was a little older than ten, he would let me have that job too. Unfortunately, I did not take up the practice of calligraphy seriously, so I could not keep up his legend.

Still, today, although my father passed away nearly fifty years ago, among East Asian countries, where brush calligraphy is still appreciated, my father's cursive style of writing still enjoys respect and admiration. His work is also collected by museums and connoisseurs of calligraphy. Both his calligraphy and his original poetry are greatly admired.

As a point of clarification, my mother often refers to her godparents' children simply as sisters and brothers.

In 1936, my brother Peng got married. He soon left for England with his new wife. Unless my father happened to be in Shanghai, other than my two younger sisters and their nannies, and a cousin, Chih Hsien *(Zhi Xian)*, there were usually no other members of my family who resided in that house. The rest of the residents were the people who worked for my father.

So, in 1937, when I graduated from the elementary school in Suzhou, I said goodbye to my godparents' family, and went back to my home in Nanjing in June.

Normally, my Number One mother would be in Nanjing. But that summer, she went back to my father's native town for some business in Shaanxi, a province nearly seven hundred miles northwest of Nanjing. It happened that my oldest sister, who was twenty-four years older than me, was managing the household. It was my understanding that years ago, she married a student movement leader in Beijing University, where they studied. After the wedding, both of them went to Moscow to study. Unfortunately, they had not been there for long, when my brother-in-law was accused of being a spy for the Nationalist Government, and was arrested and sent to Siberia. Therefore, my sister came back and stayed at home, together with her son, my nephew Bei Da, who was four years older than me.

That year, around August, Japan attacked Shanghai. Since my Number One mother was already in Shaanxi, my sister decided she and my father would stay in Nanjing with the government, but she sent her son, me, and another cousin, accompanied by a relative, back to Shaanxi, where we would be safe.

I remember the day we went to board the train. It was a stormy day. Rain and gusts of wind mixed with fallen leaves were pelting at us. It made me feel so sad to leave. Who could know that parting would last for eight long, long years?

9

At first, our train ride was very pleasant. It normally took roughly four days to reach our destination. Unexpectedly, on the third day of our trip, we came to a town in Henan province, where the whole town was inundated by flooding from the Yellow River. We were stuck on the rails, but we could not get off the train on account of the water that was surrounding us. It was in August. We did not have air conditioning then. The electric fan did not help much, and we found out that our train could not supply us with any water to drink or to use. The only food we could get was egg fried rice. Even though I was only eleven years old, when I saw the numerous people trying to flee the disaster, loaded with their belongings, carrying their old and young, it made me very sad and depressed. I had never encountered such sorrows in my whole life.

We had been delayed for about three or four days at the same spot. Everyone on the train became extremely thirsty. One day at noon, my nephew Bei Da suggested we should open up one of the bottles of our Worcestershire sauce in order to have some liquid. These bottles were meant for my Number One mother. Out of desperation, we all agreed to share one bottle. Because I was the youngest, they let me have the first drink. I can still clearly recall the sour and salty flavor today even after eighty years! Needless to say, no one argued. All six bottles, including this just-opened one, were saved.

Finally, the water receded. We were able to continue our journey. Everything on this journey was new to me, as I had been raised as a city girl so far. Shanghai was the most westernized, international coastal city, while my father's home town in Shaanxi province was far inland. Life was entirely different. It was mainly an agricultural society, even in the largest provincial capital city. So my new life was full of new discoveries.

The train arrived at Xi'an, its last stop. My Number One mother was waiting for us there. On the second day, we all headed for Sanyuan, my father's home town. There were two mule-drawn wagons waiting for us. I was the last to get on the front one. There were four of us plus the driver in it.

Everyone in the wagon was used to this way of travel except me. Even my nephew Bei Da did not show any discomfort. But I was twelve years old, and five feet two inches tall, and at that time, I had never had the experience of sitting cross-legged on a flat surface. The sitting surface of the wagon was slightly slanted with the front higher than the back. There was nothing for me to lean against to steady myself, since I was seated in the front. During the trip, my Number One mother somehow played a card game with her lady friend. We rode on rocky roads for a long while, then the two wagons had to get on a wooden ferry boat to cross a river before we could reach the town of Sanyuan. By then, I thought all my bones were about to break apart. I do not know how people who sat on the inside of an American western wagon felt, but to me, this mule wagon ride was the hardest trip I had in my whole life.

After we arrived in town, we came to the campus of an elementary school. We stopped at the rear of the campus. There was a long single-story building. It was where we would live. Later, I found out that this was a school that my father had established. He had built this row of housing for our own use.

That night, I slept with my Number One mother on the "kang." In northern China, winter was usually very severe, so people built large mud beds with a fireplace underneath to heat the whole bed in the winter season. Although it was not yet winter, we had heavy bedding covering the top, so I did not feel any hardness, and was happy to have a good night's sleep, and to stretch and relax my sore back from the ride.

11

That night, before I went to bed, my first shock was that I had to use an outhouse. For one who was trained on flush toilets and running water, it was not too pleasant or convenient. But soon, I got used to it, and that was also a good preparation for my next eight years of wartime living.

A few days after, some ladies took me to join them for harvesting cotton. I learned how to pick cotton from the dried husk. There, I was introduced to the cotton bugs and some worms, which made me shudder, while the others laughed. Years later, when I was living in the US and reading about how American black slaves had to endure the searing sun and long hours of bending for picking cotton, I could empathize with them, just from that one late August afternoon excursion of mine.

It was getting close to the end of August. Normally, it was still summer vacation time for most of the schools. However, during weekends, I noticed the students at this school were still busy coming and going in the front part of the campus, where the classrooms and dorms were located. I wondered why there were classes. Another thing made me curious, which was that many students came back on weekends. They all carried a bag on their backs, which was usually loaded with "mantou," the plain steamed bread which was a staple of the Northern people. One day, I asked a friend of my father's, why. He told me, "You know your father founded this school. He has been shouldering all the expenses for hiring the teachers and all the school expenses by himself. The students are free to attend the classes, but he just could not have the extra money to feed the children. That is why you see the students return with the "mantou" on their backs. These plain steamed breads, when they become dried, do not spoil, and that is the main food for the students for the week." He also told me that it was not quite the time for the fall harvest in the field yet, which was why classes were still on. By late

12

September, the school would then be closed so the students could go home to help their parents work the land. I wondered why I was leading an entirely different school life, and my father had never told me about all this.

One day, I went to visit a relative, whom I called "Uncle Yang." It was about two o'clock or so in the afternoon. He was happy to see me. Soon I heard him call out to his daughter-in-law who was in the kitchen, "Since Hsiang Hsiang *(Xiang Xiang)* (my Chinese given name) is here, go get four ounces of meat and we will keep her here for dinner." I thanked him, but said I should go home, because my Number One mother would be waiting for me around dinner time. But Uncle Yang insisted, and said that supper would be ready very soon. Sure enough, about a little past three, dinner was served. There were about six or seven people, including me as the special guest. That was the first time that I found out that the local people only ate two meals each day. The men would leave home early to work in the fields. By nine or ten o'clock, the women in the house would have the first meal cooked. They would deliver the food to the field for the men, then come home for other chores. The men usually would be finished with the day's work and would return home about three or four o'clock in the afternoon. At that time, the second meal, the dinner, would be served. The majority of people would go to bed around nine o'clock, partly to save oil used in lamps. I began to realize how thrifty the people were. I knew Uncle Yang was not a poor person, and yet when he was treating me, the whole family only bought four ounces of meat to share in one big pot of noodles. No wonder that I have always heard that life in northern China was poor and hard.

Another day, my Number One mother said that the weather was too hot, so we should go to the "yao" to cool off. The so-called "yao" is a cave, hollowed from a cliff or hillside. Shaanxi province was known for their cave dwellings. We were driven there but I did not know how far away it was from our town of Sanyuan. The yao that we were to use was on a steep hillside,

13

high above the road. It actually had a nice, wide, tall front door, which was already opened for us. I did not know who owned it. Perhaps it belonged to my Number One mother. The northwestern area of China was very arid. The soil basically consists totally of loess. It does not crumble, but was very densely packed, so many people would just dig out a cave, and make a "yao" to live in. Interestingly, in summer, it is cooler than the outside, and in winter, it is warmer than the outside temperatures. We stayed there for a couple of days and then returned to Sanyuan.

Many, many years later, when I was at Penn State, an Egyptian professor was doing research on cave living around the world. I was glad I had this short experience living in one, so I could help him with the Chinese material and translate for him.

Behind our living quarters in town, there was a large ball field. At the edge of it, there was a river down below, so I realized that our campus was on higher ground than the surrounding land. From the ball field, walking towards the front part of the school, the right side borderline of the field was next to a private house. I often took walks to see the river in back of us, and then walked along the borderline home. Our land was higher than our neighbor's back yard wall, and there was a tree whose branches grew over the wall onto our side of the wall. I noticed it was full of little round green fruit. At first, I did not dare to eat them, but by the second time, when I was passing through, the temptation was just too strong. So, I bent down, and picked one and ate it. It was so juicy and sweet and crisp. I could not help but pick a few more, and brought some home to show my Number One mother. She ate one and asked me where I got the fruit. She also said it was a kind of green date, the kind that when fully ripened, the fruit remained green, not turning red. But she also said that I should not pick the tree without telling our neighbor. Later, she informed the owner, and I even got permission to pick as many as I wanted anytime. Late August was a wonderful time for all sorts of local fruit. Watermelon, large sweet pomegranates, different

14

kinds of persimmons, and of course, so many different kinds of dates. People even preserved the dates in liqueurs.

One evening, my Number One mother told me that the next morning, a friend of my father's would take me to my mother's grave. Early the next morning, a car came and Uncle Li beckoned me to get in. We drove away from the town of Sanyuan towards the countryside. Soon we came to a vast area of farm land. The land was divided into all different sizes of tillable fields. We walked on the raised narrow paths between them. Then I saw, straight ahead of me, there was a small grove of low-growing trees. Uncle Li said, "That is your family's graveyard. Some of your ancestors are buried there." We approached the little wooded knoll. Uncle Li showed me my mother's tomb. I laid down some flowers and some other food offerings, and then knelt down in front of the tombstone. I kowtowed three times, as I was told, to show my respect. After Uncle Li showed me the other graves, we went back to our car, but we did not go home. Uncle Li said he was going to show me the farm that my father had donated to the local people. I then recalled one year when I was home in Nanjing, a guest came to visit my father, and he brought some red and green apples for us from Japan. My father saved half of the apples and reminded us we must not eat those, because he wanted to send those back to the farm in Shaanxi.

Half of a century later, in 1992, my brother's family and I went back to Shaanxi for the first time since we left China in 1948. For years, we had heard that our ancestors' graves had been damaged and ruined. So in 1992, we made our trip back especially to repair my mother's grave. During that trip, we also went to see the farm, and we were even served some really good apples. We were very pleased that the Communist government had not ruined it. They had made it a true experimental farm as my father had wanted. We were further surprised to find that the piece of a carved plaque that had my father's writing, stating that he was donating the acres to the local people, was well preserved and still on the wall. It was very poignant for us to see, that so many years ago, my father had written on that plaque, that if any one of his children wanted to be a farmer, he could have twenty-five acres out of the fifteen hundred acres of land.

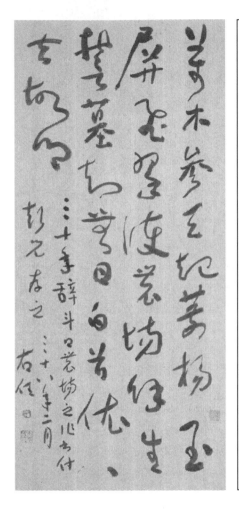

Poetry on Leaving Doukou Village Farm in Cursive Script

The famine in Shaanxi during 1929 resulted in the deaths of more than three million people. Afterwards, Yu Yu-jen used his family's property at Doukou Village in Jingyang, Shaanxi, as the start for the "Doukou Village Experimental Farm." Teaching farmers new techniques, he vowed to donate the farm for their benefit. The poetry here was written in 1941 upon his departure from the farm. At the end of that year, he left for Gansu and Qinghai on a field trip on how to establish the Great Northwest.

This scroll was written for Yu's son, Yu Peng, several months before arriving in Taiwan. At that time, the Nationalist hold on the mainland had been lost and Yu must have been racked with emotions, the brushwork and characters here clearly uninhibited and rousing. Although written in light ink, the lines are not monotonous, the areas where the ink collected revealing traces of the brush. The tones also show many variations, making this a masterpiece by Yu.

This poem about the Shaanxi farm was donated by my uncle (Yu Peng) to the National Palace Museum in Taiwan and displayed in a special exhibition during the summer of 2017 (text from exhibit).

On the day Uncle Li was taking me home after the visit to the experimental farm, there was an incident which left an indelible impression on me. As our car entered the city wall of Sanyuan, I saw a young girl, about seven or eight years old, who was walking awkwardly, while holding onto the wall. I was shocked to see that a girl as young as she still had a pair of bound feet. It was so sad to see that she still had to suffer through that cruel treatment, especially since I knew that the practice had been outlawed a long time ago, ever since the Republic of China had been established in 1912.

Soon, quietly, September came. I did not know who made the decision, or how the decision was made. I was sent to the capital of Xi'an, to be with my godparents' family again. They had left Suzhou sometime after the government had lost Shanghai to Japan. I stayed in Xi'an only for a few days, and was flown to Chengdu, Sichuan, with my sister Chi Chou, brother Chi Sun, and my godmother.

Chengdu is over a thousand miles farther inland from Nanjing, far enough away from the Japanese-controlled areas that it became a center for many evacuees leaving the more war-torn areas.

On the day before we were to board the plane, we all had to be weighed. The flight was my very first, so it was very exciting to me, especially when I happened to see right under us, outside the window, our plane's shadow on the white soft clouds below. The shadow was in the center of a round rainbow-colored circle. When we arrived in the Chengdu airport in the afternoon, my godfather's eldest son, Chi Fang, who had left days before us, was already there to meet us. We waited and claimed our luggage; then we all rode rickshaws to our destination.

Chengdu was a large city. It is also known to people as "Little Beijing." There were hardly any automobiles, and in 1938, the streets were mostly bumpy, narrow alleys. We traveled for a long while, then arrived in front of a traditional Chinese house. We all followed Chi Fang and entered the front door to a large open courtyard. The owners of the house came out to meet us. We were introduced to each other and I learned the owner, Mr. Yen, was the uncle of one of the mutual old friends of both my father and godfather. Since he had a large residence, they had prepared part of the house to be our temporary lodging until we could find our own place.

I forgot how long we lived there, but I did remember the three of us, Chi Chou, Chi Sun, and I, did not waste any time, and very quickly, we all got enrolled in schools for the fall semester.

As in Suzhou before, Chi Chou and I both went to the same girls' school. She was in senior high, and I started in their junior high class. But this time, we both had to be boarding students and could only go home on Sunday mornings and had to be back in school by five o'clock on Sunday afternoon. The majority of local students all spoke in Sichuan dialect, whereas students like us who had fled the war, who were from other provinces, all spoke in different dialects. Soon, the newcomers all learned two things. One was the local dialect, and the other was how to eat hot peppery foods like the natives.

Not too long afterwards, my godfather and Chi Fang found a house so they moved out from the Yen residence. By then, my eldest sister had already left Nanjing with my father, just before the Japanese took over the city. My father had to go with the government. My sister first went back to Shaanxi to see my Number One mother. There, she picked up her son, Bei Da, then together, they all flew to Chengdu to Mr. Yen's house.

The government moved through several places, and finally settled in Chongqing. Because of the frequent air raids on Chongqing by the Japanese, my father stayed alone there, but had us settled in Chengdu, about two hundred miles away to the northwest.

During the spring semester, Chi Fang also helped my eldest sister to move into our own house. Shortly, my Number One mother also came from Shaanxi and joined us. Before I finished my first year of study at the girls' school, the Japanese had started to bomb Chengdu. Since my father had helped a very good school to be settled in a small town, Jintang, about thirty miles away from Chengdu in a rural area, it was decided that both Bei Da and I should attend that school. Then, since it would be much safer from the Japanese bombing there, our entire family moved there too.

That small town, Jintang, was a prosperous town, unlike a great many Chinese rural towns. It even had its own hydropowered electricity. The electric power plant belonged to a Mr. Tseng *(Zeng)*, who was the elder of the largest local clan. Mr. Tseng had a vacant residence, so we became his tenants. As for the school, its Chinese name was Ming Hsien *(Ming Xian)*. It also had an English name, which was, "The Oberlin Memorial School in Shansi." *(It is now known as the Shanxi Agricultural University.)* Before the war, the school was founded with funds supplied by the Oberlin College of Oberlin, Ohio, USA. It was established in memory of those missionaries who died in the Boxer Rebellion. The head of the trustees and president/principal,

Mr. Kung Hsiang-Hsi *(Kong Xiangxi)*, was an Oberlin graduate and my father's colleague. He was also Chiang Kai-Shek's and Sun Yat-Sen's brother-in-law. During the Sino-Japanese War, Shanxi became occupied by the Japanese, so the school had to escape to somewhere farther inland. As it turned out, the elder Mr. Tseng's nephew was a good friend of my father. When my father learned that the school needed to find a new home, he introduced these friends of his to Mr. Kung, and thus, the school eventually found a new home in the three vacant properties owned by the Tseng family in Jintang. The whole school, including faculty and many students, made the trip with the greatest effort, marching nearly eight hundred miles from the old location to reach Jintang.

Oberlin-in-China Migrates

Nine hundred miles from home, Shansi students of the Oberlin-in-Shansi school have fled deep into the interior of China to Chintang, in Szechuen province, to avoid invading Japanese armies. Only meager reports have thus far come to us concerning the last two changes of location.

Students hiked for miles over mountains and plains. They slept over-night in temples, ate from the land. They used new contacts to propagandize for the National Government of China. They gave propaganda plays, educated the farmers in air raid precautions, first-aid, and general patriotism. At their destination they repaired old buildings for living quarters and classrooms, and began their studies as soon as possible.

Herbert VanMeter, '37, walked, ate, and slept with the students on their travels. He reports great pleasure in sharing student life, although he "wishes Mel and Charlotte were here at Chintang."

When my family moved to Jintang, it was Ming Hsien's second year operating at the Tseng family property. It was comprised of three separate campuses, each with its own clustered housing. These were called "The Old Fort," "The Upper New Fort," and "The Lower Fort."

The auditorium and administration, the sports field, classrooms, and the girls' dorms all were in The Old Fort. The Upper New Fort housed the male students and a couple of single teachers. All the rest of the faculty and their families' residences and an elementary school were at the Lower Fort. The three campuses were connected by narrow paths, and all were within walking distance of each other. Since more than ninety percent of the students came to Jintang with the school without their own

20

families, the teachers practically became their parents. Everyone felt that they were members of a large, loving family.

My nephew, Bei Da and I were among the more lucky teens. We could return home on weekends. There was no public transportation, except for a kind of one-wheeled wheelbarrow cart, so going home meant a four and a half mile walk each way. At school, everyone was poor, but because Ming Hsien was mainly run according to the American school system, many of the students could apply to work for the school to be exempt from certain fees. Some of our teachers were graduates from American universities. Before the war, every two years, Oberlin College would send two representatives to Ming Hsien to teach English. They were either upperclassmen or new graduates. First, they would be sent to Beijing to learn Mandarin Chinese for six months. Then they would go to Taigu in Shanxi where the school was located. After two years, they would be replaced by two new representatives. But since the Japanese attacked and occupied Beijing, and the Chinese had lost a lot of territory, the Oberlin representatives could no longer go to Beijing, but had to go to Jintang directly. The trip was not easy. When I was there, some of our representatives had to stay more than two years, because the new replacements were not coming. There were four representatives. They all taught me, and later, became two married couples while there.

The school's dining hall for the girls was also in The Old Fort. The students who traveled with the school from Taigu were all northerners, but Jintang in Sichuan was more in the south. The main staple was rice. Actually, our campuses were all surrounded by rice fields. Only every now and then, or for special occasions, we would have pastas. Then the students all would stuff themselves. It was also because of the rice fields, that malaria became our most serious problem. More than half of us all got sick at one time or another. My case lasted for three long years. During that period, I was constantly attacked by severe chills and high fever. Somehow, the quinine pills just did not help me. I became badly anemic for years, only recovering after I left Jintang.

I did not go to the Sunday services on our campus. I know we had a preacher, and there was Sunday school, too. Even though Ming Hsien was a Christian school, religious belief was entirely free. It was in that kind of environment that I was gradually introduced to a little more of the hymns of the church, Western music and Western civilization. One year, my English teacher even directed me to perform a play titled, *The Dumb Wife*. I was cast as the "dumb wife," but had to memorize all the lines in English!

Speaking of English, early each morning, the athletic field would be full of students, all holding their English books or notes in hand, walking around immersed in memorizing their English vocabulary and texts.

We had lived in Jintang for a few months. My two younger sisters finally arrived after their long trip from Hong Kong. The last time when I saw them, they were in Shanghai with their nannies. When the Japanese went to our house and searched the house for them, someone had hidden my sisters in an attic storage place above the ceiling. Luckily, they were not discovered, but they were little, so both really had a frightening experience. At that time, my father was with the government and was on his way to Chongqing. Because of that incident, arrangements were made. Swiftly, the nannies and my sisters were taken to Hong Kong, where they stayed temporarily with my cousin Chih Hsien, who previously lived with us in Shanghai. A trip through Henei, Vietnam, then entry into China via the southwestern border had been arranged. The two nannies went back to Shanghai. My sisters were accompanied by a relative to join us in Jintang. Mian Mian was nine and a half, and Wu Ming was six years old. Soon, they also started school in Jintang.

By then, my oldest sister's husband had also rejoined the family. Although he had previously been arrested and jailed by the Russians as a spy, he had been released and returned to China.

There was one incident that left a deep, deep impression on all the members of the school. I think I was thirteen or fourteen at the time. One night, during a school week, around midnight, a young male student at the Upper New Fort had a severe pain attack in his belly. We did not have any doctors with us then. There were not even any doctors in all of Jintang, other than some traditional Chinese herb doctors. The situation was extremely critical. The only hope was to send the student to a hospital in Chengdu. Chengdu was about thirty miles away, and there was no transportation. At that juncture, someone must have awakened the two English teachers, so Mr. Kennedy and Mr. Carlson, the two Oberlin representatives, volunteered without hesitation. They would use a stretcher and carry the student on their shoulders and walk the thirty miles to Chengdu. It was pitch dark. They only had a dim light held by another teacher. They reached a university hospital in time before the appendix burst. A doctor was able to operate on the student and saved his life. Ming Hsien's motto is "Learn to Serve." The two young teachers certainly showed us by their spirit how to serve others. And they taught us a lesson in modesty, which is at the heart of true service, because the teachers rarely spoke about what they had done.

Many of the alumni from Jintang during the eight years of the Sino-Japanese War eventually lived in the US and Canada. Around 1991, we formed an alumni association and went to an Oberlin College commencement gathering for the first time. Mr. Kennedy and Mr. Carlson were both there. I was surprised to learn that Mr. Carlson was the retired president of Oberlin College. We offered them some beautiful roses to again thank them for what they did that night in Jintang more than half a century earlier.

In 1942, I asked my father to allow me and my sister Mian Mian to be with him and to attend school in Chongqing. Once there, I went to a boarding school located outside of the wartime capital of Chongqing, but Mian Mian was in town. During the weekends, my father would come to school and pick me up to go home, either in town, or to my father's residence in the countryside in the hills.

As for going home on weekends, I still clearly remember that I did a very foolish thing one week. It was a Saturday. I thought my father was coming to pick me up on the way to the house in the hills, so I told a classmate, Ling Tsu Hwa, to wait with me, since her home was also in Shandong in the hills. But by five o'clock, my father still had not come. I said to Ling that maybe we should start walking to the Little Dragon Hollow to wait, since it was a busy bus stop. Little Dragon Hollow was about thirty minutes from our school. Even if my father did not come, we could catch a bus to go home. She agreed. We reached the bus stop and waited patiently. But the light was fading fast, and it was getting colder. We changed our minds, and decided to take the bus. Then we found out that the last bus for Shandong had long gone, and there were no more buses going that way. I guessed that my father must have forgotten me, and became a little anxious.

I thought about it, and then suggested to Ling that the only way out was to hitch a ride. She left it to me. It must have been because I had watched too many Hollywood movies. Hitchhiking did not seem to be that difficult. I figured in my mind that because it was during the war, we did not have that many automobiles going around. We should not try to stop the cars that were either too old or too new. The mechanics of the too-old beaten-up cars probably could not be trusted. The real shiny newer ones – their owners might be involved in some illegal activities so their owners could afford the new cars. Only the ones that were not too old or too new, yet were well kept would mostly belong to official government offices. They should be more trustworthy.

Thus decided, I started to try to stop the passing cars. For quite a few tries, none that I had signaled would stop for us. Then finally, a car passed us, but then stopped. Slowly, it backed up to us. Then the front window lowered, and the chauffeur poked his head out and asked me what did I want? Then he turned inside and talked to the people in the back seats. Then the back door opened. A man with a young girl was asking us to get in. Ling went to the front seat and I settled into the back.

The man told the driver to proceed again, and started to tell me that we gave them quite a fright, because the road was very dark, and they could not be sure who was stopping the car. When they passed us and saw it was two girls, they decided to pick us up. He asked us our names. We honestly told him, and so he asked me if I knew a Mr. Yu You Ren. I answered, "He's my father." The man said, "Oh, no wonder. When I saw you, I thought your face was a little familiar. Now I know! If you would add a handful of long beard, you would look just like your father." So I knew he must have been someone who was a high government official. In turn, I politely asked his name. He said, "Tell your father Tseng Yang Fu took you home. He knows me." Then he continued to say that we were lucky, because he was late that day in picking up his younger daughter at the same school as mine. Otherwise, he would have been at Shandong a long time ago.

He dropped us off at my door. Ling did not have too far to walk, so she bid me goodbye and left. As I entered the dining room, my father was surprised to see me, and asked me, "How come you are home, and at this hour? How did you get home then? I thought you said you weren't coming home this week?" I told him that it was Mr. Tseng Yang Fu who gave me a ride. My father started to laugh and said, "You sure got the right person to take you home. The Minister of Transportation delivered you door to door in person." All of a sudden, it dawned on me. I was so dumb while

I was in Mr. Tseng's car! I missed my chance to complain "in person" that they should have more bus runs on Saturday from Little Dragon Hollow to Shandong hills. Before Ling and I had gotten into the car, I told Ling that one day, if I could meet the Minister of Transportation, I would definitely ask for more bus service. Now, because I could not connect his name with his office, I probably would never have such a good opportunity again.

That year in Chongqing, my sister and I met our nephew George for the first time, as he was born in Edinburgh, Scotland. It was his first trip back to China. His parents, my brother Wang De and his wife, had left China right after their wedding, years ago from Shanghai when I was just five years old. Now everyone was home again and George was already more than ten years old.

I did not particularly like Chongqing. It was very crowded, and the summer was unbearably hot. However, those few years I was there, it gave me the opportunity to meet a great number of interesting people: writers, artists, poets, journalists, businessmen, politicians, young and old, rich and poor, famous and not, somehow, they all appeared in my father's quarters. Their visits definitely opened my eyes to a much more colorful, complex, and sophisticated adult world that I could never have experienced if I had stayed in Jintang.

Then in the summer of 1944, I took the Joint College Entrance Examination of five famous private universities, and got admissions from two of them. Both were funded by Americans. Originally, one was from Nanjing, and the other one, Yenching University, was from Beijing. They were both famous institutions, especially Yenching. Its campus in Beijing was so beautiful that *LIFE* magazine had a special article with pictures to show its American readers. Because of the Japanese war, many of the universities all fled and moved from the Japanese-occupied areas to inland areas where they could be safe. Among the several large universities that moved to Chengdu, they shared a lot of facilities. They practically all congregated in the same place outside the Chengdu city limits. Only Yenching University had its college of liberal arts and the student dorms in the city.

I chose Yenching and decided to major in Chinese literature. My father was pleased that I was attending college. Before the summer vacation was over, my sister Mian Mian and I went back to Chengdu from Chongqing in preparation for our schooling. By that time, my elder sister's son Bei Da had already finished high school at Ming Hsien. My Number One mother had brought my youngest sister and moved to Chengdu so Bei Da could attend college. Again, I was boarding in the dorms on campus, only returning home on weekends.

Yenching, like the other four Western-associated universities, all had Western church associations, mostly from America. Our president, Dr. John Leighton Stuart, later became the last American ambassador to China before the Nationalists evacuated to Taiwan.

Yenching University was considered one of the top universities in China. The Harvard-Yenching Institute still exists today, with the mission to promote the teaching of humanities and social sciences in East Asia, although Yenching University itself has been dissolved and assimilated by other major universities in China.

Our campus in town was rented from an American-sponsored Christian high school for girls. The men's dorm was at a vacant temple close by. We had some faculty families living close to the freshmen women's dorm. We slept on bunk beds, eight people to each room. Each of us had our own desk. I was surprised to find that a few of my old classmates from Ming Hsien and one of my good friends, Yvonne, was also my roommate.

Life in Sichuan

College life was exciting! Though it was wartime, and we were all poor students, we were a happy bunch. I regret that I was not a diligent student during the first year. The second year started. The sophomores could move to rooms in the main building. Yvonne and I were again roommates. Our room was small and simple. It consisted of only a bunk bed, one desk, and one chair.

Yvonne graduated from Ming Hsien with excellent grades, so she came to Yenching without having to take the college entrance exam. She had an older sister who was also in Ming Hsien when I was there. The older sister, Lynette, came to Yenching ahead of us after graduating. When we were not too busy and had some pocket money, Yvonne and I often would go to see movies or visit the small restaurants around the neighborhood of the school.

I remember that inflation was very serious in those years. It was common for shops and restaurants to show prices on chalkboards so that they could change the prices constantly. Yvonne and I frequently had lunch at a small food stall just outside the campus. I remember one day, after we had finished a plate of bao zi *(dumplings)* we decided to get another plate. The owner came over to apologize. He said that the price of flour was going up and he did not know how much the next plate of dumplings would cost! We would have to wait before we could order. After a brief wait, he came back to report the new price. It didn't seem unusual at the time! When it was time to pay my tuition for my sophomore year, I recall riding a rickshaw with a huge bundle of currency at my feet – it was cash for my tuition. Nobody paid much attention to the bundle of money, as it seemed that the currency was not worth anything.

Gradually, Yvonne and I learned about each other's families. Among her siblings, she adored her second oldest brother. More than a few times, she would tell me stories about this brother. She said that out of the nine children, he was the favorite one of their mother. But he was strong-willed, so their mother had to let him do what he wanted to do. He left home and went to Tibet to pursue Buddhism. At that time, Yvonne's parents were living in Xikang province, which was originally part of eastern Tibet. Her father was the official military representative of Chiang Kai-Shek for that area. She told me the town they were in, Xichang, was a scenic and peaceful place, with clear blue skies and a beautiful lake. There, her mother had learned from the French priests, how to grow grapes and make brandy.

After the freshman year, Yvonne and her sister Lynette both went to Xichang to spend their summer vacation at home. When they came back, there were more stories about this brother. Yvonne also proudly told me that her mother had gotten a baby boy home from east Tibet. The boy had such long eyelashes and was so handsome looking. It was her brother Garma's son with a Tibetan woman. They were not married, because the girls there were more socially free with their partners. Many of them still kept the matriarch system, so the child would be living with the mother's family. Yvonne's brother wanted the child to grow up and to be free as a Tibetan. He did not let his mother know about the child. But his mother found out. She was so excited that she had her first grandson. Somehow, she managed to get permission from the mother and had the boy taken home. The little boy immediately captured everyone's heart. Yvonne became a proud aunt and she even showed me the little boy's pictures.

Yvonne's parents had a nice house in Chengdu. In December of 1945, the war in Europe was already over. A few weekends before Christmas, Yvonne's oldest brother Louie, and sister-in-law Jean were giving a party in their parents' house. The couple was living there, waiting for their visas to study in the US. Yvonne invited me to go. I accepted. Then we had a surprise. Neither Yvonne nor Lynnette expected to see their second-oldest brother Garma at home. Without notifying anyone, he had returned from eastern Tibet, so he was just in time to join the party!

That evening, the people at the party were all college-aged people. We danced and also had wonderful food. We were introduced to each other, and Garma, the brother from Tibet, danced with me. Our conversation turned from food to novels. I told him I had just finished Leo Tolstoy's War and Peace in Chinese translation, and recommended it to him. After that, he surprised me and came to call on me at our dorm the very next day. I was amazed by his knowledge about so many things, be it current or past, domestic or foreign affairs, because I thought he had been in a very remote place for so long. In the following months, I learned that in order to receive outside mail and news, he established the first post office, and became the postmaster for the area. At one time, he had organized a militia group to fight the local warlord who was smuggling opium and taxing the local villagers, both in labor and harvest. He also helped the American soldiers to purchase horses. He said he needed help with his English, and I soon learned why, as he told me his story.

When he was about twelve years old, his family was living in Nanjing. He and a good friend were unhappy to see the unfair living conditions between the well-to-do and the poor. Through their reading, they felt that the Marxist theory was the more ideal way to make China more fair. So the two twelve-year-olds decided they should earn their living by their own labor, and ran away from home. But the only jobs they could find was to be rickshaw pullers. Of course, they were too young, and not strong enough to pull. At the same time, both families discovered the two boys were missing. They reported them to the police, who quickly caught them and took them home.

When Garma started the eleventh grade in senior high, he visited a friend. By mistake, he wandered into his friend's father's study. It pleased him to see that there were so many books. He forgot to look for his friend, but instead, picked up a book and sat down to read. It was a book on Buddhism. Reading it, he became deeply interested in it. He said to himself, "This is the right path for solving the problems of our world."

A few days later, in his Chinese class, the teacher happened to say that recently, he was reading a book on Buddhism. He said he was very much attracted to the Buddha's teaching. Unfortunately, the text was in Classical Chinese, which made it very difficult to read. Otherwise, he would recommend that the class read it. Garma stood up and said that he was reading a Buddhist book too, but did not think it was that hard to follow. The teacher would not believe him, since he himself found it difficult. Thereupon, Garma picked up his Chinese textbook, turned around, and threw the book out of the window. Then he walked out of the classroom. And that was the end of his formal education. And that was why, when we met, he told me that he needed to improve his English.

My father spent eight years in Tibetan monasteries. As I understand it, he studied with various masters before deciding to study with Gongga Lama. He spent six years at Gongga Monastery (page 307) studying Buddhism under his guru, the 9th Gangkar Rinpoche. See page 276 for some more highlights from his early years.

Another night, Garma was walking me back to school. We had to walk through a park. It was a very cold winter evening. The park was almost devoid of any people except for the two of us. We came upon a large old plum blossom tree. It was a famous tree, because the blossoms were in the color of pale green, instead of the usual pink or red. Plum blossoms only flower in winter. The full moon above cast moving spotty shadows under our feet. Whiffs of faint sweet fragrance from the tree permeated the air around us. We felt we were in a fairy land. Slowly, we started to dance under the moonlit tree. I knew then that I was in love with Garma.

One Sunday afternoon, I came back to school from home and saw that Yvonne was sunning herself alone in front of our dorm. I sat down to join her. She looked so lonesome. Then she laughed, but at the same time gave a sigh, and said, "You know, I'm almost sorry that I introduced you to my brother. I used to have a good friend to have fun together, and a brother who often would treat me to do interesting things. Now look, I'm minus a good friend and I've lost a brother."

Early in the following spring, Yvonne's mother came from Xichang and stayed in Chengdu. Louie and Jean had left for the US. Yvonne and Garma invited me to meet their mother. Yvonne told me that one of her mother's worries was that Garma did not want to get married, and someday, he might renounce everything and become a monk. "She would be very happy to see you," Yvonne said. I met her. She struck me as a very beautiful, middle-aged, elegant lady. I could see why all her children were so bright. She had already learned that I had lost my mother when I was young. She also knew who my father was. In spite of it being the first time we met each other, she treated me as if I were one of her own girls.

A couple of months later, her husband was appointed to be the new mayor of Chongqing. So, their whole family all moved to Chongqing, two hundred miles away. By that time, World War II was over. The Allied countries were victorious and all the Chinese government organizations had started to move back to their original locations. The universities were also scheduled to move back. Yenching University decided to move back to Beijing as soon as the spring semester was over. Garma and I thought we should be engaged. There was no problem with Garma's parents, but I had to convince my father that Garma would not forsake me to be a monk.

Engagement announcement, very colorful and bound in red silk

In early May, I flew to Chongqing to be with my father. Because my father had to be in Nanjing shortly, our parents held our engagement party on May 12, 1946 at the largest hotel in Chongqing *(Chongqing Da Xia).* Although many people had already left Chongqing, that day, there were more than two hundred guests who came to celebrate. Partly, it was a happy time -- the war which had lasted eight years was over, and the Chinese were on the side of the Allies. Partly, it was because both of our families were headed by well-known government officials. Father left for Nanjing several days later. But he let me stay behind with Yvonne's family for two more weeks. Then I parted with the Changs and joined my own family in Nanjing.

When I flew back to Nanjing, there were so many surprises to greet me. One was that we had a new rented residence in a newly developed area. My bedroom was across the hallway from my father's on the second floor. My bed was a raised Japanese tatami, the only one left in the house. The Japanese had used the newly constructed house as their officers' club. Another surprise was that my brother Peng and his whole family were back from the US. They were staying on the same floor with me. There were his two young children too. His son Victor was born in London, but his daughter, Diana, was born in New York after they evacuated from the air raids in London. My eldest sister's son, Bei Da, had gotten married and was in the fourth bedroom with his new bride. My two younger sisters were already there on the third floor. But my eldest sister and my Number One mother went back from Chengdu to Sanyuan, our native town in Shaanxi province. We had a full household of people! Some of our servants and father's old attendants even came back after the eight long years of separation. They were all very happy to see us return to Nanjing, especially to see me. When I left, I was still a child, and I came back as an adult.

Early in June, one day, my father talked to me, saying that a new governor had been announced for Xinjiang province. Xinjiang had been a problematic province for a long time. There were frequent political incidents with the Soviet Russians, and the various Muslim ethnic groups. Since my father enjoyed a good reputation with these parties in the past, he was asked by Chiang Kai-Shek to supervise the swearing-in ceremony for the new governor. He asked if I would like to go with him.

We boarded a chartered plane a couple of days later. Besides the flight crew, there were eleven of us, and I was the only female passenger. It was a long flight. We made two or three stops at some historical places on the way, and finally arrived at the capital city, Urumqi.

We were welcomed by the new designated governor *(Zhang Zhizhong)* and his party. Right at the airport, there was another surprise. There was my eldest sister with her husband. On our way to the governor's residence, I learned that this brother-in-law who had been imprisoned by the Russians as a spy all those years ago was the current mayor of Urumqi on account of his knowledge of the Russians!

This brother-in-law, Qu Wu, eventually held many high-level positions in the Communist government. A detailed listing of his many titles can be seen in <u>Who was Who in the People's Republic of China: With more than 3100 Portraits</u> by Wolfgang Bartke.

Our residence was built quite some time ago by the previous governor. It actually was built like a fort with a thick outer wall, circling around the main building. Between the two structures lay a very large, beautifully trimmed garden. All members of my father's party had their individual rooms, except for me. I was introduced to the governor's family-- his wife and his three children, who were home. The youngest son was still in elementary school. The two daughters were also college students like me, so I was put in their bedroom, and soon we became good friends.

The previous governor of Xinjiang *(Sheng Shicai)* left behind a bloody legend. The building we were all staying in was called The New Mansion, which had a large number of rooms. There was a special small office with thirteen telephones around the desk, on the second floor. The window in front of the desk faced directly to the main gate of the outer wall. Stories said that whenever the governor parted with his visitor, he would go to that small office and sit in front of the desk. If he did not like the guest or had the slightest suspicions about the visitor, he would immediately call his guard and he could soon see the guest arrested and thrown in prison or executed.

The old governor had a brother whose wife happened to be a White Russian *(anti-Communists who fought the Bolsheviks)* woman. One year, for some reason, he became suspicious of her. She was beaten to death, and the beating took place in the large room which my father was occupying. Of course, no one would dare to tell that to my father, but still, some people said that her ghost was still roaming around.

We heard so many rumors. One day, the three of us girls were taken to visit the outer wall. There were some dorms for the guards built into it. There were also a few rooms or cells at the wall. In one of the empty rooms which our guide showed us, we saw large, heavy nails along the wall that formed into a neat circle. They were higher than a man's height. Some of the nails had coarse, dirty jute bags hanging on them. The guide told us that these jute bags were used to put people in them. The bags were then hung on the wall to torture the people. Many just died in them. Suddenly, I felt the room become chilled, and I quickly backed out.

As the governor had killed so many people, he became more and more paranoid. In his later days, before he was removed as the governor, at every meal, he would ask his most favorite concubine to taste his food for him.

The governor could behave like this because the Chinese central government was preoccupied and almost exhausted with the Japanese invasion. At the same time, Xinjiang was a vast territory, very far away. So the governor had the chance to act as an emperor of a local independent kingdom.

Of course, our stay in Urumqi was not limited to hearing these terrible tales. Almost every day, we were welcomed by different ethnic groups and other parties. Although the Han *(or ethnic Chinese)* people were the majority in this province, the largest minority of the natives were all Muslims. They mostly wore their colorful ethnic attire, and they all wore beautifully embroidered caps. Girls all had long braids. Many of them looked completely like European people, with blue eyes and curly blond hair. Many of the Cossack children learned to ride bareback when they were merely two or three years old. I managed to learn to ride from them, but very poorly.

The most polite way for the local people to show their sincere welcome to their houseguests was to offer fermented horsemilk. The offering usually would be squeezed out of a leather pouch carried over the shoulder. The pouches were generally made from a whole sheep or goatskin, with the feet tied neatly to stay out of the way.

Unfortunately, when I was in China, I never drank any milk. So everywhere I went on that trip, my interpreter had to apologize for me. But the practice was that I should drink at least one sip, and then let the host finish the rest. Otherwise, it was an insult to the host. I only remember the fermented horse milk tasted really thick and sour. Now, many years later, I have to laugh at myself, because after I was in the US and was pregnant with my daughter Eva, the doctor threatened me saying that if I did not start drinking milk every day, the baby would surely suffer. So obediently, I faithfully gulped down the milk three times a day. Sometimes, I even drank buttermilk, which tasted very similar to my impressions of the horse milk. Certainly, milk does not taste that bad, and I wonder why I made such a fuss then.

Odd as it may seem, there was an ice cream machine in my brother-in-law's office. This was quite a rarity in the remote provinces! I remember enjoying eating ice cream until I watched them making the ice cream one day. There were flies everywhere. I could no longer enjoy the nut and raisin flavored delights after that. I also remember being served a customary Muslim dish of rice and raisins cooked in lamb fat. I have always disliked the taste of lamb and mutton, and the presence of the raisins could hardly add to my enjoyment. I also recall the most memorable meals included having the head of a sheep being served, facing the guest of honor.

We stayed in Urumqi for a week. My father and his party and the governor flew to visit the south part of Xinjiang. Sad to say, I had to miss that trip because I had come down with a bad case of bronchitis, and was under a doctor's care. In just about a week's time, the touring party came back, and soon my father took leave with his company back to Nanjing, while I remained with the governor's family, with the understanding that sometime later, I could fly back on a special flight with General Sung.

I returned to Nanjing in early August. School was still more than a couple of weeks away. Then my fiance Garma arrived from Chongqing. He had an offer to be an instructor in the department of philosophy at the Nanjing University. At the same time, my father wished I could stay in Nanjing to be with him. Therefore, I took the transfer test and enrolled in the same university for my junior year. Unfortunately, I did not do too well with the math portion of the test, so I was required to take a make-up class in calculus. I knew I could not accomplish that big challenge, so after explaining it to my father, I still went back to Yenching University in Beijing.

I flew back to Beijing to continue as a junior at Yenching. Because the campus was unusually beautiful, during the Japanese occupation years, they did not destroy it, but used it, just as they used our house in Nanjing. It became the social club for their officers. They also paved the walking paths on the campus. We lived in the fourth dorm for girls. Yvonne was still my roommate. In winter, we even had central heating. Life was very comfortable. In the past, people often referred to Yenching as the school for children of the nobility, even though the students might not have been all that well-to-do.

Around 1946 or 1947, Beijing was becoming surrounded by Communist forces. We Yenching students were fortunate. We paid our tuition, room and board at the beginning of each semester. A student committee in charge of the kitchen commissary arranged for the purchase of food staple supplies for the entire semester at the beginning of each semester. The students at the other major university, Beijing Da Xue *(Now Peking University)* were not always so fortunate. This school was the public university, and students depended on scholarships or money sent from home. School supplies and food were paid for by the month. With the Communists in control of the area, it became difficult for students to receive money from home. I remember that there was a student who had been starving due to lack of funds. When he finally received some money, he went to the dining room, overate, and died as a result.

Garma and I corresponded by air mail almost daily. After teaching one semester at Nanjing University, he informed me that he was going to the Tagore University at Santiniketan, India *(now Visva-Bharati University),* as a research fellow, so he left Nanjing. But the civil war with the Communist party had already started. In the summer of 1948, Yvonne graduated and left Beijing. We had some relatives and friends who were in the air force. Their flights took them to many different destinations on different missions. All the news they brought back was the same—the Nationalists were losing. Some cities were completely besieged by the Communists. At those airports, you could see discarded gold bars laying around because the outgoing airplanes were all fully loaded with people fleeing, and they could not take any extra weight other than just the passengers. Later, even Beijing became surrounded by Communist troops. Many students were hungry because they no longer could receive any financial remittances from their families. My father also was worried about me. In November, 1948, I left Beijing on one of my family

39

friends' last flight back to Nanjing. There were hardly any commercial flights available by then.

By that time, Garma had long been at Purdue University in Indiana. He had resigned from Tagore University in early 1947. He enrolled in Purdue as a special student to study Dairy Husbandry. He planned to learn some advanced technology so he could go back to Eastern Tibet after we got married. There, he had a nice small farm. He thought we could live a simple, happy, and peaceful life.

In the fall of 1948, the Tibetan government in Lhasa saw that the Communist troops were about to take over the Nationalist central government. The Lhasa government thought that they should increase their own contact with the outside world. A small group headed by their minister of the Treasury was sent to the US to explore the possibility of building up some direct trade relations. They arrived at New York City. Naturally, they went to visit Wall Street *(the financial district)*. There, they met Garma's older brother Louie, who was representing a small private bank in Sichuan, which belonged to one of his father's good friends. Louie spread the news with his business associates. Among them, there was one small company which became interested in doing business with the Tibetans, but they needed someone to help them communicate between the two parties. Louie said he knew the exact person they needed, and so he recommended Garma. Thus, Garma left Purdue University and went to New York. Garma fulfilled his duties successfully. However, due to the visiting group's limited time in the US, it was not possible to complete any deals. But the meeting resulted in the American firm offering Garma a job to go to India, where he could carry out the research work for future trade with the Tibetans.

Around the end of 1946, Garma's father was already the mayor of Chongqing. Then around the end of 1947, Garma's father was announced as the governor of Hubei province by the Nationalist government. He was pleased to return to his home town.

Therefore, in October of 1948, when I was still in school in Beijing, Garma sent me a telegram from New York, informing me that first, he was going back to his parents at Hankou *(formerly Hankow, now Wuhan),* the capital of Hubei province; then he would come to Nanjing to see my father, and we should be married in Hankou. After I returned to Nanjing, I received another telegram from him sent from Hubei. He said there was a change of plans. He asked me to fly to Hubei for our wedding first, and then both of us would come back to see my father.

At that time, after Garma returned home, the civil war between the Nationalist government and the Communists was reaching a very crucial point. People were all very anxious about the political situation. After his two telegrams, I received Garma's letter. In it, he explained that he had a job to go to India, as soon as we got married. I told my father. My father was quiet for a while, then he said to me, "I'm so happy for you and Garma, but I'm very sorry I couldn't give you any monetary dowry, only an airplane ticket. You will go now. When your date is settled, I will come to be at your wedding." I reaffirmed to him that both Garma and I would be back after the wedding. I left with a small suitcase with one gold bracelet from my brother and flew to Hankou.

We had to postpone the wedding date a couple of times, because my father telegrammed me that due to his position in the government, he could not leave Nanjing at that time, so as not to cause other people to speculate that the high officials were fleeing the capital. Instead, he would send my brother Peng to attend my wedding.

Garma and I actually did not have to do anything for our big event. My mother-in-law arranged the whole affair, so we just waited for my brother to arrive. In those days, news and rumors about the war changed day by day. Almost right after my father's last telegram, I received a telegram from my brother, telling me that the only commercial airline had stopped all flights from

Nanjing. We should not wait for him any longer. It was under the most unsettling situation that we held our wedding. Though a great number of guests were still present, there was only one of my father's old friends, who happened to be living in Hankou, who attended to represent my father and my family.

My wedding dress was a well-used gown from America. Garma's oldest sister Helena and her husband had both completed their educations in the US, and as was the custom in those years, had returned home to China. She brought her wedding dress home with her. Her younger sister Lynette also wore the dress for her wedding. And I was the third lucky wearer of the Chang family dress.

Immediately after we were married, my husband proceeded to apply for our visas to India. We stated that we were going there to spend our honeymoon. I also thought of bringing Garma's son Jeffrey, my new stepson, along with us to India, but my mother-in-law said that she could not bear to part with Jeffrey. Besides, people reminded us that it was to be our honeymoon trip, so we did not bring him.

My parents were married on December 7, 1948, anniversary of Pearl Harbor Day.

Our trip started from Hankou to Hong Kong. Then we flew to Calcutta. Even though it was our wintertime, Calcutta was unexpectedly too hot for me. We checked in at the Grand Hotel which was a well-known

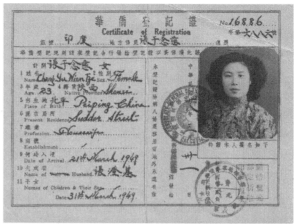

western-run hotel. All the service people were Indians. Some of them could speak some English. In 1949, India had already been independent from British rule, but the hotel still kept the English traditions for their service. The six o'clock morning and four o'clock afternoon teas were faithfully served in our room every day without fail. One day, I tried to ask a question of a sweeper who always crouched on the bathroom floor when he cleaned. Another uniformed server who came in told me not to speak to him. Later, I found out the reason at the front desk. It was because the sweeper belonged to the untouchable caste.

For the time we were in Calcutta, we were busy with all kinds of paperwork. Also, we had to decide where to live. In checking the dates, I was surprised to see the calendar was full of red-inked holidays, because they had to observe all the Christian, Hindu, and Muslim holidays and memorial days. If we were not careful, we could not get money changed at the banks because they would be closed for a holiday, and time, money and energy would just be wasted.

One day, when we were at the Chinese Consulate for some business, my husband discovered the Consul General, Mr. Tsai *(Cai)*, was his chemistry teacher from junior high. Knowing we were new in town, he kindly introduced a good friend of his to help us. The friend was Mr. C.P. Hsueh *(Xue)* and his wife Hsu.

The Hsuehs had been in Calcutta for a good many years. They loved to entertain, so they soon included us as their guests, and we became fast friends. C.P. was the CEO of a well-known private trading company from China. He also did business with the Tibetans. He gave us all the help we needed and also suggested that we should live in Kalimpong.

My husband and I followed C.P.'s recommendation and moved out of the Grand Hotel, and took the train bound for Kalimpong. The train reached the town of Siliguri. There, we had to take a three-hour uphill ride in a small bus to Kalimpong, which was situated at forty-five hundred feet high in the Himalaya Mountains. I had no idea how and when my husband made the arrangements. After traveling on the winding hairpin road for a long period, the bus dropped us at a beautiful bungalow. It was to be our rental residence. The owner was a high Tibetan government official. The agreement was that in addition to our monthly rent, we must promise to keep his "mali," the gardener, mainly because the house had a large garden surrounding it, which definitely needed constant attention.

We managed to get our luggage into the house. It was truly a beautiful place. We were very lucky that when we were in Calcutta, my husband had met a Mr. Chang *(Zhang)* at one of C.P.'s parties. Mr. Chang's family had been doing business with the Tibetans in tea, silk and other goods for many generations. He had learned that we needed help after we settled down, so he very generously let us have one of his young employees named Wang. This young man showed up at our house the next day. I was relieved of my worries, because not only was he Chinese, but he could speak Tibetan, Hindi, and Nepali, which were the most important languages for communications in that area. I said he was young. In fact, he was the same age as me.

Kalimpong was a small mountainside town with a very mixed population. The European population was not that big. The Europeans were mostly Irish, Scotch, and English from the British

Isles. There was a couple who arrived in town about the same time as we did. It was Prince Peter of Greece and his Russian princess wife, whose name I cannot recall, because we only met her once. They lived outside of town in a villa and were the owners of the only private automobile in Kalimpong. They also had a large motor home which had to be parked somewhere down the hill in Siliguri because it was too big to be driven up the steep curving mountain roads. *(See page 293 for more information on Prince Peter.)* There also seemed to be a few French priests and nuns. The rest of the people were Tibetans, Indians, Nepalese, Bhutanese, and quite a few Chinese families. The town had one long main street with a short section as its downtown area. There was even a Chinese restaurant. In front of it, you could catch the buses for either Siliguri or Darjeeling.

Wang, our new helper, was very smart and capable. Soon, he led me to the town's market on its twice-a-week marketing days. Whatever fresh produce one needs could only be purchased on those days. So, each shopping trip, we had to get enough food to last for three or four days. I only visited the market a few times, then stopped going, because I could not conduct any purchases in the local languages. Besides, I just could not lug all the grocery supplies and walk over a mile home. I really appreciated Wang, for he was not only our shopper and our cook, he also cleaned our house and washed our laundry. Sometimes, he also took care of our special errands as well. I knew he was also fond of us, because we had always treated him as one of our family members.

It did not take too long for me to shed the anxious feeling which had accumulated from the past ten long years, caused by the wars and the political uncertainty in China. Kalimpong was such a quiet, bucolic place. The house we rented was roomy and comfortable. Every day, I could look at the shining white remote peaks of the Himalaya mountain range, under the clear blue sky, breathing unpolluted fresh air. The climate was like constant spring. Our "mali" kept the garden neatly trimmed and took care of the colorful flowers. I felt truly secure and content. As for my husband, he began to make inquiries and started to visit the local Chinese merchants. Almost all of them were involved in trading with the Tibetans. He also talked to some of the Tibetans, many of whom were traveling on foot from Tibet through Kalimpong on their way to Calcutta. We found out that the Tibetan high officials and their families did not live in Kalimpong for any long periods, even though some of them owned  properties locally. Gradually, we made more new friends and my husband was able to compile lots of materials for his report to be sent to America. They contained information about the trade for tea, silk, and especially had detailed reports about the kinds and grades of wool and their available amount, both for carpets and for knitting or weaving. Days just sailed by smoothly as if we were living in Shangri-La.

For a few years, I would occasionally have a dull pain in my right side where my appendix was located. But then, the pain became more frequent and stronger. My husband thought I should be checked by a good doctor, so we left Wang to look after the house and went down to Calcutta. A famous Irish doctor decided that I should have an operation before the appendix became seriously infected. So I underwent the operation. For the few days I stayed in the hospital, my husband stayed at C.P.'s house. Later, I joined him after I left the hospital.

Soon, I was able to return back to Kalimpong. In those days, it seemed that both the doctors and the patients believed in longer rest and recuperation periods for any kind of sickness. So I actually felt that I should be pampered for a while, and did not feel guilty about it. Meanwhile, some of our newly acquainted friends came to visit us. Many started to invite us to dinner at their houses.

Our social gatherings seemed to be ruled by the old Chinese social custom that men and women guests were not invited on the same day. At least in Kalimpong, usually between the Chinese families, the husbands would be invited the first day, and their wives would be invited the following day. It might have been that most of the dining areas were small, and in order not to offend any couple, they held their social gatherings the Chinese way, with men and women on separate days. The cooking was always prepared by the host's wife. Yet, for some reason, maybe because I was a newlywed and was always seen with my husband, somehow, I was mostly invited with my husband to be included in both evenings.

As time went on, our social circle grew larger. My husband also learned that we could join the local tennis club. He had played the game before, and was quite good at it. But it was my very first try. It happened that many of the Europeans were all members. There was no formal "club" to belong to. The so-called tennis court was a very rudimentary flat surface covered with tarmac, situated in front of a small building which housed the Kalimpong Public Library. I did not see anyone use the library, except a mali who was always using it to prepare the afternoon tea for the players. The court was below the main street about a half a mile away from our house. It was there that we began to meet the Europeans and some members from the Bhutan House. They were the nobles from Bhutan. Prince Peter of Greece also came often. As for my playing, at the beginning, I had to admire the male players for their patience and their gentlemanly courtesy towards my poor playing, for whenever I missed a ball, which was very frequent, they would apologize, or they would say, "Hard luck!" instead of complaining.

Occasionally, we would have some small gatherings. Once, I recall, the two ladies from the Bhutan House invited a few of us for a picnic in their garden on a traditional Tibetan Spring Festival day. When we arrived, we saw beautiful large Tibetan carpets were spread under the tall trees. All sorts of delicious foods were already displayed on them, so we all sat down on the carpets and enjoyed ourselves. The hosts were the grown children of the owner, who were in Bhutan at the time. The second daughter was a couple of years younger than me. She had just returned from a school in England and was soon to be married to a prince in Bhutan. We admired each other's dresses. Mine was Chinese, and hers was exactly like the Tibetans, which was very colorful. She suggested that just for fun, we should exchange our dresses. She took me into their house, and went into her bathroom and we changed. When we came out, they also suggested that my husband should try Bhutanese attire. Their men's outer robe was very similar to the Tibetans, except theirs were mostly made with vertical striped patterns. Since my husband did

not wear tall boots, his legs were bare, but Prince Peter took some pictures of us. Alas, now I only have one left with me, and unfortunately, the color has also faded.

We also became friends with the elder sister of the Dalai Lama and her husband. I still have a small carpet from her which was a gift. We also knew one of the Dalai Lama's younger brothers back in China because he had studied there.

Among the Chinese friends, there was a Mr. Shen, who was the principal of an overseas Chinese elementary school sponsored by the Chinese Nationalist Government, the Overseas Chinese Elementary School of Kalimpong. Because of Kalimpong's location and the higher elevation, it was cooler than the other cities, so some Chinese families would send their children to board in this school, until they were ready for high school. Naturally, the local Chinese families also had their children study there. Soon after my recovery from the appendix operation, Mr. Shen came to ask for my help. He said he had just lost a first and second grade teacher due to pregnancy. He heard I was a college graduate and was not occupied at the time, so he had come to ask me to replace the teacher who had resigned. Somehow, I did not need too much persuasion, and courageously I just accepted the position. I remember the salary offer was 180 rupees per month. Compared to the average Indian salaries, it was very decent pay. Besides, I could also have two months' summer vacation and a one month winter holiday. How could I know that this salary would be our only income for almost two years? So I became Teacher Yu. When the school started in September, other than the regular classes, I also found out I had to teach the little kids to sing and dance as well.

The children were lovable and happy. I also had a Tibetan child in the class. Occasionally the children would tease each other, and then I had to settle their little disputes. They did all seem to like me; even the higher grade students liked to chat with me. Every time, whenever there was a holiday or a special Chinese festival, many parents would send their children to my house, delivering many homemade specialties, which were always great treats for my husband and me. During the winter break, usually we would go down the mountain to Calcutta, or do a little traveling, as that was the most comfortable season of the year.

Summer vacation time, although long, was just too hot, or the monsoon season would be occurring. With the highest precipitation in the world from May to early September, the powerful downpours just kept us staying inside the house most of the time. I did not mind the rainy season too much except for our laundry. There were no washing machines or dryers. All the large pieces of sheets and towels would have to be sent out. But when the local laundry delivered them back, the pieces were all still damp. Worst of all, they would all be permeated with curry flavor.

About half of a year after we had lived in our colonial-styled bungalow in Kalimpong, the Communist Chinese were advancing into Tibet. *(The Chinese invasion culminated in the Battle of*

Chamdo in October of 1950, leading to the "peaceful liberation" of Tibet by the Communist Chinese.) Then the usual Tibetan travelers began to dwindle. The local Chinese merchants all became very worried about their future trade with the Tibetans. Garma, my husband, knew that it would not be fair to his firm in New York to continue his assignment, since the trade situation had changed so hopelessly. With difficulty, we made our big decision, and he sent in his resignation.

Suddenly, my salary became the sole income for us. We definitely had to downsize our lifestyle. Quickly, we moved to a second floor flat on the main street, with the kitchen and Wang's room downstairs. It belonged to a Tibetan widow. While our bedroom and the living room were both fairly roomy, it had a very small study. Of course, there was no need to keep our mali anymore. Soon, we resumed our life routine. I went to school every day, returned home after classes, immediately walked to play tennis with my husband, then walked back to have our dinner. Then we would take a stroll down the hill to appreciate the scenery. We both definitely stayed very healthy.

While we were living in India, Prime Minister Nehru invited a very famous Chinese painter to visit India. Chang Dai-Chien *(or Chang Dai Ch'ien or Zhang Daqian)* was one of the most famous artists of China and the world. Since he was a good friend of my father, my husband and I paid him a visit in Darjeeling.

He decided to paint two paintings for us. Since he knew that my husband was a devout Buddhist as was he, he painted a portrait of a Bodhisattva in the Dun Huang cave-painting style and dedicated it to my husband. He also painted a picture of a woman from the rear, accompanied by a stand of bamboo. He knew that my father had always admired his paintings of bamboo, so he chose the bamboo as an element in his painting for me.

I remember that he had a white monkey that somehow got loose on the train from Darjeeling to Calcutta.

Chang Dai-Chien did not stay in India, but lived around the world. See page 294 for more details on this world-famous artist and accomplished art forger!

In that same year, 1950, because my husband was no longer employed by anyone, he thought we would go to Calcutta to see C.P. for some advice. He told me he would probably be there for a longer period this time. About three weeks or so after he went down, one weekend morning, I was awakened by a strong rocking. While still in bed, I saw the ceiling light was swaying wildly, and then I heard my landlady knocking on my door, shouting something in Tibetan. I hurriedly got up and went downstairs. My landlady pulled me outside into the courtyard. Then, Wang came to me and told me it was an earthquake. It lasted for a little while longer, and then stopped. But no one dared to go back to the house. Soon, Prince Peter came in to check on me, because he knew my husband was away. He told me he came into town in his Jeep. Somewhere on his way, he saw some farmers standing behind a cow and shouting. The cow was straddling a deep crack freshly created by the quake. He tried to help the farmers to get the cow either to cross over or to back over the crack, but to no avail. He gave up and proceeded on his way to check on me.

It was not until the next day and the days following that bits of news slowly reached us in town. We learned that it was the most severe earthquake in sixty years in India in the Assam area. All the electric wires were down, felled by the downed posts. Railway rails were hanging on treetops, washed up by mountain floods. There would not be mail, telephone, telegram, or bus traffic for at least six months. Normally, things like flour, sugar, and certain other rations were transported by the daily bus trips. Now, all these supplies had to be carried up to our town on bearers' backs, bag by bag, step by step. Luckily, Kalimpong did not have any injured people or too much serious damage, but we were completely shut off from the outside world.

Later, quite some long time afterwards, out of necessity, people started to walk down to Siliguri. Their steps had created a narrow path. The buses were still idled. Then the telegrams began to come through. One day, I received my husband's telegram, asking me to send Wang to meet him at the Siliguri train station. Because he had done some purchasing, he needed help to bring things back home. So I gave Wang some money and sent him down. But two days later, I received another telegram, in which Garma said he was not going to wait for Wang, but was coming home by himself. I was at a loss. I thought by that time, Wang must have met him already, but evidently, something must have gone wrong. So I had no choice, but to get to Siliguri myself.

Quickly, I got ready and went to the spot where travelers usually could find company to walk down the mountain. There, I met two Irish nuns who had just climbed up, and one was trying to sell her tall rubber boots, which she wore to climb up through the underbrush. I bought them, even though they were a bit too large for me, because I had heard stories about the tall grass and the leeches along the way. Then, I joined some people and began my downward journey.

When we reached the Siliguri station, it was almost completely dark. I found the station director. He said that the Calcutta train had already arrived a while ago. I searched around, but there was no trace of my husband. I had no place to spend the night, so I walked into the women's waiting room. It was clean and vacant. Without supper, but dead tired, and worried, I fell asleep on the benches. Now, when I recall it, life must have been very safe then. Just think now, to spend a night in a train station waiting room in a strange town, all alone! Danger? The thought did not even enter my mind!

The next morning, I was just concerned about what my next step should be. Should I keep waiting or go back? Then, I was surprised to hear my husband calling me outside the waiting room door. I rushed out, and there he was! He asked why I was there. I asked him how he knew I was in the waiting room. He said some of the Indian bearers saw that he was looking for someone. They signaled him and said, "Cheena mumsai, Cheena mumsai," while pointing at the waiting room, so he figured it could be me. However, he actually was looking for Wang. Then I knew Wang must have gone on to Calcutta to meet my husband, thinking that Garma must be waiting at C.P.'s house.

I didn't even have a chance to wash before we went to find some food. While we were eating, my husband told me that he also arrived at Siliguri the previous night. He thought since he did not see Wang, he would stay overnight to get some rest, and leave for Kalimpong in the morning. There was a long section, longer than ten miles, on the way from Calcutta to Siliguri, where the rails were damaged, so all the passengers all had to come down and walk for that distance. He was pleased he could get a bearer to carry his luggage, otherwise, under the strong sun, with no shade, he didn't think he could have made it.

Our homeward trek started as soon as we finished our meal and found a bearer to carry our things. Some fellow traveler had told me that the road I covered yesterday was approximately eighteen miles. I shuddered when I heard it. That meant, today we would have to climb upward for eighteen miles. I had never walked that much in any one day. It was also a good thing I did happen to buy those rubber boots from the nuns. The path we walked was indeed full of tall grass and leeches. We followed a group of Kalimpong-bound people. Slowly, we walked and walked up the steep mountain path. We both were so tired that neither of us was in the mood to talk. Finally, we arrived home. Right after we paid the bearer, both of us dropped down onto our bed. When we woke up, it was almost dark. Since Wang was not home, no one was there to cook. We really did not have any energy left to start a fire and cook something from scratch. The only way to get food was to go to the Chinese restaurant before they closed. That meant another walk of three miles round trip. Since we did not have any lunch during the day, no matter how tired and exhausted we were, we pushed ourselves and made the trip. When we eventually dragged ourselves home again, both of us were almost dead with exhaustion.

According to the U. S. Geological Survey, on August 15, 1950, the Assam-Tibet earthquake registered 8.6 or 8.7 on the Richter scale. Between fifteen hundred and three thousand people were killed. It was the tenth largest earthquake in the twentieth century.

Before the fall of 1950, a couple, Mr. Hsueh *(Xue)* and his wife, who used to be a teacher, came up from our embassy at New Delhi. They brought us the news that the ambassador, my Uncle Loh, had closed the embassy and was about to leave India. They came up to Kalimpong because Mrs. Hsueh had applied to teach the third and fourth grades. We remembered them from our previous visit at the embassy. Therefore, I had a new colleague. They also brought their two teenaged girls. Shortly after school started the fall semester, we learned that the Indian government had officially acknowledged the Communist government of China. The Hsuehs were very excited. They wanted to change the Nationalist flag for a Communist one, but no one knew exactly what the flag looked like. But the Hsuehs did some research, and made one by themselves for our school. Our principal, Mr. Shen, was not that anxious to make the change.

The political climate was looking darker for us. The Indian government had recognized the Communist government of the PRC *(People's Republic of China)*. Our uncle Loh had closed the Nationalist embassy shortly after we visited him, and had already left for Taiwan. Both my husband's and my family were connected with the Nationalist government. We were also holding Nationalist government issued passports. My husband and I began to feel the need to rethink our residential status. We debated what to do.

Having learned that my in-laws retired soon after they arrived in Taiwan, we knew the traditional Chinese responsibility of sons supporting the family was on our shoulders. Since Taiwan in the early 50s was full of unemployed people, we could not go there to make a living, while also trying to support my in-laws.

At about that time, we began receiving several letters from my father-in-law, asking for our financial support. He wanted to invest in a Thermos factory in Taiwan. He knew my husband had saved some money from doing trade when he was in Eastern Tibet. He needed at least three thousand dollars. My brother-in-law Louie in New York also was asked to send money. Louie had been writing letters discussing the issue of long-term financial support for their parents. He knew that in India, we could not earn enough money to help the family in Taiwan, so he urged us to go to the US to make a living and start a new life. Right after my husband sent the three thousand dollars to his father, we began seriously to consider our next move.

In the end, we decided to give it a try in America, knowing wholeheartedly that it would not be an easy goal to achieve, because American visas were extremely hard to get for Chinese applicants.

Yet, we had to try.

We talked to C.P. first, to see if there was any way we could make a decent living if we continued to stay in India. His answer was very negative. We then wrote a letter back to China to my husband's good friend, who had returned to China from Purdue in 1948, because his wife was there. We asked if we should return to China to offer our service, but he wrote back and said that we could serve our country by just staying abroad. Then I asked my father about the situation in Taiwan. He also encouraged us to go to the US "to further improve ourselves." We understood what they were telling us, and we made up our minds. Soon, I apologized to our principal, Mr. Shen, and let him know that I would resign my position at the end of the fall semester.

Once we had decided, we proceeded to gather all the needed documents for our application to the US. I also had to tell Wang, our faithful cook, that he should be prepared to go back to his old boss. But he said no, because he now had a wife, so he would try to find some other work to be on his own. In fact, his wife, Nima, had been living with Wang in his room, with our permission, for quite some time by then. So Wang said they would stay on until the time we left.

When all the needed papers and photos were all gathered up, my husband and I went down to Calcutta and handed everything with our visa application forms to the US Consulate. The people there were very pleasant to us, but they said that in order to prove that we would not stay in the US for the long term, we must have the certificates of "No Objection to Return to India" signed by the Indian government. We should be able to get the certificates from the Indian Police Office. We were surprised by the request, but we clearly knew we must acquire them. Without delay, we went to the police headquarters and applied. They told us to go back, and when they were ready, they would send them to us by mail.

We went back to Kalimpong. I still went to school every day while we waited. We waited until school was over, and we waited some more. There was just no news. So instead of sitting and waiting, we began to sort our things for the trip, as if we knew we could definitely go.

We only lived in Kalimpong for two short years, yet we still accumulated a great deal of things. It took us a good deal of time to sort out what things were to be taken with us. We gave Wang and his wife all the things they could use, discarded the unwanted, and held a sale of all our "imported" things, like our radios, phonograph machines, cameras, and all the other fancy gadgets. The people who came to the sale mostly were more well-to-do

Tibetans. When at last, all the saleable items were all gone, a Tibetan lady looked around, and then she saw the watch I was wearing. She pointed at it and wanted to buy it.

Well, the sale was over. We had no more things to take care of, but we were ready to leave. However, we still had not received anything from the Indian Police Office. So we just had to be patient and wait.

In front of a friend's pavilion for playing mah jongg

Some time previously, my husband and I visited my "Uncle Loh" who was one of my father's old friends. Addressing one's parents' good friends as "Uncle" or "Auntie" is a Chinese tradition. At that time, Uncle Loh was the Ambassador of the Republic of China to India. We stayed with him as his guests at the Chinese Embassy in New Delhi, India. Uncle Loh was well known for his literary talents among the Chinese scholars. One of his poems was made into a beautiful song, and it was taught in many Chinese schools to nearly all of the students. I also learned to sing it and rather liked it.

We stayed about a week. One day, Uncle Loh told me that he was inviting just a couple of guests and wanted us to be at the dinner. He wanted to be sure that we would be available for dinner that next evening.

The next day, dinnertime arrived. We were surprised to find out the only guest he invited was the Prime Minister of India, Mr. Jawaharlal Nehru. As New Delhi was always hot and humid, and there was not any air conditioning, after dinner, we all went out and had our coffee on the terrace. Later, the conversation somehow turned to poetry, and then I was startled to hear Uncle Loh asking me to sing for Mr. Nehru. He asked me to sing the song that he had written. I could sing, but I did not have any formal training. However, there was no retreating. I vaguely remembered standing up and finishing the request. How the rest of the evening ended left no trace in my mind.

Meanwhile, we were now waiting for our visas. We had my brother-in-law's financial guarantees for our stay in the US. My husband still had some savings he had invested in the US during his first visit. We also had legal passports that the US recognized. In addition, my husband did study at Purdue University before and both our families were anti-Communist. However, the American consul repeatedly told us, "You need a document from the Indian government stating that they have 'No Objection to Return' to India."

We had lived in India for a little over two years. We entered India as visitors, but once a year, we could apply for extensions. Now, since the Indian government had ceased relations with the Nationalist government, and had recognized the Communist government of the PRC, our Nationalist passports were useless in India. Unless we changed our passports to the new Chinese Communist passports, once we left, we could not return. But if we changed to the Communist passports, we would not be able to travel to the US. Yet the American consul insisted we had to secure this "No Objection to Return," even though our passports were no longer valid.

One month, two months, three months went by. There was no response to our applications. We became very anxious. To complicate matters, I was pregnant. If it became too apparent, I might not be able to enter the US. So time was running out. One day, a young Chinese friend who came out from Tibet who was studying in Santiniketin came to see us. We told him about our predicament. I also happened to mention our earlier travels and that I had sung for the Prime Minister, Mr. Nehru, in New Delhi. Our friend said all of a sudden, "Why don't you write to Mr. Nehru and ask for help?"

That suggestion excited all of us. So the three of us worked together the next day and finished a letter to Mr. Nehru, stating that I had met him at Uncle Loh's dinner and now my husband and I were applying for visas to go to the US. For that, we needed to obtain a "No Objection to Return to India." But since we had been waiting for a long time, and still hadn't heard any answers, could he be so kind as to look into this matter and facilitate it for us.

The letter was mailed with all our blessings. Soon after, we heard from the Police Office, and exactly two weeks later, my husband and I went down from Kalimpong and went directly to the US consulate in Calcutta. The very next day, we were granted the visas.

From then on, every time when I talk about how I came to the US, I always say, "Thanks to Uncle Nehru and the No Objection to Return to India."

I remember some things about living on Staten Island, New York. I must have been around seven or eight years old. Sometimes, while listening to the radio, the announcer would mention Prime Minister Nehru. My parents might comment about "Uncle Nehru" during those moments. My childhood mind did not understand why this mysterious man on the news was related to me. Of course, I knew that many of my parents' friends and acquaintances were "Uncle" and "Auntie" to me, but still, I had met them and knew how they were connected to my family. As it was, this was just another of those mysteries that I knew I should keep to myself. It was not something that I would mention to my friends at school. I knew it was too far-fetched and that I would not be believed. It was not until later when I heard this story that I understood how critical "Uncle Nehru" had been in the story of my family.

FORM OF AFFIDAVIT TO BE USED IN LIEU OF A PASSPORT

I, CHANG CHEN CHI whose occupation or profession is that of MERCHANT residing at Calcutta c/o. Pao Yuen Tung Company, P33 Mission Row Extension, West Bengal, India being first duly sworn, depose and say:

1. I was born at Canton, China on the 28th August 1920 I have lost my nationality of origin owing to fall of Nationalist Government of China.

2. I am unable to obtain a national passport or any form of travel document from the Government of the country in which I now reside.

3. I attach hereto my photograph and personal description as evidence of my identity.

4. I am urgently desirous of travelling to U.S.A. via Hongkong for business purposes.

5. I wish to leave as soon as possible I intend to return to India after a stay abroad of not more than six months' duration.

(Signature of Applicant)

Subscribed and sworn to before me this 7th day of December 1950.

Notary Public. Calcutta

DESCRIPTION.

Height 5 ft. 9 in.
Colour of eyes - Brown
Colour of hair - Dark
Special peculiarities - nil

I hereby certify that the above are the true and proper photograph and personal description of CHANG CHEN CHI the deponent of the affidavit hereto annexed.

Notary Public. Calcutta

CANCELLED
N.

Between the end of 1950 and the early months of 1951, India had an outburst of smallpox cases. During that time, my husband and I were waiting in Calcutta for our ship to come to the US. The Indian health workers were stopping people and vaccinating passersby right in the streets. Against my protests and explanations, one day I was still given a second dose of vaccine.

On February 28, we boarded a returning American ship, the Alcoa Puritan. It was a freighter chartered by the famous aluminum company, Alcoa. On the very next day, March the first, we started our trip.

My husband and I were the only two passengers on the ship. The other passengers were some six hundred Indian monkeys in large steel cages stacked on the deck at the back of the ship. They were test monkeys to be delivered to a medical lab in Boston.

The stifling air over the Indian Ocean felt better after the ship started moving. On the fourth day, we arrived at Sri Lanka (it was called Ceylon then). The ship was to be there for four days for cargo loading. We were looking forward to getting off the ship to visit the many famous Buddhist holy sites, but we soon learned that we were under a quarantine order and not permitted to leave the ship, because one member of the crew was sick and had to be taken to a local hospital. He was suspected to have caught the disease of smallpox. Later we found out it was not true, but he was to remain there at Colombo for the next US-bound ship to take him home when he was well.

For four days, we could only look at the beautiful green water at the harbor from the deck, and again to put up with the humid and hot sultry air of the Indian Ocean. Sometimes we would walk to the back of the boat to watch the monkeys. The poor animals were crowded in their cages, baking under the tropical sun during the day and were covered by a layer of tarpaulins at night. We both deeply felt the misery they had to be suffering.

Finally, the ship's engine started again. For the whole trip, we ate with the officers. I was introduced to the grapefruit they served at breakfast, and grew to like it. After dinner, they also taught us how to play the card game Canasta. I forgot how long it was after we left Colombo, Sri Lanka, when we stopped at another port. We went out onto the deck and saw a great many small local sailboats, all surrounding us in the water. People in the boats all had things in their hands, eagerly trying to sell to the people on the ship. One of the officers from the ship pointed at a faraway spot on land, and said to me, "You might be able to see the Pyramids over in that direction." Then I found out that we had arrived at Port Said, Egypt. I did buy a small pair of carved black elmwood elephants. Unfortunately, there is only one left with me now.

After Port Said, the weather began to get even hotter, but drier, as we approached the Red Sea. One thing distinctively left a strong impression in my memory. That was whenever the wind blew the wrong way, the unbearable stench of monkey air would suffocate me. Often it made me feel as if I was locked up in a monkey cell of a zoo in winter.

Sailing through the Red Sea was extremely hot. There was not much to see along the way, so most of the time, we just stayed in our room.

As soon as we reached the Suez Canal, the captain quickly processed the required paperwork with the British authorities. We entered the canal. I vaguely remembered a movie about the Suez Canal I saw a few years ago. I could hardly believe that I was actually going through this monumental masterpiece. I could not help but marvel at the hardships and the difficulties the working team must have endured and conquered through the entire task. It truly was a great achievement.

(For those readers familiar with the geography of the area, you will note that coming from Asia, the Red Sea comes first, then the Suez Canal and last, Port Said and the Pyramids. A minor detail.)

It was March. The temperature was still unbearably hot. However, the scenery of the canal area was very peaceful and pretty. There were trees and neatly trimmed lawns along the banks. It was a very pleasant experience to sail through such a well-cared for area, especially right after the arid banks of the Red Sea.

The Mediterranean Sea slid by without leaving much impression on my mind. I can only recall when we were passing the Straits of Gibraltar. My husband excitedly explained to me how important the Rock of Gibraltar was to the Allies during the Second World War.

The weather changed dramatically shortly after we got onto the Atlantic Ocean. Suddenly the air became so cold and the wind often was so strong that no one could enjoy staying on the deck anymore. Frequently we would also have high waves mixed with freezing rain which made the dinner tables into "rock and roll" stages. Lucky for us, both my husband and I were not susceptible to seasickness. But we did have to restrain our activities.

One morning, I saw several crew members standing around the monkey cages for a long time. I could not make out what they were doing there, as I did not want to venture out into the severe cold and drizzling rain. Soon, at lunch time, someone informed us that a mother monkey had given birth to a dead baby. She clutched it tightly close to her bosom and refused to let the baby be taken away from her. She held it in her arms for almost a week. In the end, she was tricked into giving it up that day. Everyone felt sad for the mother monkey and yet it was not the only sad case that happened to those poor monkeys. By the end of our trip, a few more monkeys had also died en route simply due to the fact that they were all confined in overcrowded cages and were constantly exposed to the inclement weather of the Atlantic Ocean for almost a month without proper protective shelter.

The remainder of the crossing journey slowly became more monotonous. The ship kept on heading toward our destination – New York. Between days with white heavy rocking waves or occasionally smooth sailing, the water appeared threatening most of the time. At eye level, there was no boundary between the sea and the sky. Looking down, the dark water was unfathomably black. Only two or three times, we crossed paths with other ships. When we stood on the deck sometimes, I felt hopelessly lonely and lost. Then at night, the dark starless night and the pitch black bottomless water was frightening to me, but when it was a moonlit night, the stars were scattered bright above, and they gently blinked and rocked with the ship's sway. Then the nights would transform into enchanted charming worlds, even with the cold in the air.

Thus, the days passed quietly until we arrived at Boston. The captain told us that just about everyone would be busy with the unloading. There were the monkeys to off-load. My husband and I could get off the ship to tour the city until late that evening, so we took his advice and became a pair of tourists and enjoyed half of a day in town. At first, we could not even walk steadily. We felt we were still on the ship. It took us a while until we got used to the feel of solid land under our feet again.

The next morning, we sailed toward New York City. It has been so long, I do not recall how long this last part of the journey was. I just remember that about noontime, we were urged to go to the front of the ship because soon the Statue of Liberty would be in sight.

"Statue of Liberty" did not mean much to me. All I knew about the statue was what the Chinese called her, which meant "The Goddess of Freedom." I did know that she was a gift from the French people, but I did not know anything about her true significance or the history behind her. I just stood there at the tip of the ship and admired the beautiful patina of the tall lady standing alone on a small island with a torch raised above her head. Learning to respect what she represents and deeply loving her would come many years later.

Then finally, everything came to a full stop. We knew we were about to start our new life in a new land.

It was March 28, 1951.

Alcoa Puritan, built in 1943

Ellis Island

When the crew helped us to unload our luggage on the pier, my brother-in-law Louie was there waiting for us, but we had to go through both the Immigration office and Customs before we could leave. We never expected that just a few days before we arrived, a new rule had been passed, for all Chinese passengers. It was due to a certain American immigration officer at the Hong Kong consulate. He was caught issuing visas illegally in return for accepting bribes. So now, all Chinese visitors would have to deposit $5,000 in bonds per person to guarantee that they would not become illegal immigrants.

$5,000 in 1951 was more than a year's salary. The average salary was around $3,500 at that time!

This new requirement surprised all of us. It was Friday afternoon. Fortunately, my brother-in-law worked on Wall Street. Hurriedly, he rushed to his office to arrange the bonds. Meanwhile, we were ushered into a bus which took us on to a ferry. Then we were taken to an island. The only thing I can remember from that trip was that we went into a big hall. The hall was divided into two parts. On the metal divider, there was a plaque, saying something like "Guest Room" or "Guest Waiting Room." An officer led us into the room, locked the door and left, leaving us there to wait.

There were all sorts of people there. Some looked very solemn, some were obviously very excited, especially a group of about five or six young Chinese teenagers. From their conversation which I overheard, I knew they were new arrivals from Hong Kong and were waiting for their fathers, but none of them could speak English.

Roughly about five o'clock or so, Louie came back and told us everything was settled, and we could now go home with him. Many of the other people were not so lucky and had to stay overnight, or possibly longer.

Only later, through the years, from reading and from watching movies and TV, I gradually learned about the historical background and the relationships between Ellis Island and the immigrants in the development of the US.

Sometimes, I try to recall that event. I almost always feel regretful that I did not pay much attention to the whole experience. I think it must be because at that time we were very anxious to know if everything could be settled in time for us to leave the "Guest Waiting Room." It was not the arrival that I had pictured. However, it was an experience that I would not forget or trade. After all, it was the first step of my becoming a first-generation immigrant.

See page 313 for a history of Chinese immigration over the years.

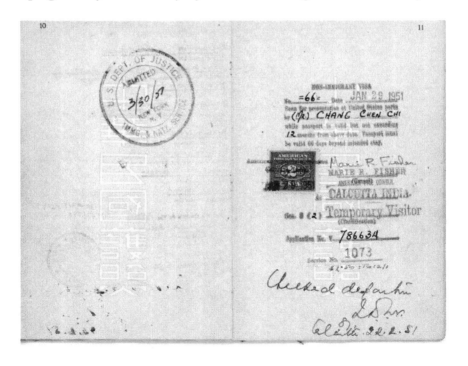

After two to three hours of driving, our car finally stopped. It was already very dark outside. Louie led us into a nice medium-sized house. His wife Jean and their daughter, Leatrice, were waiting for us. The last time I had seen Jean was in 1948 when she went back to China to visit our in-laws. We soon sat down and had the dinner she prepared for us. When the dinner was over, they took our luggage to the guest room in the attic; and that was to be our living quarters during our stay.

For the next couple of days, my husband and I did not do anything but rest. Because it was a weekend, Louie could stay home and be with us. Our conversations were mostly about the situation in mainland China and Taiwan, and how the brothers were going to share the responsibilities of supporting their parents' household expenses in Taiwan.

Louie also showed us the house and its surroundings. They bought the house, 14 Fiddler Lane, in Levittown, Long Island, in 1950 with $8,000. It sat on a corner lot with two bedrooms but no garage. It was one of the thousands built by a Mr. Levitt shortly after WWII, mostly for the returning veterans. Levittown was supposed to be a self-contained residential development with its own churches, library, school, fire department, hospital and parks. It was a very desirable housing area, except it was too far from the city and one needed to have a car in order to get around.

We did not have much money, just like most of the new immigrants. We urgently needed some income. Though my husband still had about $20,000 in a bank account from his trading activities in Tibet, without a job, it would not last long. On top of that, I was pregnant. Of course, there would be the inevitable medical expenses to be considered too. Unfortunately, both of us held visitor's visas. That meant we were not supposed to work. Yet, we could not stay with my brother-in-law forever, so we decided my husband must first buy a car and then immediately look for a job, any job.

Louie had just bought a new car. He kept his two-year-old car, a Chevy sedan, purposely for us. My husband talked to him and settled for a delayed payment. Thus he became an "illegal immigrant worker." While he was gone during the day looking for work, Jean was very kind to me. She  taught me how to become an "American housewife" because she knew I was exactly like her. We grew up with servants and maids. Now suddenly, we were faced with all household chores: the cooking, washing, cleaning, and shopping. Life certainly would be overwhelming. She also took me to find a doctor, then accompanied me to get some maternity clothing. I truly was very grateful to her.

Two weeks or so passed. One day, Louie told us that he had been negotiating with a grocery store in Miami, Florida. Now he had reached a deal, so my husband should go down first to accept the store and Louie would join him shortly. I did not participate in the decision-making. When informed by my husband, I just packed, loaded everything into our car, and started our journey to the south.

To me, the trip going down to the south was interesting and exciting. My doctor did tell me that I should get out of the car and walk a while, every now and then. Since we followed his instructions and also because I did not know how to drive, it took us a little longer than usual for our journey.

When we went through the Carolinas, the dense dark green pine trees in those states looked so beautiful to me. I was beginning to have a little problem understanding the local accents. Whenever we stopped for gas, I would see six or seven "Negros" who would come to clean our car and attend to us. Their speech was like a different language which I could not decipher. Especially in Georgia, be it a white or black speaker, I found I was always at a loss when following a conversation, even though it seemed I had no problem making myself understood by others.

It was May when we arrived in Miami. As soon as we settled in a hotel, we contacted my brother-in-law Louie's friend. He came over to greet us with Louie's telegraph addressed to us. It simply said, "Change of plan. Store contract cancelled."

Those few printed words in the telegraph suddenly made us feel like a kite being cut off from the string. We did not have a home, a job, nor any destination. We were confused and completely at a loss. My husband became fairly indignant about the whole situation. After we thought it over and over again, we decided not to return to New York, but to go to El Paso, Texas to visit his sister, Yvonne.

Yvonne had been my classmate and roommate through my high school and college years and had introduced me to my husband. She was studying in El Paso with my husband's financial help during her last year there. She later married an American-born Chinese fellow student, and she was very pleased to see us.

The weather was already very hot in the south, though it was only in May. We kept on driving west without any air conditioning in the car. Fortunately, along the way, we could buy watermelons to quench our thirst and heat. Sometimes, during a whole day, we would not encounter any other traveling cars. Finally, we reached Yvonne's house. I was deeply impressed by the vastness of the country, in spite of the fact that I had come from China and India, both of which are also large countries.

Naturally, during our visit, her husband George joined us, and we often discussed what we could do to make a living. I think, partly because El Paso was such a dry desert area, and also because it was a small border town at that time, chances were not too good for us to find a decent future there. So, with my physical condition beginning to change more quickly, we bid Yvonne and George goodbye and reluctantly started our journey back to New York.

Levittown in the 1950s, the forerunner of suburban sprawl in America

We drove back to Louie's house on Long Island. The very next morning, my husband went to the city to look for a place for us. In the afternoon, he came back and picked me up and took me to the first residence of our own in the US. It was a furnished one-room apartment, sharing a kitchen with two other families. Rent was paid by the week. It was conveniently located at 110th and Broadway. I remember we had to purchase all the basic kitchen utensils from scratch. We also had to buy baby things, and especially a carriage to use as the crib.

Every day, my husband searched high and low in the paper, trying to find some work. He worked as a busboy in a Chinese restaurant, sold Howdy Doody ice cream from a pushcart in the street, and also did some odd jobs. Finally, one day, his application was accepted by the Voice of America as an announcer for their Asian program. Meanwhile, we also found another apartment further uptown, but we had to wait before we could move in.

On the weekend before my baby was due, he drove me back to Long Island to stay with Jean, because my doctor and hospital were all there, and then he went back to the city for his new job. Two days later, on September 10, my daughter Eva was born in Nassau County Hospital, in Mineola, Long Island. She was a healthy 7 lb, 14 oz. baby, but I had a fever for a few days afterwards. I remember one morning there was quite a commotion in the hallway. Soon, the nurse and a few people all crowded into my room. She held my daughter high and showed her to the others. Everyone admired my daughter, and then I could see that the nurse had combed my daughter's black hair and tied a pink bow to it. When all the excitement receded, I learned that Eva was the very first Chinese baby born in that hospital. Furthermore, she was the first baby born with a full head of long black hair.

In those few days that I remained in the hospital, I was asked all sorts of questions about the baby, concerning the changing of the color of eyes, the hair, etc., which were all strange questions to me, because the Chinese never expect the baby's eyes to change into blue or green, or the hair to become wavy or straight, or to turn dark brown or blond. We  always have eyes that are brown, and hair that is black and straight.

One week later, my fever was gone, we took the baby home to the city, and started our life as a pair of new parents.

When Eva was about one month old, the apartment we were waiting for became available. This apartment was located at 135th St. and Riverside Drive. It was a one bedroom, one bath small apartment with a shallow kitchen which barely fitted in the original coat closet. We could only see the sun when it was reflected into our room from the opposite building's window in the afternoon.

We bought the furniture from the previous tenant – that consisted of two studio couches and a small dinette set. We put the baby in the small bedroom in the back, and we slept on the couches in the living room. It was small, but it was our home. And, the rent was affordable.

I don't remember how the elderly Mrs. Gordon became my husband's student. She studied Tibetan with him. She was a volunteer at the Metropolitan Museum, in charge of the Tibetan collections. One day, my husband informed me that he had invited Mrs. Gordon and her husband for dinner. It was the first time since our marriage that I had to prepare a full dinner without a cook. Also, it was in such a small kitchen and dining space.

Somehow, I managed to accomplish the mission. Both our guests were very gracious and kind. They even bravely enjoyed my cooking. Much later, I happened to learn that Mr. Gordon was a rather active realtor in New York, and they were millionaires. However, the friendship between us lasted for many years until they passed away.

My father later introduced Uncle Louie to Mr. Gordon, which is how my uncle got started in the construction business. He ran this business successfully until he passed away at a relatively young age.

Soon afterwards, my husband was transferred to San Francisco to work for Radio Free Asia. He had to report there in short order. This endeavor was rumored to be sponsored by the State Department or the CIA. He hurriedly drove to the West Coast with the understanding that I would join him after taking care of selling the furniture and transferring the lease to a new tenant. It took me a fairly long time to accomplish the task.

In order to maintain the rent at the same low price, we followed the general practice of what people did in New York City at that time – the transactions were done quietly without the knowledge of the landlord. It certainly made the deal more difficult since I could not advertise openly. Luckily, after a month and a half, through a friend's help, I was able to leave with my baby. One late evening, a friend of ours took us to the airport, and there I bought a red-eye flight ticket, and with Eva in my arms, I boarded the plane for San Francisco.

My father broadcast in Tibetan for Voice of America, and in Chinese for Radio Free Asia!

My husband took us from the airport and drove straight to our next home—a hotel apartment on Polk St. I cannot recall how long we stayed there, but I do recall that every day we discussed how we could supplement our income so that we could afford to send the monthly support checks to Taiwan for his parents.

In the end, we decided to run a rooming house. Neither my husband nor I had any experience that would help us in running a rooming house, but since we made the decision, we plunged our efforts into finding a place. With our limited funds and capabilities, we leased an old rooming house on Divisadero St. Of course, we did not know it was an area that was going downhill. We moved in and discovered I was pregnant again.

The building itself was a two-storied structure with a fenced back yard. All together, there were eight units, six of which were single rooms, and two units that were two-bedroom units. There was a communal kitchen on each floor. When we took it over from the landlord, it was fully rented except for the unit we were to occupy on the first floor. Under the building, the walk-out basement was rented to a plastics lab. So, when Eva was about six months old, I became a landlady.

I was told by the original landlord that my responsibilities included supplying clean sheets by the week, cleaning all the common areas, and supplying all the utilities, plus a coin-operated public telephone in the hallway. We were there for about two years. There, I gave birth to my son Leo, and I met people who were all from low income groups. I learned about the strange behavior of alcoholics. I had tenants who sometimes had to sell their blood to get by. I found out how single mothers struggled to make a living. But the worst of all my experiences was that I had to lie to "Negroes," to refuse them while the vacancy sign was hanging on the door, all because I was warned by the other residents that black people were not welcome.

However, no matter how difficult and how their own lives were troubling them, they were all very kind and courteous to me. Since I did not know a single thing about fixing anything, and my husband was hopeless with his hands, they always offered to help us in repairing things when needed.

I was also very impressed by their attitudes. They reflected to me the true American spirit, that everyone is born free, poor or rich, and that people are all equal. Both my husband and I came from a very privileged class in China, where most people would not think that the rich and poor should have equal rights.

One year later, the Radio Free Asia station was ordered to be closed. The authority decided to transfer some of the employees to the Army Language School in Monterey to teach the Chinese language. For different reasons, some people did not go, but my husband went, and left me with two young babies and a rooming house to run.

He commuted weekly for a period of time, and then we made plans to ask one of our long-time tenant ladies to take care of the place. We would pay her for the work. She was happy to step in, so we were able to be together again, and we moved into an upstairs flat in the nice peaceful little town of Pacific Grove.

I was released from all the chores of the rooming house, but I was worried about the residents living there. Would there be any vacancies? Would there be any accidents like the time one of the residents tried to commit suicide?

We lived in Pacific Grove for half of a year. One day, my husband received a letter from his brother Louie. Louie told us that he had just bought a grocery store and that my husband should go there and work with him.

While my parents lived in San Francisco, my aunt Helen (Mian Mian) paid them a visit. My mom was expecting the delivery of my brother Leo at any moment. It was Christmas, and my aunt decided to come for a visit during her holiday break. She was attending a school in Kentucky at the time, which was run by nuns. She did not let my parents know ahead of time that she was planning her visit. Instead, my parents came home from dinner with a friend and found a telegram at their door, informing them that she was arriving on the train that evening.

My father drove from San Francisco to Oakland to meet her. It was long past midnight when they arrived back at the apartment. Since it had been six or seven years since they had seen each other, they stayed up late, talking. But at five a.m. the next morning, Leo decided to make his appearance, so my parents went to the hospital. In those days, women stayed in the hospital for several days after delivering a baby, so my mother was in the hospital for several days. I was not allowed to see her, but she tells me that she would wave out the window to the car to greet me.

On one of my father's visits to the hospital, he told mom that my aunt had been crying, but he did not want to pry as to the reason for her tears.

After mom returned home, she asked her sister why she had been crying. "I was so upset that my brother-in-law had to sweep the floors. My sister married someone who has to sweep their own floors," she lamented.

My mom asked my aunt, "How many servants do we still have at home?"

"Just a minute, I have to count...Including the chauffeur, only eight now."

My mom just laughed. My aunt had yet to learn for herself the contrast between the old life in China and the realities of life in the new world.

My husband had a strong commitment to be a good and obedient son, combined with the traditional teachings of filial obedience and respect for one's elders ingrained in him. Therefore, maintaining his respect for his older brother Louie, he readily resigned his language school position, and without any further questioning about the proposal, he took our car and soon was on his way back to New York. That again left me alone to tie up all the loose ends in San Francisco. If I wanted to leave the rooming house, first of all, I had to find someone to take over the remaining lease we signed with our landlord, and only then could I tend to the packing and moving with two young toddlers by my side.

It was not particularly easy to transfer the rooming house properties, as the housing values of the area were falling much lower, partly due to the "beatniks" who were slowly moving in, and partly because we had a few vacancies. Daily, my husband would send a letter to me, telling me what a blunder the grocery store investment was, and how hard he had to work. Each day, he had to do a great deal of physical labor to fix the store. Each day, he had to put in twelve to thirteen hours of work without rest, even on Sundays. I, for the longest time had no good news to report to him either. I could only tell him how the children were progressing. We missed each other terribly, but there was just no offer for the rooming house.

It went on like this for a few months, and at last, I succeeded in handing over the rooming house to a new owner. Finally, in May 1954, happy and exhausted, the three of us rejoined my husband and moved into our new home back in New York again.

This time, my husband had found a two-bedroom apartment for us. It had a rather spacious dining room and a living room, so we decided to use the master bedroom as the study, and occupied the dining room as our bedroom. The two toddlers then were comfortably put in the second bedroom.

The apartment was on the fifth floor. The building itself was on West 119th St. between Amsterdam Ave. and Morningside Drive. Columbia University was within walking distance, while on the sidewalks of Morningside Drive, there were nice sandboxes for the children to play in.

We soon met some other Chinese couples there who also had small pre-school-age children, including the Nobel prize winner Dr. T. D. Lee, who had two young sons who became playmates. It did not take too long before we all quietly settled down. *(According to the Nobel Prize website, "...at age 29, Lee was then the youngest-ever full professor in Columbia University's faculty history. In 1957, when awarded the Nobel Prize at barely 31 years of age, Lee became the second-youngest scientist ever to receive this distinction.")*

Soon after we had settled in our new place, I wanted to see the grocery store, thinking I could be of some help to my husband, but my husband refused to let me go, especially because I had the two children. Time after time, he just would not let me go. I kept on begging and begging, and then he told me the reason. The store was a very small one, and it was located in the infamous area of Harlem.

It happened because by chance, his brother saw the store, and close by, there was a new skyscraper cluster up for rent. He thought the store could surely get good business from those residents. He told my husband that each week, he would come and work a couple of days, and the rest of the days, he would still be working on Wall Street, figuring with the income from the store, they would be able to support their parents. So, without discussing it with my husband, he bought the store. That meant my husband would be the main person to stay at the store, just like the first Miami arrangement.

Fixing up the place took almost three months. When they opened, they had to hire a Mr. Henderson to help out. Of course, for all that time, there was no income, only expenses. My husband did not want me to go, because he said there was not even enough room for me and the children to sit.

I insisted that I should see it with my own eyes, so one afternoon, he took us in our car and headed for the store.

We drove through some crowded and very dirty streets, and then stopped in front of our store. I do not even recall if it had a name. Mr. Henderson welcomed us. He was a slim black man in his late 50s or so. He spoke softly to my children and they immediately liked him. I looked around the store. It was small, but it was kept very clean, in contrast to the outside. There were different glass cases for meats and seafood. There was also a wall lined with vegetables and fruits. However, with the five of us inside, there was hardly any more room for any customers. Evidently, we could not remain there for long. I told my husband I would take the kids and slowly walk home. He told me it was too far to walk, so he told Mr. Henderson he would be back later, and drove us home.

Days went by. Every morning about eight a.m., my husband would leave after breakfast, walk through Morningside Park, down the steps to the store. He stayed there until about eight p.m. in the evening, then again would climb through Morningside Park to come home. He would carry home whatever food they could not sell before it went bad, for us to eat.

The route was more or less a shortcut between the store and our home. Since parking was always difficult, he always walked to work. Unfortunately, the park was a dangerous area. It was known that even the double patrols of policemen would not venture in there at night, so every night I would be worried and anxious about his trip home. By then, I also learned that Louie was not coming to the store regularly, and furthermore, the store was not making any money at all.

Since I arrived from San Francisco, my husband started to stay at home on Sundays. Usually before noon, he would try to write some lectures on Buddhism in the study. Then in the afternoon, most of the time, we would take the children to Central Park to ride the merry-go-round, or visit the museums when the weather was bad.

Although it was very hard work, as neither of us had very good command of the English language, he slowly compiled a few lectures. Then an incident happened. One day, when he was alone in the store, a black man dashed into the store, and with a shiny knife, demanded money. My husband had to open the register for him, but as soon as the man grabbed the bills and ran, my husband took chase. Not only did he not get any money back, he got a deep slash in his right hand. After that, I insisted that he take Saturday afternoon off in order to have some free time to find some other way to make a living.

He then contacted Mrs. Gordon to resume her Tibetan lessons. He also tried to give talks on Buddhism at different gatherings. Gradually, he established himself as a Buddhist scholar, and eventually was able to offer courses at The New School for Social Research. *(See page 310.)*

Meanwhile, at this time, he still had to work at the grocery store.

Among his audiences, a lady who was studying the *Egyptian Book of the Dead* also became interested in the *Tibetan Book of the Dead*. She somehow learned of my husband's situation, and advised him that he should apply for a fellowship from the Bollingen Foundation. I never had the chance to meet her, but my husband told me she was Natacha Rambova, a ballerina, costume and film set designer, and the last wife of the famous movie star, Rudolph Valentino. *(See page 297.)*

Bollingen Foundation was founded by the Mellon family mainly to publish the works of Dr. C. Jung. At that time, being new to this country, we did not know any of the prerequisites for getting into the academic world in this country. Neither did we have any outstanding achievement credentials whatsoever. But Natacha encouraged us to apply.

Thus, my husband first had to decide what project he wanted to work on. It took him only a few days to reach a conclusion. He told me, because he had always wanted to introduce the most famous Tibetan yogi, Milarepa, and his songs to the outside world, this would be a good chance to fulfill his dream. With that decided, we started to work on the Tibetan text of Milarepa's songs. I said "we started." I could not read Tibetan, but my husband needed me to help him with his English translation. As it turned out, some time ago, when he was at the grocery store, a young black man sold him a very old office model of an Underwood typewriter for one dollar. Somehow, I managed to turn myself into an amateur typist for his manuscript during the times when he was not using the typewriter.

We struggled for quite some time on the first ten chapters of the Tibetan text named *The 100,000 Songs of Milarepa*. By then, my husband was under really heavy time pressure: he still had to work at the grocery store, he was preparing lectures for his New School classes, tutoring Mrs. Gordon's private lessons, and on top of that, he had to put his best efforts into the translation of the Tibetan Songs.

It was hard for me to feel so helpless, and unable to do more. Finally, I asked him to tell Louie that we wanted out from the grocery store, even knowing that we would be losing money. Grudgingly, Louie agreed, and they closed the store in August that year.

After the sale of the grocery store, I did a calculation of our financial situation. We had a grand total of $300 left in our account, out of which our monthly rent was $90 and my in-laws in Taiwan would receive $60. We were without health insurance. And we still had to eat. The future certainly looked gloomy, but I was relieved that my husband would not have to go back to the store anymore, and could concentrate on the translation.

Finally, one day, I finished typing our best efforts for the manuscript of the first ten chapters as a sample and sent it to the Foundation. We just prayed and waited patiently with blind faith for the Foundation's grant.

(See page 308 for more about the Bollingen Foundation.)

Days of waiting were not spent in ennui. On the contrary, my husband focused all his available time on the translation of the Milarepa text. Fortunately, among the people who attended his lectures, there was a gentleman named George Currier. George was doing some editing work for a small publication. He volunteered to help my husband's English. I was very happy about it, because I knew that the work my husband was doing definitely needed help from someone whose command of the language was far better than mine.

George would come during weekends. He was a bachelor, so he could stay as long as he wanted to, and my job was to keep the children somehow occupied, and also to make sure I served a good meal at the end of the day.

At last, I think it was in November, the long awaited and prayed-for letter arrived from the Bollingen Foundation. It granted my husband a three-year fellowship with a $3,600 a year award. Three long years! We never dared to dream of such luxury. Just to think that for three years, my husband could have his full effort focused on what was his dream work, and not to be distracted by worrying about where the money was coming from for the next month.

Around that time, news came from the Tibetan settlement in India that the Communist government of China was carrying out a systematic scheme of burning all the Tibetan Buddhist books. The Tibetans do not have much Tibetan works other than the Buddhist texts, which are all printed by wood block prints. Now that the Chinese government was burning these wooden prints, sooner or later, there would not be many Buddhist books left.

A few years ago, back in China and India, we were friends with the Dalai Lama's elder sister and two brothers, although not very close friends. Through the one brother who was teaching at Berkeley in California, we confirmed that the book burning was true. My husband was alarmed and began to plan how to save some of the most important Buddhist texts.

About the same time, a young Hungarian friend, Peter Gruber, who we knew when we were in India and who loved to discuss Buddhist practice and philosophy with my husband, also had left India and came to the States. He first worked at a Wall Street brokerage, but soon afterwards, he started his own little firm. Somehow, he found us. He introduced us to his American wife and two children. Often, when he could get away from his office, he would drop in to be with my husband. Following the traditional Chinese custom, he became my children's "Uncle Peter." *(See page 283 for more on this great philanthropist.)*

The trip to go to India to save the Tibetan books was a frequent topic between the two of them.

It was early in 1956. One day, I came home from outside with my children. I was surprised to see my husband was at the door, seeing off a well-dressed gentleman. He was wearing a hat. My husband introduced us, and said, "This is Harvey." When Harvey left, he told the children to play, and wanted to talk to me. As we went into the study, he said, "What do you think, should I accept Harvey's proposal or not?" Then he told me, Harvey called him for an appointment, then came to see him, after he verified that my husband was indeed a Tibetan Buddhist scholar. Then he said he was from the CIA. The agency was looking for someone who had good knowledge of both the Chinese and the Tibetan cultures and languages, because they wanted to collect information about the activities that were going on in the region, especially the border areas among China, Tibet, and India. My husband told Harvey that he was fully occupied with the Milarepa project, but he did have a wish to go to India, in order to bring some important Tibetan texts back. Harvey said it would be a good cover for him to go, and of course, there would be some stipend paid for his trouble. Finally, Harvey also said, "I know you and your wife are applying for the permanent resident status. If you go, I will see to it that the procedure will be completed without delay." My husband then asked me again. "Harvey is waiting for my answer. I should let him know soon, because he said there would be some training involved."

Of course, with the prospect of permanent residency status available, we decided that my husband should accept Harvey's offer.

My husband's lectures would occasionally bring different people to visit him. Dr. Muses was one of these.

I still remember that day: we were having dinner. He knocked on the door and came without an appointment. We invited him to join us, and soon, we learned that he had just come back from South America. It was the first time I met him. He probably was in his late 40s. His dark tan made him look like an adventurer. Within a short time, he told us that he was the president of the Falcon's Wing Press which was located in the suburbs of Denver, Colorado. The Press was interested in publishing old exotic texts and at the present, he personally was especially interested in a Tibetan text on Tantric teaching which he had acquired during one of his travels. On his way out, he said he would bring the text to show my husband on his next visit.

The next time he came, exactly like the first time, he just showed himself at the door without any previous announcement. He wanted my husband to translate this text for the Press. At the same time, he surprised us by offering my husband a lifetime position to work for the Press. Immediately, my husband told Dr. Muses that he was fully occupied with the Milarepa translation and that he was also planning to collect some Tibetan works in India. It was impossible for him to handle any additional work. But my husband's refusal was not accepted. Dr. Muses was very persistent. He insisted that it would be so good for him to have my husband as a member of the Press. I was stunned by his generous offer.

He said the Press would give my husband a permanent position. They would supply a furnished house for our residence, free. The salary would be starting at $300 a month. We could move to Colorado, get settled, and then my husband could leave for India. As for the work, my husband could do as much as he could. Definitely, the trip to India would not present any problem. He would give us a few days to say yes, because he was about to leave for another trip.

To us, a young family from a foreign country, without any roots in a foreign land, to have a permanent position sounded so attractive. In addition to a job, we could even have our own residence. We debated the opportunity with its pros and cons for two days, and then finally told Dr. Muses that we decided to accept his offer. Then he told us that we should inform the Press about our arrival time, as he would not be there in person to receive us. Instead, the owner of the Press, Mrs. Howell, would be there to meet us. *(See page 288 for more about Dr. Muses, a most intriguing person.)*

Since we had also asked our good friend Peter Gruber for his advice, we immediately informed him of our decision. He was very happy for us, and further surprised us with some financial help to purchase the Tibetan texts.

In my younger years, I read somewhere about Kalimpong and Darjeeling as centers of intelligence activities. I used to kid around and say that maybe my father had worked for the CIA. It was not until my mother wrote down this story that I found out that my wildest speculations were indeed true, although not during the time frame when my parents actually lived in India.

In April, a couple of our friends wanted to take over our apartment. That was a big worry off our minds. By then the training my husband underwent with Harvey had already been completed. He kept hushed about the training, so I had no idea what was covered.

Our main obligation was to the Bollingen Foundation, but it was a long time away. In order to find time to do the new work for Dr. Muses, my husband made all the necessary arrangements and ended all his other previous engagements. When the month of May came, we figured the weather should be nice and pleasant, so we started our journey towards Colorado. We thought this would be a good chance to combine some sight-seeing with the trip. The AAA showed us some of the spots en route where we could stop, so when we were in West Virginia, we stayed at Cacapon State Park. It was too early for the touring season. The kind park ranger let us use a brand new cabin at a very reasonable fee. We could also go to the lodge for meals if we did not feel like cooking for ourselves. My children had never seen a fireplace before, so they excitedly picked up the already split wood to start a fire. In the mountains, the nights were still chilly, even in May. We surrounded the fireplace and all felt so secure and content.

Before the end of May, we found ourselves climbing higher and higher. The vista gradually changed from large spreads of farmland to vast stretches of mountainous pastures and plateaus. Soon after we crossed the border of Colorado, the view became more colorful with deep green pines and reddish earth. However, our car was slowly losing power for climbing. We started to worry, but happily, when we stopped to get gasoline, the attendant at the station solved our puzzlement. Laughingly, he said, "Oh, you must adjust your carburetor for this high country. New York air pressure is different."

We kept on climbing like a snail, following the instructions given to us by the Press. The Falcon's Wing Press was located near a summer resort area southwest of Denver. We drove past Golden, the famous light beer brewer's headquarters town, and then past the famous Red Rock Theater, and finally arrived at Indian Hills. There, we called the Press from the post office to inform them of our arrival. Soon, the caretaker, Ed, came in a Jeep and led us to our new home.

We followed Ed for about ten minutes or so while gently climbing upward. Soon we came to a chain-link fence gate. Through the gate, we proceeded along a big curved road and then we stopped on the dirt driveway of a two-storied house. There were five tall mature pines lined up in front of the house. Ed said, "Here you are." We all scrambled out of the car and entered the house. It was a solidly built structure with two bedrooms, a living room, one bath with laundry supplies and an eat-in kitchen. There was also an attached garage. Ed informed us that Mrs. Howell wanted to refinish the upstairs, so there would be people coming to finish the work on the second floor. He said when we had settled down, we should contact the Press, which was nearby.

It was to our pleasant surprise that the house was indeed fairly well furnished for us, even having flannel sheets for the cold weather. In the kitchen, there was an old red traditional square Chinese dining table with fine lacquered carvings. Ed also told us where we could shop for groceries. He warned us that due to the persistent drought, even though the house had two wells, we should watch our supply of water.

The next day, Mrs. Howell called. Later, she came to see us. She was an elegant looking lady, probably in her 50s, straightforward in her manners, but very considerate. She welcomed us and offered her help if we needed it. She also wanted us to meet the other members of the Press when we were ready. We enjoyed the meeting and I promised to invite her for a Chinese meal, since she expressed her liking for Chinese food.

Getting settled did not take much time other than getting to know a little about our surroundings. We only needed to unpack the books that we had brought with us, since the house was already very well furnished for us. Soon, my husband started his old working schedule during the days. In the evenings, we would drive to explore the area around us. Indian Hills was a small town. The main street only consisted of a post office and a store called "The Trading Post." There  we could get a few basic grocery items and newspapers from Denver, which was about thirty-five miles to the northeast. Otherwise, we had to go to our closest neighboring town, to Evergreen, to get our regular groceries.

Our house was built on a small plot of ranch land. I think it was about two acres. If I wanted to meet my next door neighbor, it was a long walk to go over. However, for all the time we were there, we never did meet them. There were two horses that often came and grazed on our land. One day, two young girls came to see us and told us the horses were theirs, and politely asked us for permission to let the horses continue to come to feed. My husband readily consented to their request.

Then one day, we were introduced to the other members at the Press. There weren't too many employees. They even had a small party to welcome us. It made us feel pleasantly at home. We also learned that all this while, Dr. Muses was still away on his trip.

The caretaker, Ed, surprised us one afternoon. He brought us a border collie puppy, three or four months old. Everyone fell in love with it. Ed said it was for us to keep. But he said the puppy did not like to sleep in the house. We should try to make a bed for it in the garage. My husband named it "Shabo," which means "dog" in Tibetan.

91

It was 1956. Colorado was in a very dry period of drought. Soon I found out that the good habits of flushing the toilet, which took me a long time to teach my children, needed to be unlearned. Flushing the toilet became a critical problem. Both Eva and Leo were very confused by their mother's inconsistency. We had to save our bathwater for flushing. In addition to that, I discovered that it took only one load of laundry to empty both wells. After I called Ed a few times, they ordered water to be delivered to the two wells. It ended up that I was always the last one to use the bathwater. First the children, then my husband, then me. I imagined then that this was what it was like for the American pioneers.

Sometime in September, Dr. Muses came back from South America. He was even darker tan, and looked more like a tropical large animal hunter than someone who was interested in exotic religious texts. My husband showed him the typed manuscript he had been working on up to that time, and also brought out the topic of the long-planned trip to India. November to April was the more ideal time to go, on account of the monsoon and extreme hot season which usually started in May.

Since Dr. Muses knew about the trip when we were back in New York, all he asked of my husband was to keep on sending back his translations from India, as they had previously agreed upon. He said that my children and I would be well looked after during his absence.

As far as I can remember, through our married life, my husband constantly busied himself with reading and writing. He kept on reading, mostly the classic works written by famous scholars and other writers on Western religions, as well as works of philosophy, because he was not trained in those fields. As for writing, it was completely out of necessity. He needed to prepare all his lectures in writing first, and in order to have better readable translations, he needed to be more lucid with his written English.

For the first few years after we lived in the US, he never had any time to relax, simply because of his strong sense of filial responsibility and his role as the breadwinning head of family. Only at this time, our financial situation was finally beginning to improve somewhat. We had income from three sources: the Bollingen Foundation, "Harvey," and the Falcon's Wing Press. However, all these results came not without prices.

My husband was an extremely bright and fun-loving person. We enjoyed dancing, theaters, music, and travel. We gave up all those enjoyments for many years, partly due to lack of funds, and partly due to the pressure of time. He needed all the time available for his work, while under the pressure of worrying about our status of staying in this country. But the worst price he paid for our security was his eyesight. Now this trip to India relieved us from worrying about our immigrant status, because Harvey had told us so. We knew as soon as he arrived in New York, Harvey would give us the approved permanent residency. Then he could apply for the visa to India on his US affidavit document. But his eyes had begun to give him trouble, and that lasted until the last days of his life.

Even at the very beginning of the time when he began his Buddhism lectures, he felt a deep need to understand Western philosophy, Christianity, and Indian religions. The nonstop reading and writing caused his eyes to tire out easily, and he could only proceed in his work with frequent rests. That of course slowed his progress a great deal. However, he managed to keep up the work according to his schedule. When the departure date came, he asked the manager and the caretaker, Ed, to keep an eye on me and my two children. He left in early September.

A few weeks passed, then my husband's first letter from India arrived. He was back at Kalimpong again. Most of our old friends were still there, but he said there were definitely more Tibetans coming out of Tibet than before. The majority were refugees fleeing the Chinese Communists.

After he left, I was idling at home. Eva had just turned five years old, and on her birthday, September 10, we went to a portrait studio and had a portrait taken to be mailed to my husband. Leo was almost four. Shortly afterwards, I was getting restless. I thought I should improve my typing skills in order to be more efficient for future work on my husband's manuscripts. I started to inquire about a babysitter for the children, so I could go to classes. Through the Trading Post, I found Mrs. Brown. She and her family had just moved from Iowa to Indian Hills. Mr. Brown worked at the Post Office in Denver. They had a rented house, so I could take the children to their house in the morning and then attend a secretarial school in the city of Denver. By four in the afternoon, I would pick up the children and go home.

Soon I discovered that late at night, there would be horses running outside our house. The work on the second floor had long been finished by the time my husband was about to leave. The workers had stopped coming. Only Ed was our occasional visitor. Other than that, I was always alone with the children. The weather was getting colder. I tried to move our dog Shabo's bed into the house but failed. He would rather sleep outside under the window of my bedroom. Whenever I heard the horses running down the slope at night, Shabo would be barking frantically at them. I had no way to know if there were riders on the horses because the outside was so dark. There was only the light of the stars and the moon for light. The nightly visits of the horses really frightened me, so I moved the children into my bedroom without telling them the reason, and I slept with a broomstick by my bedside.

Sometime in late October, I received a letter from Dr. Muses. It enclosed a copy of a letter he wrote to my husband in India. The letter to me was very simple and clear. It just informed me that he was sending me a copy of what he was writing to my husband.

But that letter to my husband shook me so badly that I could not eat or sleep that night.

First it alleged that my husband's trip to India was not in our understanding for our coming to Colorado. Secondly, he accused my husband of failing to fulfill his promise of sending back his translations. At last, he told my husband that he was not a responsible person, that he not only neglected his work, but also left his family behind, uncared-for. Therefore, from that time on, the Press would use their welfare funds to support me and the children.

The truth was that I knew that all of Dr. Muses' charges were wrong. He was well informed about the trip to India before he even offered my husband the job to work for the Press. As for the translations, my husband had regularly been mailing me the carbon copy of all the work he was sending to Dr. Muses. Therefore, I knew he was not neglecting his responsibility to the Press. To be on someone's welfare list made me angry, ashamed, and full of indignation. Yet, since I did not know what caused Dr. Muses' sudden change of mind, I could only wait for my husband's response.

I kept on going to school during the day. At night, I would consider how I could get out of this dilemma. Soon, as expected, my husband's responding letter came. He also included a copy of the letter he addressed to Dr. Muses. He explained the facts, and refuted Dr. Muses' accusations in a very calm tone, but in the letter to me, he told me to be tolerant of the situation and wait until he returned home to make further decisions. Long distance telephone was nonexistent then, so I waited quietly for further development.

Then, communication between Dr. Muses and my husband turned uglier. I wrote to my husband that I had made arrangements with Mrs. Brown to stay with them temporarily. He replied to me that since our coming to work for the Press was based on good faith, we took Dr. Muses' word with complete trust. There was no way for us to prove that we were mistreated. He had second thoughts about coming back to Indian Hills. By November, we both decided to go to Taiwan to visit our parents and to leave Denver for good.

I cleaned up the house and returned the keys to the caretaker. With Mr. Brown's help, we took Shabo and moved to the Browns' residence.

We began boarding with the Brown family. They gave us a room and fed us. I rode with Mr. Brown to Denver every day. My children played with the Browns' two older children, and in two weeks' time, I finished the school. Then I began focusing on preparing for the trip to Taiwan. It had been eight years since we had been married. We had not seen our families in all that time. I was excited about going home. The first step was to apply for my permanent residency. I went to Denver's immigration office to apply. They told me that they would have to transfer my files from the New York office first. For the time being, they could not do anything. I went back and started to gather information about the ships going to Taiwan. One Taiwan freighter was leaving Portland, Oregon on December 8. My father in Taipei, Taiwan had asked a friend to book a passage for me and my children on it. That left me a short time to get everything ready.

The second time I went back to the Denver immigration office, I told them I really needed the certificate urgently because of my trip. They said that the New York office could not find my file, so I told them I was confident that I should not have any problem, since my husband was already traveling abroad on permanent residency status. The officer who was in charge of my case was fairly considerate of my situation. He promised to further pursue my case. Mr. Brown was kind to me. He suggested that I write to the Colorado Senator for help. Then the Denver immigration officer called me to meet him. He showed me my husband's file and said, "Look, the New York office sent us your husband's file without yours. In your husband's file, it listed his wife's name as Yolanda, but that's not you. Are you sure your husband doesn't have another wife?" I told him I was 100% sure I was his only wife, and that it must have been a mistake. Fortunately, the officer was very sympathetic towards me. He said "OK, since the New York office could not find your file, I will just establish a complete new file for you and I will issue the permanent residency certificate to you." Thus, a few days later, I went in and picked up my papers.

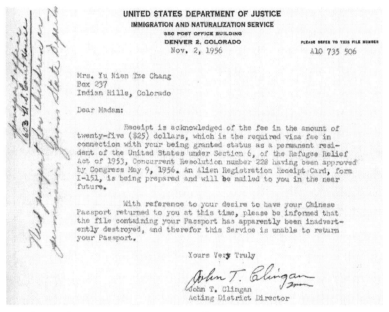

Once I had the necessary traveling documents in my hands, the schedule for my departure immediately became more pressing. First, I had to find a place to store our belongings. Most importantly, that meant storing all our boxed books and a lot of household things that we would not need while in Taiwan. I was very happy when the instructor at the business school offered her basement to me and said she could just ship them to me when I returned to the US. Then there was our car to be disposed of. Mr. Brown helped me to sell it and also arranged the transaction date so I could use it until the day I was leaving. I learned that we could take the train to go to Portland, Oregon, where the Chinese freighter was docked. When I inquired of the ticket clerk, "How long is the trip?" he told me, "The next morning, you will be there." The very last thing left to do was to find a good home for our Shabo.

Well, about three days before we were leaving, we found a family that wanted to love our Shabo. They lived fairly close by, so after a teary goodbye, Shabo was led away. However, in the evening the next day, the new owner of our pet called, and told us that Shabo would not eat or drink for the whole day. Then I remembered that even when we were staying with the Browns, I had kept feeding Shabo Chinese food. I hurriedly made something and brought it over to the new owner, and suggested they could probably mix my food with the regular dog food in order to smooth the traumatic change for Shabo and make it a little less painful. The next day, I made more food for them to keep in the refrigerator. After I watched Shabo start to eat, I quietly sneaked away. That was the last time I saw Shabo.

On the last morning, my children and I said goodbye to Mrs. Brown and their two children. It was hard to part with them after living together for so long. Finally, Mr. Brown and I each drove our own car, and went to deliver my car to the dealer and picked up my check for the sale. Then, all three of us rode Mr. Brown's car to the train station. Mr. Brown left after he helped us settle in our seats. Shortly, the train carried us towards a future that was both exciting and full of unknowns.

It was the first time I traveled by train in the US. I found it was a very different experience compared to what I remembered of all the different train trips I had taken in China and India. The train that we were riding was not at all fully occupied. All together, there were only six of us. Besides my children and myself, there were only three young soldiers. By dinnertime, I wondered where the dining car was, but the soldiers said there was none. They told me, when we arrived at the next station, I should go down to the waiting room and get some food from the machines. The food that came from the machines made such a hit with my children because it was a completely new experience to them. Then, night arrived. We didn't have beds or anything to soften the seats. Somehow, we made do with our winter coats. The children slept all right, but I sat through the long night.

The following morning, I had two more discoveries. I was surprised to be informed by the train conductor that instead of arriving at Portland that morning, actually we had one more day to be on the train, one day longer than what the Denver clerk told me. The other discovery was to find out that among the three soldiers, two were in handcuffs. The third soldier was the officer who was in charge of escorting the two to jail in Oregon. By then, I had resigned myself to the situation. The soldiers already started to play with my children. They entertained them with stories and games for which I was very grateful. I only knew they were deserters. They were caught and were being brought back to be punished, but they were all very friendly and well-behaved young men in spite of the handcuffs.

When another day of machine food and another night of sitting up was over, we reached Portland, Oregon.

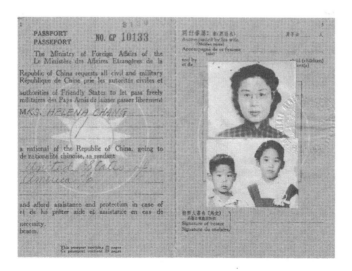

The ship was an old US war surplus vessel, later purchased by a Chinese maritime shipping company. It was docking at a pier in Portland for loading. My children and I were the last passengers to board. It must have been through a special arrangement, because we were given an officer's cabin instead of sharing a room like the others. Since it was a freighter, all together, there were thirteen passengers. When at last the wheat was loaded, we sailed toward Taiwan.

It did not take all the passengers long to get to know each other, especially for me, because of the two children. Most of the passengers were newly graduated Masters or PhDs, returning home to Taiwan. I was the only housewife and mother. The voyage took close to two weeks, sailing smoothly in the Pacific Ocean. However, when we sailed into  the Strait of Taiwan, the waves suddenly became savagely strong. The ship tossed and rocked for the longest time, and only became calm again as we neared the south tip of Taiwan.

We had gradually shed our winter clothes days before we arrived at the city of Kaohsiung. When we docked, in the midst of the excitement of parting with my fellow passengers, I was met by my husband's youngest brother, Edward. There was also a cousin of mine who my father had sent down from Taipei to welcome us home.

Since the return train to Taipei did not leave until late in the evening, the harbormaster treated all of our family members to a full Chinese banquet with ten or fifteen courses. It was the first time my children had ever had a Chinese meal of this type, and they eagerly gorged themselves from the first appetizers, through the Peking Duck, to the last Chinese Eight Precious Rice pudding dessert.

We rode the evening train to go to the north of Taiwan. I tried to catch up with all the happenings I had missed for the past eight years, from both of our families. I also learned that my husband was still in India, and that he would not be with us for a few more days yet.

Around eleven o'clock, late at night, we arrived at the Taipei train station. I was so surprised to see my father standing there waiting for me. I had not seen my father since I had flown away for my wedding at the end of 1948. Now I was meeting him, in a foreign land. His long beard had almost all turned white. He was close to eighty years old, and I knew standing was hard for him, and yet he waited until almost midnight to welcome me home. I went up and clutched him, my tears streaking down my face. Sadness, love, and happiness choked me to wordlessness.

A short while later, I said good night to my father, and saw him slowly walk away with his attendants. My brother-in-law Edward then took me and my children to my in-laws' home.

My father-in-law and mother-in-law were both standing, waiting for us at the front door. They were so happy to see their two grandchildren for the first time. They told me because they knew my father was going to meet me, they did not want to intrude on his joy of the reunion; that was why they stayed home to wait for us. I was very grateful for their consideration.

A room was already prepared for us. By the time we went to bed, it was almost dawn. The next day, we enjoyed breakfast without me having to prepare it. The grandparents and everyone else were all happy and pleased that my children could talk to them in perfect Chinese. My mother-in-law told me that I should find an "amah" to help with the children so that I could go and stay at my father's house more often.

Soon, my husband wrote me from Hong Kong to tell me of his arrival date, but at the same time, he told me to prepare for a month-long trip to Hong Kong sometime in March, because a Buddhist group there had invited him to give a series of talks. Meanwhile, relatives and friends from both sides of the two families had already started in arguing who could invite us first, whether it was breakfast, lunch, or dinner. Having fled eight long years ago from mainland China to the island of Taiwan, as a whole, the mainlanders' economic situations had improved a great deal by then, and the cost of living was reasonable. Also, food was abundantly provided by the richness of the local soil, so most of the people were fairly well off.

On my in-laws' side, there were more relatives waiting to treat us, whereas, from my father's side, it was mostly his old friends and some close associates from work. By the time my husband came back to join us, our days were fully occupied with breakfast, lunch, and dinner engagements.

Shortly after I was back, my mother-in-law took me to a tailor to have some Chinese dresses made. In order to make them fit, they wanted me to have a fitting appointment first. In one week, when it was time to go back, the dress made according to my body measurements had become so tight that I could barely squeeze in; that of course, was the direct result of one week's banqueting.

My days were divided between my father's house and my in-laws. I did hire a nice amah to help my in-laws with the children. Luckily, American dollars were worth much more than Chinese dollars then, so I could afford it. I was pleased to see that the children could bring some happiness to their grandparents.

As for my husband, other than at mealtimes, he mostly kept his own schedule for working and meeting with others. I enrolled the two children in a Chinese nursery school. My mother-in-law knew a rickshaw puller fairly well, so he was hired to take the children in the morning and take them home after school. It worked out quite well for a while, until I found out that the children were not happy to go to the school, so I took a friend's suggestion and enrolled them in a Filipino-run private school where they spoke English and where the great majority of children were either Americans or other foreigners. To my surprise, that change made my children eager to go to school again, even though we never spoke English at home.

One day, Leo told us that in school, the teacher asked the class to raise their hand if they knew the name of the president of the country. He raised his hand quickly and the teacher asked him, "Who is it?" He said he gave the answer, but the teacher laughed and said it was wrong, so we asked him what he had said. "Eisenhower, Ike." The teacher was naturally expecting Chiang Kai-Shek.

Most of the people on Taiwan accepted Buddhism as their faith. One day, we had a visitor in a light blue western suit, who wanted to talk to my husband. He introduced himself as Mr. Lin. He was a native Taiwanese, but what puzzled me was that he said he was a Buddhist monk at a local monastery and was the regional head of a large Buddhist association of Taiwan. I had never seen any monk in attire other than the usual Buddhist garments. He came to invite my husband to offer a lecture tour around the island. He also invited my mother-in-law and me to join the trip. We asked for a couple of days to think it over. Being practically strangers to Taiwan, we needed to learn more before we could make the decision. Some of our Buddhist friends told us that because Taiwan was under Japanese rule for fifty years, many of the traditions in the Buddhist practices were strongly influenced by the Japanese. Hence, Mr. Lin's blue suit was not all that unusual. Our friends also suggested that it would be a good opportunity to meet more native followers while touring the whole island. So we decided to go.

My mother-in-law was happy to travel with both of us by her side. The children were happy to be left with their doting grandfather,

103

who had claimed the right to spoil them as long as we were in Taiwan. So, we started with Mr. Lin, or I should say, the  Reverend Lin, because by this time, he had changed into the traditional Buddhist garments. The journey started from Taipei in the northern part of the island, and progressed southward along the coast. The Reverend Lin arranged everything for our group. Sometimes we stayed overnight in temples, other times in local people's houses. We were treated with vegetarian banquets everywhere we went. The talks were given, sometimes at formal lecture halls, sometimes at monasteries, but occasionally the talks were given at market gatherings on open stages. As we went further away from the north, we became more dependent on our interpreter, who was a lady originally from the mainland, but who was fluent in the local Taiwan dialect. Many a time, my husband would just start a talk in the Mandarin dialect and then let the interpreter take over the whole speech in the local Taiwan dialect, mostly because he had found out a lot of the times his talks were too philosophical, too intellectual for the audiences. It happened that our interpreter was a very enthusiastic preacher. Therefore, almost half of the later trip was covered by her, especially when the audiences were from small towns and rural areas.

Amongst our group, there was a young French monk who had come to Taiwan to study Buddhism. He was also invited to come along by the Reverend Lin. He could only speak very limited English, and no Chinese at all. He could barely communicate with my husband and me in English. Due to that fact, we were an oddly organized group, and the tour certainly had various unexpected episodes. Thus, he had a phrase for it. The trip became our "Adventurous Expedition" with the last syllable rising up in his French lilt.

The trip offered a wonderful window for us to understand more of the local culture within a short time. Soon the month was over and we had made a complete circle of the island. When we went back to Taipei, it was time to prepare for the arrival of the Chinese New Year. For almost ten years, we had just let this holiday slide by, but now suddenly, we were again back amidst the fervent atmosphere. Everything was fresh and exciting to us, especially for my two children, because for the first few years after we arrived in the US, we were hardly in the mood to celebrate any holidays.

On New Year's Eve, families were all having reunions. Men would have had their haircuts and women would all be beautifully made up. Good food would first be offered to the ancestors, and then be enjoyed by the families. In the old days, the Chinese did not use the weekly calendar system, so many people would only get a long vacation at Chinese New Year time. Most of the stores, offices, and schools would be closed for at least five to ten days. Some even had rests as long as a whole month. At this time, people still kept some of the old traditions, although officially, the holiday would only last for three to four days.

People young and old will try to stay up for the arrival of the New Year. So we also stayed up until late in the wee hours. Early the next morning, everywhere was full of the sound of firecrackers. For the first time in my married life, we were home for this occasion. My husband and I formally bowed and wished Happy New Year to my in-laws, then the children kowtowed to their grandparents and then to us. Following the tradition, we each had prepared a little red envelope containing some money and gave them to the children.

After breakfast, my husband and I brought the children along to my father's house to wish him a Happy New Year. As in the past, the custom is for people to visit their family and friends to exchange New Year's greetings. Due to my father's age and his position, his house would always be crowded with greeters.

Later, my husband left and I stayed on with the children. On the third day of the New Year, in late morning, I remembered that an attendant came into the living room where I was talking with my father. He announced that President Chiang Kai-Shek and his wife were on their way in. We hurriedly stood up to meet them. They came and greeted my father and my children, and after a brief conversation, they parted.

The children and I stayed with my father for a few more days, then we went back to my in-laws' house. Then came the Lantern festival, which is the day of the first full moon of the New Year. All kinds of lanterns were selling in the street. The day before the festival, my father suddenly came and brought two lanterns for my children. One was a rabbit, and the other was a tank. Both were on wheels so they could be towed.

The Chinese New Year went by. Soon it was time for my husband and I to go to Hong Kong. Our hosts, Mr. S. W. Lee and his lovely wife Nancy kept a nice apartment for us. They even employed a maidservant who cooked for us. My husband gave nightly talks on Buddhism. They were warmly attended and well received by the audience. Our hosts also took us sightseeing all over Hong Kong and Kowloon. At the end of our stay, Mr. Lee's Buddhist group presented to my husband an exquisitely carved ivory Chinese boat with many tiny people carved into it. One could even open the carved windows to see the tiny furniture inside the cabin.

I felt so guilty for not being able to be with my father in his later years, as he was often alone at this time. I remember during my sophomore year summer vacation, the Sino-Japanese War was over. My university moved back from Chengdu, Sichuan to Beijing. My father, my two younger sisters and I left Sichuan and went to Nanjing where the government was. My father asked me if I could transfer to another university in Nanjing so he could have my companionship. I did try, but it could not be worked out. As a result, I left him and flew to Beijing. Two years later, I finished the college work and got married. Almost immediately, both my husband and I left China and went to India, and then eventually settled in the US. I regretted not only those long years being unable to be near him, but also that this visit could only be such a short one.

In April, my husband had to fly back to the US, partly because of his work, partly because we decided that he should leave earlier so that he would have time to look for a place for us to live. I was very pleased when he informed me from the US that he had actually finished the translation of Dr. Muses' Tibetan text and had mailed the whole manuscript to Colorado in spite of the disagreement.

While we were still in Hong Kong, both my children had caught the measles. Fortunately, my mother-in-law took very good care of them, and they did not even let us know about it. When we came back, I learned that my in-laws deliberately kept the information from us to spare us the worrying. It went without saying that I was deeply grateful.

April was coming to an end. The happy family reunion was also coming to its end. Again, it was time for me to check the dates for our returning ship. After considering our financial situation and other factors, I booked our passage on a ship which was sailing in the early part of May. I picked this freighter because it would take a very long time to reach the US, which would give my husband enough time to prepare the new place for us. At the same time, this ship was sailing from Keelung, which is very close to Taipei, which made it much easier for us to board.

Again, the days were packed with farewell party banquets. Finally, we bid goodbye to all our loved ones and boarded the ship. This time, besides me and my two children, there was one man who was in his thirties who was studying political science, and a young college graduate girl as fellow passengers. Both were going to the US to start their graduate studies.

The first stop was at the Philippine islands. As soon as we docked, one of the crew members, Mr. Huang, who served us in the dining room, came to ask me if I wanted to buy any mangoes. He said that everyone on the ship was buying some. I asked how much I should buy. He said, "Oh, I think two dollars should be enough." I've always enjoyed the Filipino mangoes: they are sweet, juicy, smooth, with no stringy fibers. The next day, Mr. Huang came back to inform me that he already had my mangoes stored in the ship's walk-in refrigeration room. I could not understand why the fruits were not brought to my room. He answered, "They would go bad. You have eighty-four mangoes." The truth was that this little harbor was a famous mango exporting village! The mangoes lasted us for quite a while. Leo loved them so much, not only did he eat our own, he was also fed by a friendly officer's share. By the time the ship reached Honolulu, all the mangoes were practically all gone.

We arrived at Waikiki Beach late in the morning. The crew told us the ship would sail late that night, so we all disembarked on shore and visited. For dinner, we ate at a club. There was a variety show for the tourists. Leo was so fascinated by a fire-dancer that he imitated the dance on my bed for a long time afterwards.

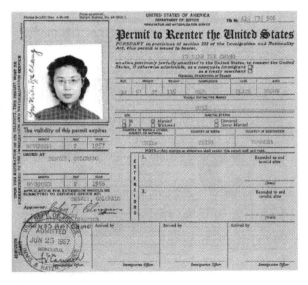

After we resumed our journey, the following days passed mostly in smooth sailing. During the day, while the children were happily entertained by some of the officers of the ship, I had the chance to be left to read all the novels written in Chinese that I found in the little library. I really did not mind the long trip. It was very peaceful to be just by myself after almost seven months of being constantly with people. No phones, no mail, and only to be surrounded by the vast ocean and boundless sky!

Then we arrived at the Panama Canal. The night before we approached the actual crossing, our attendant, Mr. Huang came into our room and warned us to be sure to put everything out of sight and to lock up. The ship would also seal all the storage. I wondered about all the commotion. Mr. Huang explained that they had bad experiences in the past. They often found that things disappeared after the local workpeople's and customs inspectors' visits.

The following morning, a group of Panamanians came aboard. They went through the ship and left. When this inspection was over, we then proceeded to wait in line for the actual canal crossing. By the time we sailed into the famous docks, I watched many people on our ship hurriedly equipping themselves with all kinds of fishing gear. When the water level started to rise, all these fishermen kept on busily dropping their lines into the water and amazingly, it seemed that everyone caught some fish. They didn't even bother with hooks. They just tied shrimp on the lines and caught fish. We certainly had more than enough fish to fill our appetites for the rest of the trip.

The water in the locks kept on rising and rising. Slowly, we passed through the canal. On the warm waters of the Caribbean Sea, we saw many sea turtles with shells as big as large round table tops floating on the surface. Many sea birds peacefully sunned themselves on the turtles. Even now, I still marvel what a great engineering marvel the canal was. And that was the last event on our trip back to the US until we reached Baltimore.

We arrived early in the afternoon. My husband was already waving to us from the pier. We bid goodbye to the other two passengers and the officers of the ship, and left the ship. It took us exactly two months to complete our voyage.

My husband drove a second-hand Ford sedan. We loaded our luggage, then happily started the journey to our new address that he had found for us. It was an apartment on Staten Island, he told me. After a long drive, at last the car climbed onto a high terrace. We arrived in front of a house which must have had about a hundred steps further up on a hill. Then my husband said to me, "It is the whole flat on the third floor." Having been on a rocking ship for two months, my legs were not very steady on land, but I remember I struggled to help my husband with all the luggage, piece after piece, first climbing up the front steps, then eventually climbing up to the third floor.

My husband had bought some necessary pieces of furniture for us. We were glad we did not have to sleep on the floor that night. Early the next morning, I toured the new apartment. It was bright and cheerful. The spacious living room had many windows on two sides. There was an eat-in kitchen, one bath, two good-size bedrooms, plus a large master bedroom with a large bay window. However, my husband was already using it as his study.

My husband took me downstairs to meet our landlady, Mrs. Speroni, who was an elderly Italian lady in her 70s. She was living alone in the large three-story house. She spoke English with a heavy Italian accent, but one could sense right away that she was a very kind and lovely lady.

Being on the third floor on top of a little hill, and on high ground, we had very nice views looking out, but when I registered the two children at the local school, P. S. 48, I found out that all those steps and the slopes weren't that fun to climb. Leo and Eva had different school hours, so that meant I had to make the trip four times a day. Unfortunately, the school was too close for the school bus, but too far for the children to walk by themselves at their age. On days when I had to get groceries, it always kept me huffing and puffing, although, looking back now, I think those four years residing there must have kept my family healthy and trained us to be good walkers for life.

When the things that we stored at my friend's place in Denver were retrieved, our life became normal again. Later, at the end of the summer, the children started school. Both had wonderful teachers. We still kept the rule in the house: no English was allowed. I did have a hard time keeping the children on the quiet side in view of the fact their father worked at home and also because the landlady lived downstairs.

Sometime later, Mrs. Speroni's daughter and her family came, and lived beneath us on the second floor. No one ever complained about the children. They even called us by long distance after we moved to Wisconsin to invite us to move back after we had been gone for quite some time.

My husband resumed his daily work routine: writing, reading, and lecturing. Through his lecturing, he met a kind lady, Mrs. Dorothy Donath, who was a professional editor for a publishing company. She liked the translations of the Milarepa manuscripts so well that she volunteered to do all the necessary editing for free. Thus began her weekly weekend visits to our house from Friday through Sunday. The arrangement lasted almost for the whole duration of time that we lived there. She was such a diligent, meticulous, hard working person, we all admired her. It was my job to type or retype their finished papers for the final copy. *(See page 302.)*

At that time, the Verrazano bridge had not been built yet. Whenever we wanted to go to Manhattan, we would have to go to the St. George pier to take the ferry. Still, it was very convenient. It was a half hour or so ride. In summer, gentle breezes coming over the water made it very pleasant. On our way home, if we were driving and waiting in line to board at the South Ferry in Manhattan, then we could enjoy the famous two for a nickel soft pretzels. Our good friend Peter Gruber had his office on Wall Street. Frequently, he would just get on the ferry and would drive to our place.

Life on Staten Island was like living in a small town, much more tranquil and peaceful than in the city. Many of our neighbors were related to Mrs. Speroni. All around, people all knew each other in the friendly Italian neighborhood.

One day, my husband told me that he had learned that there was a well-known Mongolian lama, who had the highest Buddhist rank and title of "Hutuketu" (in Mongolian). He had come to the US upon the invitation from a Professor Lattimore. His Holiness had been living in Boston for quite some time. My husband said we should invite him for a visit. My husband somehow got in touch with the Hutuketu and we went to New York and brought him home to Staten Island.

When we first saw him, he was standing upright in front of a building, wearing a traditional monk's robe. He was a lean figure with a dark complexion. Two dark eyes glistened above his high cheek bones. When he saw us, he swiftly moved toward our car and got in the passenger seat. Before we pulled away from the curb, he said to my husband, "Could we stop at a bank?" Since he did not specify which bank he wanted, we just stopped at a bank on our way. He went in while we waited. Shortly, he came out and smilingly said, "Now let's go."

On our way home, I sat in the back of the car, trying to guess his age. Evidently, he was older than us. He seemed to be in his late sixties or early seventies. When we arrived, I warned him about all the steps we had to climb. But he went up the sixty-some steps up the hill to the house, then entered the house and climbed the three stories without huffing and puffing!

We showed him his room. He took his robe off. Underneath it, he was wearing a bright flowery Hawaiian shirt. He saw our looks of surprise, and cheerfully explained, "Oh, I have a lama student in Hawaii. He sends clothes to me. Whatever he sends, I wear it." He was so appreciative, so grateful that he did not have to worry about mundane matters like what to wear!

Soon, school was over, and I went and picked up the two children. When I took them to meet him, the Hutuketu beamed, and with a big smile, he took something out from his pocket. He took the children's hands and put a shining silver dollar into the palm of each child and blessed them. At that moment, I realized why he asked to stop at a bank before we came home. But I am not sure how he knew that we had children, or how many we had.

That evening he talked with my husband. Their conversation was carried on in mixed languages—English, Chinese, and Tibetan, since his main language was Mongolian.

Early the next morning, I got up to prepare breakfast for everyone and to get the children up. I tried to keep quiet so as not to wake the Hutuketu. But he surprised me by appearing in my kitchen, coming up from the stairs, and told me he had already been outside the house to give some offerings to all sentient beings. He also apologized for taking some rice and fruit without asking me. He actually kept so quiet that none of us in the family had heard him at all. Meanwhile, I thought about all the steps he had to climb!

He stayed with us for another day. He enjoyed my "Chinese food home cooking." On the third day, we took him back to New York City.

Days afterwards, our house was still filled with an indescribable peacefulness and calmness. Even the children were unusually quiet and well-behaved. We all felt so blessed as we never felt before. Only after a long while, the serenity gradually dissipated.

Years later, my husband always said to me that it was so unfortunate that because of the language difficulty, they kept the discussion on Buddhism at a more simple level, and he was not able to learn more from the Hutuketu. Both Eva and I both still remember that short visit from the holy enlightened free spirit in 1957. *(See page 305.)*

Sometime in the later part of 1958, my husband's eyesight worsened seriously. It became hard for him to focus, either for typing or reading. He had to break his work every now and then to rinse his eyes with cold water in order to relieve the dry and burning sensation. He began a whole series of visiting famous eye doctors, but could not find any help. During the day, he would keep on his translating work and prepare his lectures as best as he could. At night, after I had put the children to bed, then I would read the books on Western religions and philosophy to him while he rested his eyes. Meanwhile, Mrs. Donath still came on weekends to work with him.

My husband went through various kinds of eye tests, and yet none of the doctors could find anything physically wrong that was causing his symptoms. He complained to me that he could not carry on any decent conversations with others because he could not look at others for long. Light, running water, all made his eyes smart. The feeling of tearing was constantly there, but no tears could come out. I deeply sympathized with his frustrations and suffering, but I could only feel hopeless and worried.

In the early 1950s, Buddhism, Taoism, and Indian religions were not that well known or popular in the West. Most of the Buddhist teachings in the US were introduced by the Japanese professor Dr.

D. T. Suzuki and his wife's books on Zen. Also, there was Dr. Evans-Wentz's writings on Tibetan Tantra.

Then Mr. Alan Watts' talks and his books on Zen made the Zen school of Japanese Buddhism very popular among the people searching for their spiritual liberation. More people were gradually introduced to Oriental thought and philosophy. Many people started to talk about Buddhist Enlightenment and how one could be freed from conventional burdens and become enlightened. The famous Jack Kerouac and many beatniks probably misinterpreted the Koan teachings in the Suzuki works, and thinking that Enlightenment could be easily or quickly reached by living a freewheeling lifestyle, ignored the serious study of the disciplines and practices of the basic teaching that is needed before anyone could reach the stage of becoming truly Enlightened.

This gave my husband great concerns, so he decided to set the translation work aside, and started to work on his book, which he entitled, *The Practice of Zen*. Day after day, he struggled with his tired eyes, as Mrs. Donath edited, and I typed. I often typed for several hours past midnight. Things went on like this for a few months, until he finished the book. One night, I also finished typing the last page of the manuscript, except the page for the Table of Contents. It was about midnight, and I was very tired. My husband stopped me from typing the last few lines. He insisted that I could do it the next morning in just a few minutes, so I left everything and went to bed.

The next morning, after I took the children to school, I sat down in front of the typewriter, ready to type, but for some reason, my eyes just could not focus. I knew the book only contained five chapters, but no matter how hard I kept on typing, the words on the draft page all remained like little ants marching in lines with fuzzy figures. I thought maybe after a little rest, I'd try again, but who could know that from that moment on, I had lost my good eyesight, exactly like my husband.

When Mrs. Donath came that weekend, she finished typing that one page. Both my husband and I were in deep despair because of our eye problems. Mrs. Donath comforted us by saying that it was time to pick a publisher for the book, and not to be in such dark moods.

So, we collected our low spirits, and we discussed and compared all the famous publishers. In the end, we decided that Harper & Brothers publishing company was most suitable for the work. The next step was for my husband to write a letter and to mail the manuscript to them for consideration. In the letter, he said he expected an answer from the publisher within two weeks. I did not know how we survived those two weeks. All the while, we did not know what a difficult task it could be for a first-time writer to find a publisher. We did not take our own lack of formal qualifications into consideration. After all, my husband did not have any academic credentials in this country. He had no idea about the process for getting a book published. Normally, it first must be approved by at least two distinguished readers. Usually, this step alone could not be accomplished within the two weeks that my husband had demanded. But, my husband was very confident in his work. Indeed, at the end of the two weeks, we heard from Harper's.

It was my husband's fortieth birthday *(1960)* when he signed the contract with Harper & Brothers *(later Harper & Row, then HarperCollins)*. He was also paid a grand total of $500 for his advance from Harper's. I remember that we first went to a fancy restaurant, then we went out and bought an expensive German-made Telefunken hi fi.

When Eva was in the fourth grade, I was asked to go to the school one day for some consultation. I became a little worried, not knowing what the meeting was about. But then it turned out that her teacher and the principal wanted to inform me that they had considered skipping Eva one grade but had made the decision to keep Eva at her grade because the school did not approve of students skipping grades, in spite of the fact that Eva's ability was above her class level. Not being raised in the US, both my husband and I were not that familiar with the American school system, so we just followed their decision. However, at the end of the semester, they met with us again, but this time, they said that they felt they should let Eva skip the second half of the fourth grade and the first half of the fifth grade. Therefore, after the winter break, Eva was put into the new class with all new classmates. She came home in the first couple of weeks and was confused with her math lessons because her new class was already in the midst of studying fractions, which she was not ready for, due to her skipping a grade. Fortunately, it was still at a level both my husband and I could handle. Every day, one of us would try to help her to catch up with her new work. We showed her how to solve the problems the way we learned back in China. Soon she was able to do her math with ease. Meanwhile, she was puzzled about why she could always reach the same correct answers as her class, but the method we taught her was different from the teacher's. We had to tell her, as long as she could solve the problems, it was perfectly all right. She did not know that we never knew what the "new math" was.

She loved to read. She would read anything she could lay her hands on, whether it was on her level or not. She often surprised us with her grasp of grammar and vocabulary. I found my husband and I frequently asking her for the correct spelling of certain words and how to express ourselves in more idiomatic English. We appreciated her help very much. Even today, I still depend on her for help.

One day after school, I was at P. S. 48, picking up the children. The principal came by and saw me. He came over and said, "Are you the mother of Eva and Leo?" Then he continued. "You must have been reading to your children a lot, is that right?" I told him I had been doing that every night since they were tiny babies. "You see, it definitely shows in your children!" he remarked.

Then he paused a moment and said, "Mrs. Chang, I heard from your daughter that you had taught school in India. Have you thought about teaching again?" He followed with some of the attractive reasons for me to go back to school to pursue an educational career and ended our conversation by saying, "Do give it some serious thought!"

That night, when the children were asleep, I related the principal's suggestions to my husband. He felt since the children were already in the third and fourth grades, they no longer needed my constant attention. If I could study and acquire twelve credits in education courses, then I could do as the principal suggested – to start as a substitute teacher and then work towards becoming a full-fledged teacher. By being a teacher, I could still spend time with the children when they had vacations or holidays. Also, career-wise, there would always be a need for good teachers. The reasons all seemed very ideal and too attractive for me not to give it a try, but I had some grave doubts. First, by then, I had been out of school for many years. During all those years, I never seriously tried to improve my English. Was my English capable of handling the study? With my husband's eye problems and my own eye problems, could I manage the reading and writing? Another question was that I fled from China in a hurry. There was not a single document to prove that I had done any work at the university level. How could I apply for admission to any school? Yet if I did not try, I would never find out. One thing I did not have to worry about was my children. They were both well-behaved and good students. They were then at the age where they could spare me the time needed for studying. Besides, my husband had also volunteered to see them to bed, so gradually I started to compare and select schools to call.

My first choice was the Teachers College at Hunter College. Fortunately for me, the school said that I could register for two three-credit courses, and if I could earn those credits with a grade of B or above, then I could become a regular student. With that information, I began my night school student's life. I was then thirty-five years old. The night school classes were designed to fit the students' lives, most of whom were adults. Some of them already held some kind of day jobs or were housewives and mothers. Therefore, each three-credit class would only meet once a week in the evening. I was glad I only had to go to the city two evenings a week. As I recall, at that time, even though I was commuting alone at night on subways, ferries, and buses, I did not have any safety concerns at all.

Through these two basic education courses, I became further aware of the differences between the Chinese and American educational systems and philosophies. Other important discoveries to me were the many problems the American public schools were facing, especially in the larger American cities. These issues included race, slums, religions, languages, smart and slow students, handicapped students, and also what a teacher could or could not do to discipline students. Some of these problems did not seem to be problems I had ever considered in China. I also was very surprised at the light schoolwork load compared to the Asian courses I had completed, and the casual respect paid to the educational profession in society. But interestingly, at that time, the budget for education never came up as a topic, not even once.

We lived on Staten Island for four years, during which time my husband would occasionally go off to some quiet place where he would concentrate on his writing, translating, and meditation.

I think it was in the winter of 1958. My husband was granted a fellowship to reside at the famous MacDowell Colony for artists in Peterborough, New Hampshire. It was our friend Peter Gruber who drove him up. It was too far for us to visit. I learned about his daily routine only through his letters. He wrote that all the fellows stayed in the same large main building. They were all required to dine and socialize at the same time together in the evening. In the morning, all residents then went separately to work at the individual studios to which they were assigned. My husband was assigned to a studio which housed a grand piano that was used by the famous American composer, Aaron Copeland, when he was working there. New Hampshire could be very cold. Sometimes, the heavy snow and ice would give my husband a hard time getting to his studio. On those days, while the outside was like a glass world, the lunch would be delivered to the residents.

He wrote about some of the new friends he met. It seemed that all the people there were very talented and hard-working. There were writers, artists, and musicians. Some of them had to work hard to save up enough money and leave their jobs in order to be able to get the time to concentrate on their work at the Colony. A couple of the people he befriended there later came to Staten Island to visit us. I especially remembered one lady who was an accomplished writer of children's books. She complained to me, saying, "I don't see why we can't adopt your Chinese concubine system. Wouldn't it be nice if my husband had four or five wives? If I want to write and do not wish to be disturbed, I can just send him to one of the other wives." *(Virginia Sorensen, winner of the Newbery Medal and Guggenheim Fellowship for Creative Arts.) (See page 311 for more on MacDowell Colony.)*

Another time, we rented a small cottage in upstate New York by a small lake *(Copake Lake)* for two months. Now and then, I would drive up with the children to visit him on weekends. That year, my father-in-law passed away.

Brothers in the Dharma Garma C. C. Chang and Peter Gruber at retreat for meditation.

The next winter, my mother-in-law came from Taiwan to see her two sons and daughter. She divided her time between Connecticut at Louie and Jean's house and our house. She also visited my husband for a week at the small cottage and even cooked for him while there. She managed all this with only the tiniest paring knife!

Picture from the newspaper, *The Staten Island Advance*, on Wednesday, February 15, 1961, showing traditional "hong bao" red envelopes with money being given to Eva and Leo by Grandma Chang

After my husband came home from that retreat, while my mother-in-law was in Connecticut, we took a short trip during the children's summer vacation. We rented a cabin in a New York state park close to the New England border, and used that cabin as our base and toured the surrounding areas. We ventured to listen to the Boston Symphony Orchestra playing concerts at Tanglewood, and we watched a classic Indian dancer performing at Jacob's Pillow. I can still clearly visualize some of the beautiful scenes even today. That trip remains as one of my favorite memories. We also learned that traveling like that, we could have more freedom than being confined in hotel rooms, while at the same time, it was more economical too.

One day, a friend, Dr. C. Y. Chang, came to visit us. He had just recently published a book on Chinese Taoism. We had not seen him for quite some time. As soon as we talked, he noticed that my husband had trouble looking at him naturally, so he asked if my husband's eyes were all right. After he heard our story, he said it was too bad that he did not know about it earlier. Then he started to tell us of his own experience.

In the year 1948, he was about to finish his PhD thesis at Columbia University. The political situation in China was getting more tense between the Communists and the Nationalists. Already, many students had returned to China. It was his fourth year working on his degree in the US. He discussed the situation with his wife back in China and both decided that he should stay a little longer and hurry up to finish his paper in the US, and then return to China. Unfortunately, by the time he was close to the end of his research work, his eyes gradually gave out due to overuse. Somehow, he managed to complete his thesis, but the completion was done at a much delayed date. He did eventually get his degree. However, by that time, China had already changed hands. He had also exhausted his funds and was cut off from his family. With no funds and no way to return to China because all the transportation had ceased, he desperately needed to find a job, but he knew he could not hold a position on account of his eye troubles. The symptoms were exactly the same as ours. He could not look at people, he could not look at things moving, he was afraid of light, and could hardly focus. He spent his last bit of money visiting eye doctors, but only became more despondent.

One afternoon, he went to the seashore. He walked to and fro for quite some time at the beach, debating whether he should end his life in the sea. He was so deeply lost in thought that he completely ignored the beautiful sun, sand, and people on the beach. Suddenly, an elderly lady came up to him and said, "Young man, is there anything troubling you? You look so dejected. Would you like to talk to me?" He was so startled by this kindness, he could not help but unload all his problems which had been gnawing at him for the last few months. Soon after he stopped talking, the lady patted his shoulder and said, "It is your lucky day today. You see, I am the mother of a doctor who can help you. But you will have to trust me, because the method he uses is not approved by the American Medical Association. But I do know he has helped people like you. I will give you his phone and address with my recommendation. I'm sure he will see you."

So Dr. Chang started his treatments. Slowly, he was able to regain his normal eyesight.

After hearing our story, he immediately wrote down the phone number for Dr. Jacobson, wished us good luck, and took his leave.

That night, we went to bed with mixed emotions. We were excited to have found a doctor, and yet, we were also worried. What if he still could not help us? The next day, when Dr. Jacobson heard that Dr. C. Y. Chang had referred us, he quickly said that he could squeeze my husband in right that afternoon. When my husband returned home, he could not wait to tell me, "I am sure he is the right doctor and he can help us."

According to Dr. Jacobson, he felt that Asian people were more prone to have this kind of trouble. He told my husband that he once treated a high Chinese official and was able to help him. The medicine that he used to treat his patients was some kind of enzyme that he made by himself. That day, even with only one injection, instantly, my husband felt some relief in his eyes. The doctor wanted to see him twice a week. The treatment was $25 a visit *(equivalent to about $212 in 2017 dollars)*.

After one month, I also started to visit the doctor. Shortly afterwards, we talked to Dr. Jacobson to see if there was some way to help us with some discount for payment. Without hesitation, he said he could teach us to give the injections to each other. We could call into his office and report our progress, and then he would send new vials of medicine to us. We only needed to visit him once a month. We thanked him for his kindness and generosity and faithfully followed his instructions from then on.

Slowly, a few months went by, and our eyes regained about half our original sight. Still, we could not efficiently work like any person with normal sight. It was necessary, therefore, to continue with Dr. Jacobson's injection therapy treatment.

One Friday afternoon, shortly after I injected my husband with the new medicine which had just arrived through the mail, he complained that his heart was having unusual palpitations. I asked him to lie down in bed and thought that it should soon be over. Half an hour passed, and he was feeling worse, so I hurriedly called Dr. Jacobson. He assured me not to worry. He asked for our pharmacy's telephone number and told me to pick up the antidote as soon as the new prescription was ready, and told me to inject my husband immediately with the antidote. He also told me that with the antidote, I should let my husband sleep. I followed his instructions, and afterwards, my husband settled in to sleep.

Soon after, Mrs. Donath arrived for her weekly visit, so she just worked by herself while my husband slept. My husband fell into such a deep sleep that he did not even stir, so we all retired early that night. The next day, he remained in the same position, motionless. We watched him constantly and tried not to disturb him. Saturday went by. Sunday, by late morning, Mrs. Donath had done all the work she could alone, and left after lunch. I started to become concerned. I thought of calling Dr. Jacobson, but gave up the idea because it was Sunday. The children also sensed that something was very wrong, and stayed close by me. They were not interested in playing and both kept very quiet. Around the children's bedtime, my husband made some noise and turned in his bed. He slowly opened his eyes and motioned us to come near, and asked, "What time is it?" No need to say that after his long sleeping spell, his recovery brought such relief to us all. We never learned what went wrong. However, since Dr. Jacobson's treatments were our only hope to recover our eyesight, we continued to remain under his care.

We continued to be his patients for some four more years. Luckily, that kind of reaction never happened again.

Dr. Chung-yuan Chang became a Professor of Philosophy at the University of Hawaii at Manoa, and authored several books on Taoism and Asian philosophy, including <u>Creativity and Taoism: A Study of Chinese Philosophy, Art, and Poetry</u>, Julian Press, 1963 and other books.

I remembered Dr. Jacobson's first name, and on a whim, looked him up on-line. To my shock, he was a famous (some might say infamous) doctor who treated President Kennedy and many Hollywood stars. He was also known as "Dr. Feelgood" to the Secret Service and his clientele. Read more about him on page 291.

Dr. Richard Robinson

Sometime in late September of 1960, a Dr. Richard Robinson came to our house. He was the chairman of the Department of Indian Studies at the University of Wisconsin at Madison. He came to invite my husband to give some lectures there. The invitation was cordially accepted by my husband. I could not remember when he made that trip. When he came back, he told me that under the Indian Studies Department, there was also a newly established Buddhist Studies Department. A good number of their graduate students were PhD candidates for Buddhist Studies. The campus was beautifully located next to Lake Mendota. His lectures were well received. Dr. Robinson had offered him a position as a lecturer starting in the 1961 to 1962 academic year. Then he said to me, "Their Chinese program is looking for an instructor. Why don't you try to apply for it?"

This information came so unexpectedly, I was fully taken aback. I, a plain housewife with only a BA, how could I teach college students without any formal preparation? But for a couple of days, he kept on urging me to apply, so finally, just like before, when I was applying for Hunter College, once again, I sat down and started to compose my application. I thought it over, and figured perhaps I had some advantages for this teaching position. For one thing, I did major in Chinese Literature as an undergraduate. For another, I speak the Beijing dialect, which is the national standard dialect, which, even today, is still the most desired dialect for any Chinese language teachers. After all, I was born in Beijing, and I spent the final two years of college in Beijing after the school relocated back to Beijing from Chengdu. My college was the Yenching University. Yenching is the ancient name for Beijing.

My finished product was not what most people would consider a formal resume. I had to present my case in the fashion of a letter, because I had to explain why I did not have any documents to prove my academic history. Fortunately, I had learned that the President of my University during the wartime years, Dr. Yi-Pao

Mei, now resided in Iowa *(Professor and Head of Oriental Studies at the University of Iowa)*. I knew he would remember me, since the enrollment at the University during the war years had decreased to a small number. In particular, there were very few who majored in Chinese Literature. I also have a very unusual Chinese name, and had a very famous person as my father. Indeed, he soon kindly sent a letter to the head of the Chinese language program at Wisconsin.

To my biggest surprise, a letter soon came back from the Chairman of the Linguistic Department of the University of Wisconsin, which was the Department where the Chinese Language program was housed. It informed me that they were appointing me as an instructor and expected me to start for the fall semester of 1961. I just could not believe this truly unexpected development. It was beyond my wildest dreams. In order to get settled before the school year started, I immersed myself in the planning and packing for our big move with my husband, with both apprehension and excitement.

Since I would be working soon, we knew we definitely would need a second car. Our friend Peter Gruber generously offered one of his cars to us. Our plan was to leave in May, taking my mother-in-law who was visiting us at the time, and drop her in Chicago, where she wanted to visit an old friend before she flew to El Paso to visit my sister-in-law Yvonne.

We thought we would combine some sightseeing along the way, so as to break the tiresome long-distance driving.

In May, we said goodbye to our landlady, Mrs. Speroni, and left Staten Island in two cars. The trip was fairly uneventful, but we did not stop at too many tourist stops on account of our two loaded cars. In Chicago, we delivered my mother-in-law safely to her friend, and not long afterwards, we crossed the state line of Wisconsin.

A friend had remarked to us before our departure, "You will know when you are in Wisconsin," but he did not tell us why. Soon after we passed the border, we found out the reason. You sure could tell by the smell in the air!

It was late spring when we arrived. There were dairy farms along the highways, and cows were scattered all over the farms. Farmers also were busy adding horse manure into their freshly tilled land. No need for further confirmation; we knew we had arrived at "America's Dairyland."

When we reached Madison, the first thing we did was to check into a hotel. We quickly cleaned ourselves, bought some local papers, and then we went to a restaurant. That evening was spent on searching for a place to live. On the third day, we happily rented and moved into a house just on the outside of the city limits. It was a four-bedroom house in a newly developed area. We were pleased. It was not like New York City. Here, we could conveniently park our two cars right in front of our house.

Next, we went to the University to visit our departments. The summer vacation had already started, but the campus was still full of activities because the summer school was in session. My husband led me to a small independent building on State Street, and there I found out that it was the School of Library Science Building, and both the Indian Studies and the Linguistics Departments were both housed upstairs.

I found my way up to the Linguistics department and met Dr. Fowler, the department chairman. We talked briefly, then he took me to see the Chinese program head. As soon as I walked in her office, I thought to myself, "Do I know this lady?" Dr. Fowler introduced me to her, and said to me, "This is Dr. Chou, your program director." Immediately, my memory turned to my freshman English Class 101 in Sichuan. Dr. Chou was then our "Miss Chou" and was our most strict English teacher. However, she did not remember me, because she just welcomed me and said I could go in tomorrow and she would then show me my responsibilities.

The following day, I was given my teaching materials and was told that I would be teaching an upper class with mostly graduate students. I was also given a nice office. When I had a chance later, I asked Dr. Chou whether she recognized me as one of her former students at Yenching. Her answer solved my puzzlement over my quick appointment. She said that she did not remember me as she had taught so many students. She remembered either the best or worst students in her classes, but she did see that I was a Yenching student. Besides, she also had received our President Dr. Yi-Pao Mei's letter about me. She knew she could trust Yenching's training and standards. A native speaker with a Chinese Literature major would most likely be qualified to teach the current courses they were offering; therefore, they accepted me without hesitation. Thus, I started my new life as an instructor at the University of Wisconsin at Madison.

One weekend, Dr. Fowler stopped by our place. He was a kind, elderly gentleman. He said his house was not too far from us. He wanted to see if we needed anything. He asked us what made us choose this house, and if we had any garages. We were curious about the questions. Then he said he could live out of town because he had two garages. He gave us a serious warning that in Wisconsin, winter could bring really severe commuting problems.

Before that Labor Day, I had registered both Eva and Leo for their school. It was nice that they could ride the school bus. Time went by fast. I began my teaching. However, my husband got very upset because Dr. Robinson's oral offer to him as a lecturer at the University was simply "forgotten." Dr. Robinson just denied that he had ever made the offer.

This was the second broken promise that my husband had encountered. The first time was with Dr. Muses in Colorado, and

129

now here again in Wisconsin. We were both disillusioned that people with such high academic credentials could still swallow their words so easily.

Alas, we were both physically in Madison, and I did get a teaching appointment. There was nothing we could do in our situation other than to just accept what reality dealt us. Certainly, we both did learn a good lesson. From then on, we learned not to take only verbal agreements. We learned the hard way about the American phrase that one "must get everything in writing." Unless an agreement was written in black and white, it is not legal.

The children adapted to their new environment without any problems. As for my husband, he did not want to waste his time there. Besides his regular work, he registered in some courses he felt would be useful for his own field. For a couple of years, he chose courses in Sanskrit, Pali, Western Philosophy, and Symbolic Logic. Those courses kept him rather busy. I learned a great deal about my own language through the English speaking students. I could see the two different cultures of the East and West reflected and contrasted in these two languages.

Our days went by routinely. Without much notice, the days shifted into winter. The weather suddenly turned colder and colder. For two weeks, it remained below twenty degrees F. Every morning, the outside world was like a world made with glass. Sad to say, neither one of our two cars could be started. I could not even open the doors of my car. Taxi service was out of the question because none could come to my location out of town. For days, I had to walk about a mile in the knee-high snow to get to the outskirts of town, and then hitch a ride to school, much against my husband's admonitions. Yet I couldn't miss my classes. By then, we understood Dr. Fowler's warning about not having a garage. As soon as winter vacation began, we found an apartment in town, on the city bus line, and we quickly moved. Oh, what a relief it was to all of us.

One day, a friend called and asked my husband about a newly published book of his. It surprised both of us. The friend told us the title of the book was *The Exotic Teaching of Tibetan Tantra,* published by the Falcon's Wing Press, with my husband as the translator. The friend had seen it in Europe. We were completely in the dark about this. It must have been published by Dr. Muses, but the manuscript my husband sent him was only the very first draft. It needed much detailed editing before it was readable. Our friend mailed a copy to us. We saw that it showed Dr. Muses as the editor. My husband thought it over carefully, then decided just to let it go, since the full responsibility for preparing the book in its final form rested with Dr. Muses. The failings and imperfections of the book as published were the responsibility of Dr. Muses. Therefore, my husband did not make any protest about the publication. However, a few years later, out of the blue, we received a letter with a check for $1,000 from the Falcon's Wing Press. Included was a letter from Mrs. Howell, the owner of the Press. She apologized formally for the unfair treatment of us years ago, and told us that the check was to compensate us for the work my husband had done on the Tibetan Tantra book. Most importantly, she said that Dr. Muses was no longer associated with the Press. He had been fired. We happily deposited this little windfall, and acknowledged Mrs. Howell's belated apology.

I taught for two years. During the second year, the number of our students increased. Also, there were more universities adding independent Chinese Language departments in the US. Dr. Chou and Dr. Fowler both felt it might be time for a large university like Wisconsin to have our own department with a graduate program. The dilemma was that if there were no students applying, there was no reason to have a graduate program. Then they decided to ask me to apply for a graduate degree to solve this problem. After discussion with my husband, I became the very first registered student in our brand-new department. So, as soon as the school year was over, I took two courses in summer school to fulfill the requirements for graduate school.

After we had moved to the city, our good friend Peter Gruber would come to visit us sometimes. We would find a quiet hotel room for him, where he could study and practice Buddhism with my husband for a few days. During the same period in Madison, our other good friend, Dr. C.T. Shen also came to visit. He was an extremely busy person. A few times, he also took time out from his work and asked my husband to find a place for him to stay for a short study and retreat. In the US, I think these two friends were truly my husband's dearest friends. The friendship with Dr. Shen, our children's "Uncle Shen," would especially impact both of our two families in the years to come. *(See page 285 for more information about this generous and humble man.)*

It was in this year, 1963, that my husband and I both passed the immigration test and were granted U.S. citizenship. We were formally sworn in at the courtroom in Madison. With our new status, the Chinese Department also surprised me.  Because I had gained citizenship, I was qualified for a scholarship, which they awarded me.

Over these two years, my husband and I were often included in the various faculty activities and parties given by our departments. But now, as a graduate student, I had to depend on these vacation days to catch up with my studies, my papers, exams, and household chores. And I had my children's interests to look after. Though my husband and I still attended these holiday parties, I found myself constantly pressed for time.

One winter, Leo told me he wanted to be a paperboy. I did not want to completely discourage him. He was eleven, going on twelve years old. I knew being a paperboy was a good training for building strong character, but I also worried about the hard Wisconsin winter weather, so we compromised. He would only deliver weekend papers. The first time when the papers were dropped at our entrance for Leo to deliver, it was about five o'clock in the morning. It was both dark and freezing outside. I was up with him. At that time, the different sections of the paper were not stacked automatically by machines, so I had to help him to sort out and insert the papers properly for his customers. When sorted, the piles were even too heavy for me to carry. Bicycling was out of the question on the slippery icy streets. So, I drove him in our car. It was a good decision, because the route that Leo had was not all on level ground, but also included slippery slopes. I did not know at the end of each month how much money he actually had collected, but I was very happy at the end of the fourth month when he gave up the venture.

Earlier, my husband had promised the Minister of Education in Taiwan that he would teach for one year. So in 1964, he went back to Taiwan and was pleased to have the opportunity to be close to his mother. It happened that our friend C. T. Shen was the owner of a shipping firm. Because he just recently built a huge oil tanker, which was having its maiden voyage to Taiwan, he invited my husband to be the only guest for the trip. However, he would have to board the ship at the dock at Bayonne, N. J. My husband thought our whole family could drive him there and make a summer vacation out of the trip. We could have a chance to visit my youngest sister whom I had not seen since she went back to Taiwan and got married when I was still living on Staten Island. Therefore, when the schools were over in the summer, we did exactly that. We traveled leisurely eastward. Just before the end of the trip, we went to see my sister, Natalia *(Wu Ming)*, and visited with her husband and her newborn baby in New Jersey.

We then drove to the Bayonne Pier, and unloaded all of my husband's luggage. The children and I reluctantly bid goodbye to my husband and slowly turned back homeward. The first night, we stopped in Pittsburgh. I was worried about the long drive home, but fatigue finally overtook me and I fell asleep. The next morning, we had a good breakfast, bought some snacks, and continued on our trip. We were in the Chrysler that Peter Gruber had given us. It was long and heavy, well suited for highway driving. We did not make any stops until noontime, when we took a break at a service area in Ohio. Leo said he did not have to use the restroom, so Eva and I went to the ladies' room. When we came out, Leo was nowhere to be found. Then I saw a group of people crouched together and busily talking about something. Eva and I went over to look. It was Leo! There, he was, unconscious and lying on the ground! I made my way in, and luckily, a doctor was already attending to him. The doctor said to me, "It was just too hot and he had heat stroke, but he is all right." By then, Leo had slowly recovered. We helped him up and let him sit up. The doctor got some water for Leo. Leo became embarrassed because other people were watching him. He insisted on leaving. I wanted to thank the doctor, but he refused to accept anything and just left. I asked Eva to keep Leo company and quickly I went to buy some lunch for us. After we got into the car, Leo asked me not to make any more stops. I did not want to upset him anymore, so I kept on driving, straight for Madison. When we arrived home, I checked the odometer in the car. It showed we had covered more than six hundred miles. It certainly was a record for a day's long-distance driving for me.

At home in Madison, I was alone with my two children. It was a great blessing that both Eva and Leo were good students, so I never had to worry about their schoolwork. I only missed spending more free time with them. While my husband was in Taiwan, he occasionally would go visit my father. We could not afford to call each other, but did write frequently and regularly. In one of his letters, he informed me that my father was admitted to a hospital because he had some teeth pulled and somehow got an infection. Immediately, I wrote to my father to wish him a quick recovery. All through his life, my father had enjoyed excellent health. Earlier, when I told him I was going back to school to study, and later, to teach, he was so pleased he wrote back to encourage me. I think I made him very happy. He was pleased that both my husband and I did not stop improving ourselves. I was deeply sorry I could not visit him in the hospital now that he was sick.

During my husband's long absence, I managed to keep both my own study and my teaching proceeding according to schedule. My students knew I was fairly demanding, yet I think they all enjoyed the work. One class even gave me a silver bowl when they graduated. I still have the bowl with me after all these years, through all of our moves. I finally earned my Master of Arts degree in 1964.

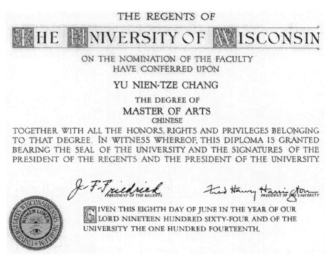

THE REGENTS OF

THE UNIVERSITY OF WISCONSIN

ON THE NOMINATION OF THE FACULTY
HAVE CONFERRED UPON

YU NIEN-TZE CHANG

THE DEGREE OF
MASTER OF ARTS
CHINESE

TOGETHER WITH ALL THE HONORS, RIGHTS AND PRIVILEGES BELONGING TO THAT DEGREE. IN WITNESS WHEREOF, THIS DIPLOMA IS GRANTED BEARING THE SEAL OF THE UNIVERSITY AND THE SIGNATURES OF THE PRESIDENT OF THE REGENTS AND THE PRESIDENT OF THE UNIVERSITY

GIVEN THIS EIGHTH DAY OF JUNE IN THE YEAR OF OUR LORD NINETEEN HUNDRED SIXTY-FOUR AND OF THE UNIVERSITY THE ONE HUNDRED FOURTEENTH.

One early afternoon in November, I was in my office preparing for my afternoon class, but for some unknown reason, I was nervous and restless. I could not concentrate on anything. Finally, I asked the secretary to go to my classroom and cancel my class for me. This was something I had never done before. I picked up all my papers and books and went to the car. I have never enjoyed just driving, but that day I just got in the car and drove aimlessly for a couple of hours. Then I decided to go home. When I opened the door, the first thing I saw was a telegram on the floor. It was from my brother Peng in Taipei. He wrote: "Father passed away this morning." Father was eighty-six.

The next day, people in my department all sent me sympathy cards because they had seen a small news item about my father's death, with his picture, in the New York Times.

A few years later, when I was able to go to Taiwan, I went to visit one of my father's close friends at his office. Soon, someone asked permission to see me. He asked me, "Are you the second daughter of our old president? Is your name Hsiang Hsiang *(Thinking Thinking)*?" I answered yes, and he continued to say that at the very last day, he was attending my father at his bedside in the hospital. He heard my father repeatedly murmuring, "Hsiang Hsiang, Hsiang Hsiang." As he later found out, it was the name of my father's second daughter, and that day, when he heard I was actually visiting there, he decided to see me in person. I know I will always regret until I die that I could not be with my father in his last moments. But I was so far away with so many obligations—children, school, teaching, and worst of all, since my husband was in Taiwan at that time, I was completely tied down and could not leave the US. This sad loss left me with a deep grief; I shall live with it forever.

In late spring of 1965, when my husband fulfilled his one-year appointment, he immediately came back from Taiwan. Doctor Robinson told my husband that he had recommended him to teach at the University of Nebraska at Lincoln. By then, I had almost finished all my courses for the semester. I was about to start my third year of study, so before his school started, our whole family drove in two cars to Lincoln, Nebraska, to help him get settled in an apartment. We stayed about a week, and I drove back with the children in one car. When the fall semester started, Eva was going on to her sophomore year as a high school student, with Leo about to begin his second year in junior high.

By this time, our son Jeffrey had grown into an adult. Since my husband and I had gained our citizenship, we could apply for Jeffrey to come to the US. So while my husband was in Taiwan, he applied for Jeffrey to come and join us. Though my mother-in-law dreaded the separation, she  knew it was best for Jeffrey's future, so she did not protest. After a long wait, he finally arrived in Madison.

With the new member among us, Eva and Leo were happy their "big brother" was with them. However, the adjustment to a new culture, new life routine, and the practice with a new language and customs all became extra areas of concern for me. Plus, we worried about how best to find a suitable job for Jeffrey. Fortunately, Jeffrey told us that as soon as his father informed him of his application to come to the US, our brother-in-law Shu Shi, Lynnette's husband, had discussed with the family and decided Jeffrey should learn a kind of skill quickly so he could be independent. Therefore, he had been trained to be a chef. With that, we soon found a job for him. He was very quick and smart, and soon afterwards, he also learned to mix drinks and became a bartender. This enabled him to earn better pay and to work fewer hours than working as a chef.

As for myself, I had just earned a Master's Degree in Chinese Literature. It was time for me to start working on the outline for my PhD thesis. I remember that almost every night, Eva would be working across the table from me on her French language assignments until late. I tried to put in some extra hours of work in collecting and selecting the research materials for the thesis. It often lasted way past the early morning hours. In December, my husband came back from Nebraska for the winter vacation. We made some plans. The thought was that when I finished my studies, I might want to teach at Nebraska too, since they had not offered any Chinese classes yet. That winter, we had a very merry Christmas time, because we were all together.

The long Wisconsin winter slowly loosened its grip. Sometime before the spring break of 1966, my husband called me and told me that he was invited to give a talk at the Pennsylvania State University in Pennsylvania. The trip only took a couple of days. As soon as he returned back to Lincoln, he immediately called me, saying "Penn State is very nice. Their Religious Studies Department already has offered me an associate professorship for me to teach Oriental Philosophy and Buddhism courses. I have accepted it and will start in the fall term. Please make arrangements and we shall go to Pennsylvania during the spring break to look for a place. I will explain the details later." This unanticipated development took me completely by surprise, because this was so unlike him. There was not the slightest indication that he was considering changing his job, and he never even discussed it with me before he made up his mind. But our spring vacation was right around the corner, so I had no choice, but made arrangements for the children, and in April, the two of us flew to State College, Pennsylvania.

He did provide some explanation to me in his following phone calls. Mainly, he noted that Penn State was on the East Coast. It was closer to intellectual activities, while in Nebraska, he felt he was rather isolated in his field. Plus, our good friends were all in New York. Penn State's location would shorten the distances between us, especially for Peter Gruber and C.T. Shen. Besides, the Pennsylvania winter would be much more preferable, compared to the Midwest winters.

He told me that he had discussed his move with Dr. Robinson. Dr. Robinson supported his choice by saying that among all the state universities, the Pennsylvania State University was among the top ones. Their Religious Studies Department was growing steadily in recent years. It should be a good place to go.

Our plane landed at a small airport. We entered a taxi, and went into the town. I was confused by the name of State College. At our hotel, they explained that the town was first established as a state college of agriculture. Through the years, it grew into the present Pennsylvania State University, but the townspeople were used to the old name, so they kept it. Nowadays, the post office has divided the town into two major zones – the borough of State College, and University Park, where Penn State is located. During the first few years after we moved there, we always had to explain to others that State College is actually the name of the town. Not until some years later, after the famous Penn State football coach, Joe Paterno, had made the town famous with his team, only then could we drop the explanation.

State College was a sophisticated little town. The school's enrollment of twenty-six thousand at that time was larger than the town's population. Through the broker recommended by the University Housing Department, we found a house after a few days' search. It was outside of the borough, but only about five or six minutes of driving distance to the campus. We liked it because nearby, there was a quiet, pretty creek. We could walk along its banks. Within walking distance, there was also a very nice park with tennis courts, picnic tables, and nice playgrounds. The Spring Creek, famous in the Eastern states for its trout, runs through the park. We could see the town was growing rapidly. Both the town's junior high and senior high schools were close together in town, and both had good teachers on account of the University. The transaction for the sale of the house was scheduled to be sometime in the summer. Then quickly, we flew back to Madison.

With the move on my mind, I had to work harder than before. Unfortunately, my eyes could not withstand the long hours of work, and began to fail. Soon my old problem of not being able to focus well came back, so I had to slow down. It was close to the end of the school year. I had two papers waiting to be completed, but my eyesight still continued to deteriorate. Soon, I reached the stage where I could barely manage to handle my teaching and go over the students' papers. I was in the midst of this desperate situation and could not think of any way out. Then the University of Nebraska ended their semester and my husband came home. He watched me for a couple of days and said to me, "Instead of struggling with your condition, why don't you apply for an Incomplete for your classes. You know, we each only have one pair of eyes. Eyes are more important than anything! Please go tell your professors and you can finish your work later. Now you need to rest your eyes."

With only two more weeks left for the semester, I knew in my heart I could not honestly do my work satisfactorily, so I went to both Dr. Chou and my committee advisor and explained to them why I had to file for an "Incomplete" for my courses. Because in the past, they had learned the story of our eye troubles, without any further questions, they let me withdraw.

Then there was the question about Jeffrey. We knew that he should be with us at least a while longer, but from what we learned about the town of State College at that time, it would be

difficult for a young man with Jeffrey's background to find a suitable job. My husband and I were very concerned, but then somehow, he got a job in Chicago. So that settled the matter for us. However, I felt I was failing my responsibility in preparing Jeffrey to face a new world, so I tried to squeeze in all the basic things a young bachelor ought to know.

I talked to him so much within the limited time he was still home, I think he must have felt that I was treating him as a child!

The children's school was over in June. We spent the whole month of June packing and getting ready to move. Before we rented a U-Haul truck, we sold one car. At the end of June, we loaded everything onto the U-Haul. My husband took Eva with him in the front, and Leo and I followed after them in our old Chrysler. On the second day after our lunch break, we continued on our way. Suddenly, my car skidded. I quickly steered my car to the shoulder and stopped. I got out of the car, and found one of my rear tires was flat. Unfortunately, my husband's truck had already sped away. Leo came to my side. He looked at it, studied it, then he said, partly for me to hear, partly to himself, "I guess I have to fix the flat now that I'm the man here." His words moved me so that I could not help but hug him, and thanked him. He was not fourteen yet. I told him not to worry, we would work together.

As we opened the trunk and tried to remove things to reach the spare tire, a truck pulled up and parked behind us. The driver said he saw us and that we could use some help. Without much talking, he got the spare tire out and exchanged the flat. He then helped us to put everything back in the trunk. We were just about to shut the trunk, when my husband's truck came from the other direction. They had turned around to look for us as soon as they realized that we weren't following them. We thanked the truck driver who helped us. He refused any payment, wished us good luck, and drove away. I was sure that the driver did not know how deeply grateful I felt, because he had saved my husband's aching back from the heavy lifting and bending.

We arrived in State College on the first of July. The ex-owner moved out a few days prior and had left the house keys with our broker, but we still had to check into a hotel first, because there were all the procedures and documents for purchasing a house that needed to be completed. Besides dealing with the banks and the lawyers, there was also the national holiday. Somehow, things went quite smoothly and we were able to move into the house only a few days after our arrival.

It was our very first house, bright and roomy enough for us. Eva and Leo each had their own room on the first floor. My husband and I had our bedroom and our study upstairs. It was a modest house on a corner lot with a back yard. The yard had been planted with a dozen dwarf fruit trees and a vegetable garden. It was fenced in with chain link fencing.

Then the real work of settling down began. Again, we needed a second car. We needed all kinds of furniture, since we had gotten rid of our "graduate student" furniture before we left Madison. So, for days, we drove around the town and also visited many of the neighboring towns looking for things we needed. Due to our limited funds, we just did the best we could and quickly furnished the house. *(Much of our furniture came from "Hall's Salvage," a warehouse for items damaged in trucking and shipping.)*

The house was like a new house, except the two baths were painted in aqua and flamingo colors. I could not stand the combination, so Leo and Eva helped me paint the bathrooms an off-white color. When all the most immediate chores were taken care of, my husband was ready to report to his department.

His chairman, Dr. Luther Harshbarger, gave us a welcome party at his house, so we could meet all the members of the department. Mrs. Harshbarger soon made us feel very much at home and part of the department.

The next step was to have Eva and Leo registered for the coming semester in their new schools. Leo was in junior high, and Eva was in senior high. Both had to ride the school bus because we lived outside of the borough.

In the past five years, other than vacation days, I had spent all my days on the Madison campus. With the amount of driving we covered for our moving, I could not rest my eyes. When all the schools started in September, for the first time since I withdrew from my last semester, I had the chance to really relax my eyes. No books, no maps to study, and no more shopping to do. My days went by with me only preparing meals, cleaning the house, taking care of the yard, and listening to my children's and husband's reports of their daily events. Slowly, my eyesight began to improve. I could read for a short period each day, but I did not dare to go back to my unfinished work so soon. My days kept flowing by. Weeks went, then months, without any accomplishments. Yet, I appreciated the restful break. I felt well rested, at peace with myself and had no guilty feelings.

Both Eva and Leo attended small sized classes back in Wisconsin. Now she told me her eleventh grade alone had five hundred students. The junior high also had very large enrollment. Not too long after they went to school, somehow, they both made friends who were also children of Penn State professors, instead of children from farming backgrounds.

My husband still preferred to work at home. Other than keeping his office hours and going to classes, he usually worked in the study upstairs. One of his classes that he started with had a little over a hundred students. The next year, the same class grew into a much larger one. It remained at over three hundred until he gave the class to another professor.

One day, Jeffrey called and told us he was coming from Chicago for a couple of days. It was such a happy surprise. Leo was especially happy because his big brother had brought a nice corduroy sportcoat for him. We learned that Jeffrey was doing fairly well both as a bartender and a chef of Chinese cuisine. We made time for a picnic. Sad to say, the homecoming only lasted for a short time.

Swiftly, the first school year in Pennsylvania was about to be over. I was beginning to feel restless, and thought it was about time to resume my unfinished work. Then I received a call from the Office of the Assistant Dean of Liberal Arts. They informed me that a Professor Oliver would like to pay me a visit. He wanted to make an appointment to see me. They did not say what the visit was for, but we did set a day for a meeting. That phone call left my husband and I guessing.

A couple of days later, Professor Oliver came. He had a long friendship with the then South Korean President, Syngman Rhee, and had resided in the Far East for some years. He said Penn State was planning to offer a Chinese language program. They had learned that I had taught at the University of Wisconsin. Since now I was conveniently available as a "local talent," would I consider having an interview at Penn State? My answer was that I needed a little time to think it over. His visit led me to some serious consideration. I discussed it with my husband. We listed all the possible favorable and unfavorable points and went over point by point. Our final conclusion was that I should accept for the first year in order to give my eyes a test to find out if I could withstand a full-time job. If my eyes could hold up for the teaching job, I could then consider resuming my research work in addition to the teaching position. If things did not work out, at least I could have the program set up for Penn State and then resign, so I accepted the interview.

There were three professors at my interview, including Assistant Dean Lewis. They offered me an instructorship with the understanding that as soon as I earned my PhD degree, they would promote me. My employment was set to begin in the middle of the coming summer vacation, so I should have ample time to prepare for the class in the coming semester.

For the first-year Chinese class, I limited the enrollment to twenty-five students. It was only offered under a two-year Chinese language program. I did not belong to any department, but reported directly to the office of the Assistant Dean of Liberal Arts. A second-year class was added with a Teaching Assistant assigned to me in the following year.

That summer of 1968, Eva graduated from State College Area High School. She was an excellent student. Unfortunately, by that time, my husband had already been suffering from angina for a few years. Therefore, even though Eva scored high on her SAT test, and was also a National Merit Scholar semifinalist, sadly, we made the decision not to send her to an Ivy League school. We knew my husband's heart disease was hereditary, since both his father and his older brother Louie both died of heart disease in their prime years. Meanwhile, through all these years, we had been sending money each month to my mother-in-law in Taiwan, and we would be continuing to do so for the foreseeable future. Moreover, if Eva went to an expensive school, then immediately next year, when it was Leo's turn to go to college, we would have to treat him equally. Depending only on my husband's salary as a Liberal Arts professor would certainly be too much pressure for him. But Eva was very understanding. Without any complaint, she registered at Penn State, where she received a substantial tuition discount due to our faculty status.

My husband and I felt that once the children became college students, in the future we probably could not always have them around during summer vacation. We suggested that the whole family should take a long vacation together and travel to the West Coast. But our two teenagers both protested. They prepared to take it easy and just stay at home. I argued, persuaded, and threatened, while my husband was so disappointed he was ready to give up. In the end, they agreed to make the trip.

For the trip, Leo was still one year too young to drive, but Eva was already a full-fledged driver. With the three of us sharing the driving, travel on the newly completed Interstate 80 was for the most part easy and enjoyable. We left home in the middle of May. For the first week, every morning was such a struggle to get the two teenagers up. My husband complained that our trip was not intended to pay for hotels for us to sleep in. He almost threatened to turn back home. At our breakfasts, I was caught between an unhappy husband and two half-awakened teenagers.

By the second week, the situation greatly improved. We could start the day early and drive in the fresh early morning air without much traffic. Our first destination was Chicago, mainly so we could visit Jeff, who was by then working in a Chinese restaurant. Our old friend C. P. Hsueh had left India and had come to live in Chicago and was running a nice Chinese restaurant. Jeff was helping him with his injured shoulder. We had a very pleasant reunion and then parted. We also visited El Paso, where my sister-in-law Yvonne lived with her family, and her husband George took us on a tour of Juarez, Mexico. We also stopped at Mesa Verde, the Grand Canyon, and many of the famous interesting places. The last place for our westward trip was Walnut Creek, California, where my sister Helen *(Mian Mian)* and her family lived. It was a happy reunion, since they had left New York in the 50s. But we started our homebound trip after we stayed only for a few days with them, because Eva was so anxious to go back to Madison to see her old friend.

Probably due to the month-long continuous travel plus the high altitude of many of the places we visited, we noticed my husband's heart was troubling him more than before. During our visit at Yosemite National Park, we stayed in a large tent furnished by the park. There was a trail nearby. I walked slowly with him. Eva and Leo climbed quickly past us, but it was too steep for my husband to go up. He insisted that I should go on and he would sit by the tree and wait for me. From there on, he did not always join us on the different tours. On our way home, when we tried to visit Grand Teton and Yellowstone Park, unfortunately, we could only drive through. We were not able to get out and walk because the high elevation made my husband short of breath. In the end, we created our family's private record of touring two national parks in one day!

By this time, I had lost most of my interest for more touring. My mind was concentrating on getting home so my husband could get the rest he needed. We did see Mount Rushmore and the Badlands of the Dakotas. Soon, we reached Madison and dropped Eva off with her friend as we had promised. From there, the three of us drove straight home without any additional sightseeing stops. Even though we shortened the original plan, now, several decades later, I know that trip left an unforgettable memory for all of us.

Now Eva was in college. Because Eva had passed several Advanced Placement tests in her senior year at the high school, she was exempt from taking those courses again. She had not decided on her major. When we were still in Madison, years ago, when the Soviet Sputnik went up into space, she wanted to be an astrophysicist. No one could predict only three or four years later, all physics departments would be losing their students. During the first four or five semesters, she kept on switching her majors. When each term was over, Eva was always on the Dean's List and I would be receiving congratulatory cards from the Deans of different colleges.

Those were the years of the Vietnam War. Most of the students I had contact with did not know what major they wanted to study, so I never pressured Eva. When Eva finished her freshman year, Leo graduated from high school. He participated in an accelerated program of study and was able to graduate a year early. Soon after the summer vacation started, he told me he was seventeen years old. By eighteen, he probably would be drafted to fight in Vietnam. Then he would be missing the opportunity to live life on his own, if he were killed. He said he wanted to take off for one year, just to roam and see the world for himself.

In school, I had been teaching many Vietnam veterans. I had heard a lot about the war, so I discussed this with my husband, and we agreed to let him go. Sometimes in my household, I had to look at things from my husband's viewpoint. My husband was a self-taught man who had a very strong belief in individual independence. He left home when he was sixteen years old and had chosen his own life ever since. So, to him, Leo's request was quite reasonable, just like years ago when we let Leo hitchhike to New York with a friend.

That event happened in the spring break when Leo was in the eighth or ninth grade. He was with a friend and told us that they wanted to hitchhike to New York City and come back. My husband asked them where they were going to stay, and readily Leo said, they could go to Uncle Peter's. Without any hesitation, my husband asked me to give them some pocket money and to let them go. Among Chinese families, 90% of families tend to be overprotective. I often had to remind myself not to be one of them. After all, don't we Americans all want to train our children to be independent?

But I could not just encourage him to go without encouraging him to plan ahead. I kept on reminding him to bring enough clothes, maps, and to be careful with his money. I reminded him that he should set aside enough money for emergencies and for bus fare to come home. Full of excitement, Leo and his friend left. That night, Leo called me from Peter Gruber's house. He said they had good luck and arrived in New York City with no trouble at all. They would let us know when they would be back.

Two days later, I received Leo's call. I asked where he was. "Mom, we are in Bloomsburg. Could you send us some money so we can buy two bus tickets so we can come home?" I wanted to drive to Bloomsburg to take them home, since Bloomsburg was

148

only about ninety miles away, but my husband would not let me. He said, "Leo wanted to hitchhike. He should carry it through. This is a good chance for him to learn." So, I could only follow Leo's request and sent money through Western Union.

Early the next morning, I received a call from a stranger. He first made sure I was Mrs. Chang, and then identified himself as a policeman from a certain precinct. He said, "Your son and his friend came to us last night, saying that they did not have any place to stay, so we let them sleep in our jail to be safe. This morning, they were given a good breakfast by the Salvation Army. They have already received your money, and soon we will see to it that they will be safely on the bus, on their way home." I thanked him and patiently waited for Leo to come home.

Now again, he was asserting his independence and wanted to see the world by himself. Both my husband and I knew we should let him go, because once he was eligible to be drafted, we would never know what kind of future would be waiting for him. We had seen too many young people who had become maimed or who had died in the Vietnam War. We decided he could take one of our cars for his venture. There were many children running away from their families during that period. I wrote a "To Whom It May Concern" statement, had it notarized to prove that Leo was seventeen years old, and that we gave him our full permission to use our family car, and he was not running away from us. We gave him some money, and saw him leave with our blessings. He said he probably would be back in about a year's time.

At home, life went on without Leo. Meanwhile, in school, because the trade with Japan was growing steadfastly, the Japan Foundation donated a position at Penn State to teach Japanese. Together with the Chinese program and many East Asian related courses, we formed a new major for East Asian Studies with either Chinese or Japanese as the required language. Some of my students wanted to keep up with their Chinese language studies after they had finished the two-year program. They all signed up for my individual studies courses, so that made me extremely busy. Some of my students would apply to study at other intensive Chinese language studies at other schools. I was very pleased to hear that those students all did very well at those institutions. Then a new class was added to my teaching load. Once a year, I also had to teach a class of literature in translation on Eastern Asian literature.

By that time, I realized I probably would not be able to finish my PhD thesis on account of my eyes and my teaching load.

My husband and I then made our decision. I would just keep on teaching. If the University insisted on my obtaining a doctoral degree, then I would simply give up my position. I did not know whether it was because of the favorable annual student evaluations or because they knew that I always carried an overload of class hours, or even because it was cheaper to keep a non-tenured instructor who never negotiated for a higher salary, but I taught there until 1985. When my husband's health was failing rapidly, I resigned to take an early retirement.

Ever since we moved back to the East, during long weekends or vacations, either together with me, or just by himself, my husband would often drive to New York for various reasons, but we would always visit C.T. Shen and his family, sometimes staying in their house. C.T. and his wife Nancy began to devote more time to the study of Buddhism. One year, Nancy bought an old telephone office building in the Bronx, NY, and donated it to the Buddhist Association of the USA, which had been established by C.T. not long before. They further had it remodeled into a Buddhist temple, so people could go there and attend regular Buddhist services. My husband naturally became a consultant for all kinds of matters. Thus, our two families had even more occasions to meet. C.T. was very respectful toward my husband, as his teacher in Buddhism, while my husband admired C.T.'s brilliant mind and his management skills, and especially C.T.'s eagerness to learn Buddhism. We also learned through different sources that the couple had been helping many people and many organizations, but never told others, oftentimes without letting the recipients know that they were behind the good deeds. C.T. was very concerned about my husband's heart condition and often reminded him to take care of his health.

Following the 1961 unscrupulous publication of my husband's work by Dr. Muses, we were very pleased to see that *The Hundred Thousand Songs of Milarepa,* after nine years of loving labor, came out in the following year. It was made possible with our friend Peter Gruber's help. The two-volume book came in a beautiful boxed set. Shortly after its publication, we learned it received many good reviews and comments. By this time, my husband's first book, *The Practice of Zen*, had already been translated into all the major European languages. A paperback version was also available. My husband soon became known internationally among Buddhist circles. Unfortunately, as his fame spread, his heart was slowly getting weaker. But he still kept at his writing, teaching, and lecturing to different groups. As I recall that period, I think back that because my husband was not a patient person, and he did not always know how to show his love and understanding to our two American-born teenagers, he had probably hurt both Leo and Eva's feelings without knowing it. I still regret that I could not get those years back and make up the so-called generation gap between them.

Leo mailed us some post cards along the way during his trip. One day, he called me from Los Angeles, California. He said he was bitten by some insect, but the scar was not healing. He went to a doctor, but the doctor said he was too young to be responsible for himself, and insisted he would only deal with an adult. He was having fever and not feeling very well. I thought about it, and told him to go to my sister, his aunt (Mian Mian), whom we had visited in Walnut Creek up in Northern California. Immediately, I also talked to my sister, and it was lucky for Leo that my sister could take care of him. Altogether, he left home for about three months. When he was well again, he informed us that he was coming home. Of course, we were happy to have him home again, and were relieved that nothing serious had happened to him. He said he was ready to start at Penn State.

When we went to the school to register, the administration told us that because Leo had missed his regular entrance class, he would have to wait one semester to start. Since all his friends were in school studying, Leo went to the Penn State Library to work. He waited for the fall semester of 1970 to become a freshman.

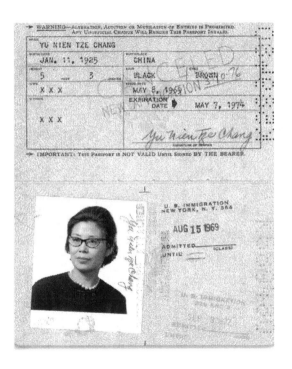

Passport for tour to Europe, the first US passport

It seemed that most of the professors' children in State College at that time all disliked the town. As soon as they graduated from the University, they all fled to other cities.

Eva did exactly the same. She went to Philadelphia where she shared lodgings with some friends. She had been a very independent girl ever since her childhood. She tried to find work there, but was unsuccessful for a long time. I did not give her much money; only when she made rare visits home, then I would give her a little money, but she never asked me for money. One day, she called and told me she found a job selling magazines door to door. I knew that not only was it a very humiliating job, the pay and the work were not really enough to make a living. Still, she did not complain. Only years later, one day she said to me, "Mom, I will never be afraid of being poor anymore. I know I can face any situation now because of that job." Deep in my heart, I admired her. I was more proud of her than before.

Then another day, she called me, saying that she was following a friend's step to enroll in a school where they trained paralegals. It was something fairly new, therefore the qualification requirements were very high and strict. That did not present any problem for Eva, so she started to go to the school and was guaranteed a job after graduation in six months' time. She chose to study the real estate business. She asked to borrow $600 from me for her tuition. When she graduated, I told her I was happy to give the money to her. She was offered a job in New York, working with a realty firm as an associate. Her first paycheck was $900. For the following two months, Eva surprised us by sending us two checks each of $100. We thanked her over the phone but did not cash the first check. When the second check came, both my husband and I were so touched by this act of love, we sent one check back and told her we treasured her thought.

We would keep the first check as a souvenir, but definitely, she should not send money to us anymore. Even today, whenever I see that check, tears will come to my eyes. It always showed me that Eva unconsciously was following her Chinese upbringing, because she saw us supporting her grandparents. She grew into a very capable woman. She changed jobs from that realty company to some insurance-related companies, to a major airline, to Ernst & Young, and to the last job when she was a partner in a software company. Finally, she was tired of the traveling and the corporate life, and she decided to do something more meaningful for herself, while being helpful to others too. So, she and her husband Doug moved from Atlanta to Florida, where she studied for three years to become an acupuncturist and practitioner of natural medicine.

When Leo was a sophomore at Penn State, Eva had left State College, and my husband was in Taiwan, so we were the only two at home. Leo asked me one day if his friend Bill could stay with us. He told me that Bill was a Penn Stater, who had just recently returned from Viet Nam as a veteran. His parents lived in Hawaii, and his father was a colonel in the US Air Force. There was a girl in the family too.

So Bill came. He was a very handsome young man, just a couple of years over twenty. At the time when he moved in, he was holding a job as a school bus driver. I did not have too much direct contact with him, on account of our working hours. One day, as I was emptying the waste basket from Leo's downstairs bathroom, I saw a syringe in it. For quite a few years, I had always kept a watchful eye over my children, because of the drug situation of the times. I asked Leo where the syringe came from, and what it was for. He said casually, "Oh, it must be Bill's. He's trying to quit his heroin habit." I did not expect that answer.

When I recovered, I told Leo solemnly that I was very sorry, but I had to ask Bill to move, because I could not have any drugs in the house. Bill was very nice. He just quickly moved out.

In the following month, February, some students of mine had schemed with Leo for a surprise birthday party for me. Usually, in the late afternoon, after classes were over, Leo and I would drive home together. That day, instead of heading home directly, Leo suggested that we should have dinner at some restaurant. But he had to make a stop somewhere before eating. I did not pay much attention, but he soon stopped at a funeral home. Then he told me that it was Bill's funeral. Bill had committed suicide because he could not hold onto any job, and could not quit his addiction to drugs! I was stunned, and I just numbly followed Leo and entered the funeral home. There, Bill lay in a coffin in front of us. So young, so peaceful looking. We stood there for a few minutes, then quietly, we drove to a restaurant. There, my students greeted me with the Happy Birthday song. However, through the whole evening, I was full of deep sorrow, and even today, whenever I think about war, I cannot forget about Bill. What a waste of a young life it was.

The war in Viet Nam was about over. Leo was lucky when, in 1969, the US Army adopted a new way to pick their needed inductees using a lottery system. Leo had a high number, so he was not drafted. In 1973, Leo graduated from Penn State, with a degree and two majors.

It took him some time to decide what he wanted to do. Then he announced that he wanted to apply to law schools. We waited for the admissions anxiously. Then we heard from Columbia University. In the summer of 1975, Leo and his girlfriend moved to New York. We did not learn about the details of his schooling, but we did know the three years of law school were tough to survive, especially living in New York. But he was lucky that he was able to move into a loft space in downtown Manhattan where Eva was already sharing living space with some friends.

In 1978, when he was about to graduate, my husband and I had planned ahead of time to attend his graduation. I had my final examinations to give on the same day. My Teaching Assistant would supervise the class instead of me, but two days before, I came down with high fever, and had an acute kidney or bladder infection. Needless to say, we had to cancel the trip. I think it was one of the deepest disappointments of my life. I still feel the hurt whenever I reflect on it.

From that time on, my son has been a New York lawyer and has never left the city.

Leo has been a partner in two law firms and is well-respected in his specialty. He married later in life and now has four children, all of whom have many achievements academically and athletically. One of the grandsons has studied Chinese and can write cards and letters to mom in Chinese!

Jeff married a woman of Polish descent, and they both worked in the restaurant industry for many years. They and their two daughters live in the Chicago area.

Regretfully, we have not maintained a close relationship over the years.

At this juncture, we are all retired, or soon to be retired, and still separated by many years of many miles.

When the summer vacation of 1972 came, my husband and I went back to Taiwan to see my mother-in-law. That year, my husband took his sabbatical leave from Penn State. While we were in Taipei, he told me that up to that time, all the publications he had done were all written in English. He felt that through all the years, by living in the West, he had acquired a great deal of new knowledge of Western philosophy, religions, cultures, and traditions and that it was time for him to write something for Chinese readers. He planned first to give a series of talks, mainly to college students, then, re-organize and edit the manuscripts to use as the draft for a book. In fact, by that time, he already had three volumes of publications in Chinese. Shortly after he finished translating *The Hundred Thousand Songs of Milarepa*, he soon started to translate the same book directly again from the Tibetan, into Chinese, with Milarepa's biography added to it. This book is still widely enjoyed by readers.

The sabbatical leave could give him the needed time to carry out his project. I agreed with his idea, so when the summer vacation was over, I left him to remain in Taiwan and returned to State College alone.

We resumed our habit of writing letters to each other almost every other day. I learned that he was hard at work in writing his lectures. Someone had already arranged dates and places for him to present the series of his talks. He complained that Taiwan's weather was unbearably hot. Some of the auditoriums did not always have air conditioning. Sometimes, the microphones did not work. Then he had to strain himself to talk louder than his normal voice. Also, the transportation was very inconvenient at times, so when he returned home, 90% of the time, he was exhausted. Sometimes, he would complain about the visitors. At that time, since not everyone could afford a telephone, visitors would just come and see him at all different hours, which was disturbing and interrupting his work. But for the most part, he was happy about the progress of the work. Then, without any reason, his letters stopped.

One day at dawn, I had a strange dream. I dreamt that my husband was standing at the head of the bed, above, and looking down at me. Then suddenly, he fell all the way down a tall cliff. I woke up and was quite frightened. As I was getting up, my mother-in-law's long distance call arrived. She said she knew I must be worried, not having heard from my husband, but everything was all right now. At that time, my husband had already left the hospital and was recuperating at a resting home. It happened a few weeks ago, when he was walking to have a haircut. He felt pain in the chest, so he went back home and the pain went away. But later, when he was going to deliver his lecture, he had a heart attack. My mother-in-law tried to comfort me by saying that I should be hearing from him soon, and hung up.

It felt like years had gone by before I finally received his first letter since his illness. All he said was that he was recovering well. He would come back home as soon as he could travel. I need not be too worried about him.

At the end of October, he called me to tell me he was flying back in November, and asked me to pick him up in Pittsburgh. When it was time, I drove to the Pittsburgh airport to meet him. He was the last passenger off the plane. I could hardly recognize him; he looked so thin and so fragile. The long flight also tired him, and made him even more haggard looking. I quickly let him lie down in the back seat of the car, then hurriedly picked up his luggage and headed straight home to State College.

When he regained his health and went back to teach, in the same year, he was promoted to full Professor. At the same time, I practically assumed responsibility for all of the family's affairs. His health never did recover fully. In 1974, C.T. Shen suggested that my husband undergo open-heart surgery. Since it was not that widely practiced an operation at that time, we hesitated for quite some time before we made arrangements to meet the doctor who was recommended by one of our doctor friends in New York.

We planned for it to take place during our school vacation time so I would be free to take care of him. But first, he must have a catheterization operation to see exactly how damaged his heart was. At that time, this was a procedure with significant risks as well. The doctor in St. Luke's Hospital at Columbia University discovered that my husband's three main arteries were all about 90% blocked. He needed a triple-bypass for his heart. The heart attack he had in Taiwan left the tip of his heart permanently damaged. We only waited for one day in the hospital before it was his turn to be operated on.

On that day, I went to the hospital very early in the morning and waited for the news. I learned that there was another patient being wheeled into the operating room with my husband at the same time. Around 1:00 in the afternoon, the other patient was wheeled out on his bed, but I heard that the poor man had a heart attack right on the operating table. Now he was dead. That horrible thought immediately occupied my mind. I thought, "What if..." Yet my husband still had not come out. I was very pleased that Eva and Leo both could be with me for the difficult wait. Our friend C.T. Shen also came. Much later in the afternoon, the doctor came out and told me that the operation was successful. I would be able to see my husband later after he was released to the Intensive Care Unit. I had never seen anyone who was hooked up to so many tubes. He looked so pitiful. That night, the hospital people did not want me to go back to C.T. Shen's house in New Jersey. They said for the sake of security, they would let me sleep in the nursing quarters.

After one week in Intensive Care, finally, my husband was transferred to the regular care unit. C.T. had arranged for him to be in a private room, thinking he could recuperate more

159

comfortably in more privacy. I offered to stay the first night there, because he was still hooked up to all kinds of tubes. But he refused, saying the service should be fine in a private room. But the next morning, when I walked into his room, he complained that the whole night, no one responded to his need for a bedpan. He fumbled up in the dark, but fell by the bed. He was lucky none of the surgical incisions were torn. I protested to the hospital, and had him moved to a semi-private room, where there were more nurses. After several days, he was released from the hospital. We stayed with my sister in New Jersey. Ten days later, after the post-operation check-up, the doctor said we could go home and be seen again in three months.

Gradually, my husband recovered from the operation. However, he was living with a damaged heart, and we also had to live with the knowledge that for a heart patient like him, every year, the heart would be less efficient by 5%.

We treated every day as a newfound gift. After a recovery period, he not only resumed his teaching, he also insisted on continuing to finish the work on his Chinese project.

Generally speaking, I am a very healthy person. However, in January of 1976, Pennsylvania had a severely cold winter. One day, I was going to a class by walking down a fresh snow-covered slope. I slipped on a hidden piece of solid ice. Immediately, a sharp pain shot through me. I found I could not stand up. Fortunately, there were students passing by, and they sent for help. When the campus ambulance came, the nurse said it looked like I had broken my left ankle. Our own infirmary said they could not do anything about it, and I was taken to the hospital. The pain was severe and a nurse had to hold my left ankle to prevent me from moving and causing more damage. The doctor had to operate as soon as my husband could be there. Soon the nurses prepared me and pushed me into the operation room, and I gradually drifted into unconsciousness.

When I woke up again, it was night time. My left leg was all wrapped in bandages except the toes. An icebag was resting over the ankle. It was a miserable night. The next day, after examining it, the doctor told me he had to re-treat it by putting screws into the bones, because I had broken every bone in the ankle. Over the night, the joined bones without the pin had shifted their positions, so I had to go through a second operation. Fortunately, that year I had a very good Teaching Assistant. He helped me so much with my teaching until I improved and could attend school with a cast. The cast lasted more than two months, so I had to be on crutches going from building to building. The worst was that some buildings did not have elevators. Every day, my husband had to give me a ride and then pick me up to go home. It was a horrible time. Luckily, at least my husband was home, and not in Taiwan.

Meanwhile, C.T. had started an Institute of World Religion. He had bought the former site of the Faculty Club at the State University of New York at Stony Brook on Long Island. He arranged to have the Institute's library housed at the University's Stony Brook campus. Then, in Taiwan, under the Institute, C.T. also started a group to translate some of the more important Buddhist Sutras from Chinese to English. My husband was frequently consulted about the projects of the institution. In 1976, the Taiwan translation institute developed problems, both in the actual work and with their personnel. C.T. repeatedly asked for my husband's assistance and asked him to travel to Taiwan. Even though we could foresee that it would be a very demanding job, he could not refuse C.T.

Therefore, after C.T. negotiated with the Religious Studies department, and the Dean of Liberal Arts at Penn State, C.T. established a chair and changed my husband's status into a research professor and promised the department that he would

161

sponsor a new position of Assistant Professor. Thus, my husband could leave for Taiwan to assume the position as head of the Buddhist Institute of Translation. That fall, in 1976, after our summer vacation together in Taiwan, I came home alone. However, we did let C.T. know that whenever it was the Penn State summer and winter vacation times, my husband would be back to spend time with me.

I must say that 1976 to 1977 and 1977 to 1978, those two academic years, were the hardest times of my married life. Classes and student papers could not fill my loneliness. I was constantly worrying about my husband's heart condition. Long distance telephone calls and letters could not warm up the severe long winter months of those two years. Only after I came to meet Olivia and her husband Ken Kuo, with their friendly weekend invitations, I managed to survive those long and depressing days.

The Kuos are younger than me. Ken came to Penn State in the 70s to teach in the mechanical engineering department. Olivia was home with one young girl and one child on the way. I met them when they joined our potluck group. This group consisted of Chinese faculty and local professionals, who met once a month for dinner and conversation. It became the center of our social lives over the twenty years we lived in State College.

Knowing that I was alone without my husband, Olivia invited me almost every weekend to have dinner with them. Once, after a heavy snow, when I drove home after school, I could see high piles of snow pushed by the city's snowplow totally blocking my driveway which had already been cleared by my snow removal company. It was late. Desperately, I drove back to town and invited myself and stayed overnight at Olivia's house. Soon we became very good friends. I am truly grateful for their kindness and friendship.

The work in Taiwan kept my husband traveling between home and Taipei. Finally, by the end of 1979, my husband came home, exhausted. He informed C.T. that the first phase of the translation project could soon be completed. Whatever final editing work was still needed, he could do at home in State College. Therefore, he could finally come home from Taiwan.

I was so happy to have him home for good; only now I could see that my husband's health had suffered during these long periods of separation. Yet it was not until 1980 that he was able to hand over the Institute of Translation to a successor.

At home, later, my husband was busy proofreading his own Chinese work on Buddhism. He already had promised one of the Buddhist publishers in Taipei to print it. Due to my husband's weakened heart condition, they decided only to print the part of the book that had been finished so far as the first volume. The rest of the remaining chapters would be finished later in the second volume. At the same time, he was also negotiating with the Penn State University Press for the publication of the translated Buddhist Sutra texts, which he was just about finished editing.

While he was attending to these works, C.T. had sold the Long Island club property and had acquired a large piece of land in Putnam County in upstate New York. He was planning to construct a new site for Buddhists to worship. He had sold his shipping company a few years previously, but had to stay on as the President for a few more years. Knowing C.T.'s intentions and wishes, through the years, my husband had been encouraging him to concentrate on devoting more time to pursue his interest and practice in Buddhism. So as soon as C.T. fulfilled his duty with the shipping company, he and his wife Nancy immediately began their planning to build a Buddhist temple. They generously donated half their land in Putnam County for this goal. Naturally, my husband was involved in most of the discussions, either in person, or over the phone. Because of the scale of the work, C.T. knew it would be too much for my husband's health, so in 1980, my husband formally became a member of the Institute for World Religion and resigned from Penn State University. In fact, C.T. was so very concerned about my husband's health, he told my husband that he did not have any specific duty to assign to my husband. He just wanted my husband to have a less rigid academic schedule to keep. Yet, since my husband was always a conscientious person about his work, other than not going to the school, he kept working just as hard as before, as his health permitted. But clearly, his condition was deteriorating. The visits to his doctors became more frequent. He also had irregular heartbeats which made him exhausted after each incident. I learned to always keep the cars filled with gas just in case I had to rush him to the hospital.

In the following three to four years, when my husband was not suffering from his weakened heart, he would try to continue work on the unfinished second volume of his book in Chinese, but he found his effort was greatly restrained by his fragile heart condition. Much to his frustration, he realized that he could barely manage to finish the book, even though he reduced the content and included many fewer of its original ideas. In the end, the second volume was finished. In the preface, he apologized to his readers, that due to his poor health, there was a big gap of almost ten years between the publications of the two volumes.

Shortly after he finished the book, his heart was showing further weakening signs. Occasionally, he would have heart failures, although he was still able to get around when not ill. Our few close friends knew that we could not be counted on for our occasional gatherings.   Sometimes it was even hard for him to walk, because he would be so short of breath.

1976 Trip to Taiwan. Mom, Dad, Grandma Chang, and Wang Sau. I was able to join them on a trip around Taiwan, as I was between jobs.

More Health Problems

In August of 1984, exactly one week before the fall term was to start, after my husband's routine checkup, his doctor made an appointment by long distance call from his office to the Cardiology department of the Cleveland Clinic Hospital which was famous for heart surgeries. The appointment was to have a catheterization for my husband to determine whether he could be helped by a second heart surgery. Surprisingly, we were told to leave for Cleveland the very next day.

We started early the next day and arrived in Cleveland, Ohio. After checking in to the hospital's hotel, we immediately drove to the hospital to meet the doctors, who told us the catheterization was scheduled for the next day.

I took him in the following morning. By the afternoon, the procedure was over. The doctor told me he needed to undergo a second bypass operation without delay. We could go home and then come back for it, but it should not be prolonged for more than a couple of days. The reason was that it had been almost eleven years since the first operation. At that time, the average life of bypass patients was only about ten years or so. Besides, his three old bypasses were already blocked up again, over 90%. That night, we debated in the hotel, and decided we would just stay for the operation. At least, he could be saved from the thousand mile ride in the car again for no obvious purpose.

As soon as I learned the unexpected news, I immediately contacted my Teaching Assistant and prepared him for my unavoidable absence from school. Luckily, it was his second time around to assist the classes. I told him I would keep close communication with him for about two weeks, and then I would be back.

Then I phoned Eva. She immediately flew to Cleveland to be with us. Early in the next morning, we took my husband into the hospital. Eva and I both stayed to wait for the news. We waited

166

and waited. We saw some of the other patients who went in to be operated on who came back out, but my husband was still not done. By late afternoon, a tired doctor came out to talk to me and said the operation was successful. However, he could not do the fourth bypass as originally planned, but only did three, because the old scars from the previous operation were in the way. We thanked him and followed his direction and went to the Intensive Care Unit to see my husband. As we were led to my husband's bed, as soon as I saw all the tubes and different gadgets dangling all over my husband who was motionless in the bed, while his face was completely colorless, I fainted. Quickly, I was helped out of the room, leaving only Eva by her father's side. When we went back to our hotel, it was late. I could not remember when we went to bed. About 4:30 in the morning, I was awakened by a phone call. It was from a doctor in the Intensive Care Unit. He hurriedly asked for my permission to operate again, saying that my husband's old bypass scars could not be stopped from bleeding, and therefore, he needed to be rushed back into surgery for another operation.

I stayed awake, and waited for the results. A few long hours passed, then the doctor called to let me know my husband came through it ok. I should be able to visit him some time in the afternoon.

Eva and I managed to pass the day and eventually the visiting hour arrived. We saw that my husband was still under sedation but was sleeping peacefully. I was a little relieved from the helplessness and worries I felt since that early morning phone call.

Halfheartedly, we found a hospital cafeteria, then we went back to our hotel as Eva had to leave the next day to go back to work. On the average, most of the open-heart patients would stay in the ICU for five to seven days, and then they would be transferred to the regular patient rooms. But my husband was just too weak to be released from the ICU. While there, I could only visit him twice,

167

briefly, each day. All I could do for the rest of the time was to either sit in the waiting room or the cafeteria. I usually would sit in the cafeteria with a cup of coffee. Perhaps because I was there so often, and most of the time with a heavy heart, some people would come over to chat with me and comfort me. Some would tell me their own worries about their loved ones who were there at the hospital for treatment. Mostly, they were all heart patients.

Finally, about ten days later, my husband was moved to the regular patients' quarters. I was very pleased that his doctor gave me permission to be with my husband anytime I wanted. By then, I knew I could not be back to school for my classes anytime soon. I had to depend on my Teaching Assistant for everything. We had to go over the classwork every two or three days. I was tired from the long hours of sitting by my husband's bedside. Every morning, I had to revive myself with a strong hot shower. I remember the water drops were so powerful it almost hurt like being pricked by hundreds of needles. Then I would do my best to get dressed, as I only brought a small suitcase of summer clothes, prepared for what I thought would be a short trip. Each day, I would walk the ten or so minutes to the hospital, and stay there until eight or nine in the evening before returning to the hotel.

My husband was slowly gaining some strength. He was put through a series of recovery activities. He began to feel hungry, yet he could not eat much. Thus, after three or four days, the doctors were wondering why he had not gained any weight, so his hunger was getting more attention from the doctors. Then they ordered him to have an X-ray test for his stomach. My poor husband was given a large amount of powdered drink but no food was allowed for the test. He was taken downstairs in a wheelchair. I accompanied him there and we were left there for more than three hours, until they said it was too late to do it and we had to go back the next day. The waiting was both cold and uncomfortably tiring for my husband. But the next morning, he had to put up with the same procedure again.

Finally, the testing ordeal was over. But there was some new bad news. The intestinal doctor found two bleeding ulcers in the upper part of my husband's stomach. He explained to me that Orientals have higher risks of having this kind of ulcers. Also, his ulcers were located where cancer was often found. These ulcers were probably brought on by the two traumatic open-heart operations. He concluded that my husband needed to be watched in the ICU of the Intestinal Department because if the ulcers were to start bleeding, it would be very dangerous. And that was the reason why he was hungry but unable to eat.

Therefore, my husband was moved to the ICU of the Intestinal Department. The next morning about dawn, a doctor informed me with urgency that they were moving my husband to prepare for an emergency operation, as the ulcers were about to burst. I was most numb with this sudden twist. All I could do was pray and wait.

Around noon, a nurse led me to visit my husband. He was already resting in the ICU. He was half awake but gave me a faint smile. I held his hand for a brief moment and quickly was led out of the room.

Half a week passed before he was released to be in a semi-private room. The nurses started the rehabilitation exercises for his heart again. His weight was so low that the doctors talked to the dietician about feeding him anything that would increase his weight, including Ensure, eggs, and ice cream, even though they were normally forbidden foods for heart patients. But salt was still strictly forbidden. Unfortunately, my husband was missing the food that he had grown up with – Chinese food. Every time when his food tray was served, he just lost his appetite. The daily American diet was either too sweet or too rich compared to Chinese home-cooked meals, especially for a sick person. One day, out of desperation, I went out and bought an electric pot, and managed to cook up some simple Chinese food in the hotel and

169

brought it over to the hospital for him. With this "comfort food," he was able to eat and begin to regain strength.

The recovery seemed to progress very slowly. He also hated the large amount of pills he had to swallow every day and he was growing more impatient by the day. He began to badger his doctors and was so annoyed that he had been confined to the bed for so long. He wanted to go home and rest, even though his condition was really not that strong. But he kept on bargaining with the doctors and told them that he could not improve in the hospital, period. In the end, he showed the doctors he was able to walk in the long hallway on my arm. The doctors reluctantly signed his release. It was exactly one month after his heart operation.

For our trip home, we followed the instructions given by his doctors. Every now and then we would stop the car so my husband could walk for a few minutes to help his blood circulation. It took us almost the whole day to cover the five hundred plus miles back to State College, but as soon as we got into the house, our tensed up nerves miraculously felt much more relaxed.

I did not go to classes the next day, as I had to find a nurse to come to attend my husband, and arrange all sorts of things before I could resume teaching. I was able to hire a man through a home health agency. After I showed him how to care for my husband, I went back to school. I was pleased to find out that the classes were progressing fairly well, but when I came back home the first day after school, and relieved the nurse aide, my husband complained to me and told me he had thrown up twice during the day by the side of the bed, and the aide just took some newspaper and paper towels and covered the spots, and did nothing to help him or to clean up. He adamantly told me he definitely did not want anyone to help him and preferred to be alone by himself. I knew him too well to argue with him, so from then on, every day, I went to school in the morning. When I finished with the necessary work, I would rush home. Slowly but surely, with some of my friends' help, especially my friend Olivia, with her home-cooked food and "lending library" of Chinese paperback books, my husband regained much of his health back, though not completely.

During this period, I could not help but feel guilty, for I could not fully concentrate on my school responsibilities. I felt it was not fair to my students, so I talked with my husband and we agreed for me to take an early retirement and resign at  the end of the semester, which ended in the summer of 1985.

My retirement brought some relief from the mental stress I had been under for a long time. My companionship also further helped my husband to improve his health condition. I could drive him out to the mall for our daily walk in the morning as the doctor prescribed. In the evenings, I no longer had to work on student papers and prepare the next day's classes. Life became much more relaxed than before. Then winter came. Our activities naturally were limited by the severe coldness. By the time March arrived, my husband started to suggest that we should move to a warmer location. We tossed the idea about a few times at first, but after more serious study and comparing the pros and cons, we reached our decision to move.

California was our first choice, but we also liked the Carolinas because of the universities, research communities, and the weather. We took a short trip in April and visited North Carolina. Leisurely, we looked around. Almost everywhere, spring was in full bloom. We spent about one week there and then drove back home. Later in May, my husband said we should try to sell our house while we fly to California to look around. Quickly, we found a real estate agent to put the house on the market, and we flew to Northern California. Once there, we rented a car and started to go southward. California had become more crowded than when we were there thirty-some years ago. We went along the coast and proceeded slowly, while visiting old friends and some relatives along the way. The last city we stayed in was San Diego. It was a very attractive place to retire, but on our return drive, I told my husband that I did not want to live in California. My main concerns were the traffic. Since I had to do all the driving, I did not care to rush on the freeways. Secondly, we would have to worry about earthquakes, drought, fires, and lastly, the price of houses was unreasonably high. With these reasons, we just drove back up north, returned the car, and flew home.

The house in State College was on the market only for two weeks or so, exactly the same length of time as our trip to California. It was sold two days before we reached home. I was not prepared to receive the news from our realtor so soon! The new owner wanted the closing date to be in August before school started. That left me without much choice but to plunge into the heavy task of cleaning, sorting, and packing.

We had lived in this house for so long. It was the only one that either of us had stayed in for twenty years. Both my husband and I had extensive volumes of books. I decided to start the packing with our library collections. I brought all the necessary packing materials home first, and then went to Olivia to ask if I could get her older daughter Phyllis, who was about thirteen years old, to help me.

We were busy for days finding empty dumpsters to discard all our journals, magazines, and old papers. It took us so many days and trips to get rid of those before we could even begin the actual packing of the books we were keeping!

It was a good thing that we had an extra-large two-car garage, where the things we did not want to bring or could not bring could all be stored. Looking at the amount of things piled there, I was deeply ashamed that our life had become so filled with material things.

Besides the packing, the most important problem had yet to be solved. Where were we to live? When we were touring North Carolina, we actually had found a townhouse in Durham that we liked, so we called and made a deposit for the rent. The management told us the townhouse we liked would be finished on August 1. That fitted our schedule perfectly. Then we informed our realtor that we would accept the closing date for our house on the 16th of August.

With an exact date, I had to speed up the selling of some of the household furniture and goods. My good friends Olivia and Pat Hu both offered to help me with my garage sale. We hurriedly marked prices on the numerous items and had a three-day sale. The leftovers were taken by Olivia and donated to the Salvation Army.

In the last couple of days, I tried my best to give the house a thorough cleaning. I was just too exhausted to cook. During those packing days, because my husband could not do any physical work, most of our meals were either bought or eaten in restaurants.

Finally, the moving company came. They started to load the long van. Even without the books that I had donated to the Penn State Library and all the books we had discarded, our books still filled a large area of the van. By the afternoon, the two movers finished loading the van. They joked that I had packed so well that I should work for their company.

When the moving van left, my husband and I gave the house our last look. Twenty years! Both our children had grown up in it and had left. So many of our memories were attached to it. Still we had to bid goodbye and we drove away. When we arrived at Olivia's house, she had already prepared beds for us and dinner was all ready to be served. The evening was spent with Ken, Olivia and the two girls. We later excused ourselves and retired early.

The next morning, Olivia drove me back to the house to pick up our Toyota from the garage. The plan was for my husband and I to drive down in the large car first. Then I would fly back to State College to pick up the Toyota from Olivia's house and drive it down to North Carolina.

The trip to North Carolina was pleasant enough after the hard work of packing and cleaning. But when we arrived at our new address, the office told us they had to put us in a different apartment temporarily because the house we rented was not finished yet. We found ourselves led to a two-bedroom apartment. We had barely settled down before our moving van arrived. There we had to live with all the big and small boxes piled up in most of the available space. It indeed was crowded.

After I made sure my husband was all right in our new place, I flew back to pick up the car in State College. I could not make it in a one-day trip, so I finished the driving back to Durham on the second day.

It was in the middle of August. It was impossible to do anything for those first two months in Durham, with everything still packed in boxes. We mostly spent our time exploring the town, and venturing to different eateries. Also, we inquired about finding a good cardiologist for my husband. Through a medical information directory, we were recommended to a specialist. After a short wait, we got an appointment. For the first meeting, because my husband still had a lot of the medicine that he was currently taking, the doctor just asked about my husband's health history and made an appointment for our second visit. When we were in his office the second time, he advised my husband to change to a new medicine. Immediately, my husband told him that he could not use anything that belonged to the calcium channel blocker family, but the doctor insisted that he should try it because he said that 95% of his patients were all benefiting from this new medicine. He even prescribed only fifteen pills just for my husband to try.

After more than a year's time of recuperating and resting, I was so pleased that under my care, my husband had regained most of his strength back, even to the point that we could do some light traveling. But that night, the night after he followed the doctor's instruction and took one of the new pills, about 9:00, I had to drive him and try to find the hospital, where the doctor said he'd be there to see us. It was dark and it was a strange town to me. Luckily, I did find it somehow. There the doctor took him and treated him and kept him in the hospital for the night. From that time on, I don't remember how many times I had to rush my husband to the general hospital while under that doctor's care. Soon, when my husband was getting on his feet again, something would go wrong and he would be back to the hospital. It went on about one year.

Once, during which time my husband was again in the hospital, my back gave out. The pain kept me in bed for almost a month. I'm sure it was partly due to the constant worry about my husband's condition, and partly due to my physical exhaustion. My orthopedic doctors could not cure me but told me the only way to cure me was to operate on my spine. Luckily, at that time, I already had been able to find a household helper, who was a Chinese professor's wife. She could drive and she herself was an engineer before she left China. She could do some cooking, and most importantly, she could go and attend my husband in the hospital every day after she checked with me.

I thought about my options, and instead of surgery, I found a good chiropractor who was able to relieve my pain with the first visit. I began to visit him, from every other day in the first weeks, to once a month as I improved. From walking hunched like a shrimp to completely standing straight again, it took me a few months to be fully recovered. Even until today, I have been free from back problems.

In the midst of all these happenings, we finally moved into our newly finished townhouse on October 1.

When my husband came home from the hospital, he was so weak I had to rent a medical bed so he could sleep downstairs in the living room. A few days before my husband was released from the hospital, my back was much better, and I was able to visit him. That night, it was getting late. Because my husband was struggling for his life, the doctor stayed there, checking on him. He signaled me to come outside the room and told me it was about time for me to inform my children to come, because he was not sure that my husband could survive that very evening. I did not want to go home nor contact my children. I just stayed by my husband's bedside for the night.

The next morning, my husband revived somewhat. The first thing he said to me was, "I want to go home." When the doctor came in for the morning visit, I told him that he must let me take my husband home. My husband did not want to die in the hospital. And that was the last time we saw that doctor.

I also moved downstairs, to keep company with my husband. I slept on the floor beside him, so I could strengthen my weak back. Home probably is the best place for any sick person to recuperate and recover. My husband, little by little, was able to get well enough to move around in the house after a month or so. Meanwhile, I had learned from some Chinese acquaintance, of a very good cardiologist, Dr. Kong, who was a Chinese doctor in charge of the catheterization department at Duke University. Soon we made an appointment and met the doctor. He was very kind and patient with us. He gave my husband a very detailed examination and explained his true heart condition to us. He told us that my husband's heart function capacity at that time could only amount to one third of a normal person's. In addition, he said if my husband became any weaker, there would not be any doctor who would operate on him or to help him anymore. Still, he kept very careful watch on my husband, and paid full attention to my husband's medical reactions. We were sincerely grateful for Dr. Kong's care.

At about the same time when we moved down to Durham, Eva had resigned from American Airlines and began working for Ernst & Young in Atlanta. Due to Dr. Kong's meticulous care, my husband's condition had been fairly stabilized. By Thanksgiving time in 1987, with Dr. Kong's assurance, we accepted Eva's request and drove down in our van to visit them.

Eva and Doug had bought a large house with a so-called mother-in-law suite meant for us to live with them. It was a beautiful house with a large lot. They did their own landscaping and kept a charming yard. We had a wonderful time with them for the holiday. Before we were leaving, Eva again suggested we should come to Atlanta to be near them. We seriously considered the situation and thought indeed we should leave Durham.

In Atlanta, we did not move in with Eva, but rented a nice house only five minutes away from her. We had a partially shaded deck at the second-floor level with a tree that grew through the center. We often sat there and enjoyed the peacefulness and quietude. The weather was cold when we first moved there. During the day, we would leisurely have our breakfast. Afterwards, partly for my husband's exercise, and partly to have something to do, we would drive out to tour the different newly built houses to pass the time. Sometimes we would eat lunch at some small restaurant if my husband was not too tired from the morning exertions. Otherwise, we would have some simple lunch at home and then he would change and get into bed for the rest of the day. At that time, his heart only had about 30% function left. His evenings were spent either reading Chinese or English novels or watching television, but mostly he would silently recite prayers in bed.

Winter was short in Atlanta. Soon, February and March brought along all kinds of spring flowers. Pansies, daffodils, and azaleas could be seen all over the city. By early May, both the pink and white dogwoods made the city look like a colorful world of the fairies.

My husband suggested that we should revisit the famous Callaway Gardens, which both of us were very fond of. It was not too far from our house, but my husband knew he could not make it as a day trip, so we made reservations and stayed overnight at the gardens. It turned out to be the most memorable trip for me because only two weeks later, I lost my dearest husband.

I always ate much slower than my husband. Since living in this house, usually after he finished eating first, he would leave the table and wait for me in a rocking chair I had placed close by for him. When I was finished, then we would go upstairs to prepare him for his nap. That day in May, he had a very light lunch, so he got up and sat in the rocking chair to wait for me. As I was still eating, he suddenly said he could not wait for me, but needed to lie down. So, I dropped my food and quickly followed him upstairs. He went into the bathroom but told me to call the doctor. It was noontime and the office was closed, so when he came out from the bathroom, and while he was lying down, he said, call 911. I immediately dialed 911, but before I could hang up the phone, he was already gone. I tried and tried to resuscitate him, but I could not bring him back anymore.

I called Jeffrey and Mary in Chicago, Leo in New York, and my sister-in-law Yvonne in El Paso. They all came to Atlanta immediately. I had made arrangements with the hospital to keep my husband there for the family members so they could say their final goodbye. Since we did not know anyone else in the local area, soon afterwards, he was cremated.

From the day that I met him till that day of May 24, 1988, our life together had only been forty-two years. On Memorial Day, Leo, Eva and I flew to New York. C.T. met us at the Chuang Yen Monastery in Carmel and we had a simple ceremony, and there, my husband's ashes were permanently encased in the mausoleum.

Before returning to Atlanta, I visited our dear friend, C.T.'s wife Nancy. She was gravely ill, and was in the last phase of her life. Sad to say, in July, Nancy also passed away.

At the end of July, I moved to Eva's house and stayed in their guest room, but stored my furniture in the extra apartment space. Then in August, my younger sister Helen *(Mian Mian)* became sick, and her husband asked me for help. When I arrived in New Jersey, I found out she was suffering from cancer. Her doctor tried to operate. Alas, it was already too late. I did my best to make her comfortable. Of course, all my efforts were made in vain. Soon, she died in September.

Shortly, her husband arranged her funeral, and afterwards, with a heavy heart, I went back to Atlanta.

Our last family Christmas, 1987

Doug, mom, Eva, dad, Leo. Leo just back from Jeddah, Saudi Arabia, looking tan!

179

For weeks, I just let days pass without any focus. I was not capable of thinking or feeling. In a brief five months, I lost three of the most dear people in my life. Slowly, eventually, I gathered myself together and started to take care of the neglected business which needed to be taken care of. One of the most important things I had to attend to was to decide what to do with my mother-in-law's old maidservant and the house they lived in, which was in Taipei.

Earlier, in 1983, I had made a trip to see my mother-in-law in Taipei and stayed with her for a month, but a year or so later, at ninety-three years old, she passed away. Even then, my husband was so weak that we could not go to Taiwan together.

Since I was still responsible for the expenses for the maintenance of that household, a trip there was unavoidable. Therefore, one day, in November, I flew over to Taiwan. I arrived late at night. The next morning, I made a phone call to surprise my brother, Peng. But the surprised one was me. Over the phone was my brother's choking voice. "Your sister-in-law just passed away this morning." When I hurried over to his house, I was met by my niece and her husband. They had just come home from the US to see their mother. I also learned that my nephew and his wife also were on their way home. I don't need to say how I felt during the following days. It was the fourth death within a half year that I had to bear. My sister-in-law's death hit my brother so hard that when his children left for the US, I spent almost every day with him to try to console him.

Yet at the same time, I needed to take care of my mother-in-law's house. Our maidservant *(Wang Sau)* came to Taiwan from mainland China with the Chang family. Her husband, a doctor, passed away shortly after they were married. Her in-laws tried to marry her off to someone, but she ran away and tried to work as a maid to support herself. She ended up with the Chang family, where for decades, she served everyone loyally and faithfully. She actually took care of three generations of our family. She came to the Changs even before I was married. Now that my mother-in-law was gone, and she was getting on in years herself, I could not let her stay in the house just by herself. Before I visited some retirement homes to find an acceptable place for her, I talked with her to see if that was what she wanted. But when I told her there was a well-known place, she told me that she "definitely wanted to die in the old home." So, I had to employ a woman companion to look after her, and still keep the house.

As for the monthly expenses, I would still remit them every other month to one of my sisters-in-law's husband, as before.

I returned to Atlanta in the spring. Eva and Doug were occupied with their own busy work. I was mostly home alone during the day. It was the first time I could rest and think clearly since my husband's last operation. It was a lonely undertaking to plan my own future life without my husband.

Before we moved to Atlanta, I had started to have problems with my eyesight. Night driving became difficult. By the time we were in Atlanta, even with glasses, I could not see street names clearly when driving. I visited three different eye doctors, but none could find anything wrong with my eyes. Living in Atlanta, no matter where we went, I had to depend on my husband to find the streets that we wanted. Now that I was by myself, driving presented a great problem for me. I debated with myself whether Atlanta was the place for me to stay. I do love the city, and besides, Eva and Doug were both close to me. But because of my fading eyesight, I suspected I was developing macular degeneration. I thought about State College. It is a small college town. I knew the whole area so well from being a resident there for twenty years. Certainly, I could drive freely without trying to read all the street names. It is also where my good friends were living. I thought I should go back and pay a visit to State College.

Since we had left, over the ensuing four years, State College had changed a great deal. There were new housing developments all over the town. I stayed with Olivia, and daily, she accompanied me in looking for a suitable place. I was surprised to find out that those leisurely trips to open houses in the south had unconsciously helped me to accumulate all kinds of references for considering a new house. We looked at numerous places, and one day, I saw a new condo. It was an end unit, roomy, bright, and close to parks, and the price was reasonable. So, within twenty minutes, I bought the place. In July 1990, I moved in, back again in State College.

The new unit was numbered "13," but in it I spent twelve peaceful and pleasant years. During the time I was there, I only had to go to Taipei once due to the death of our old maidservant. I also had to sell the old house and take care of some of the legal matters. Mostly, I was happily back in State College among my old friends. Our condo owners were friendly with each other, because the community only started with ten units. When we had heavy storms or snow days, someone would always call me and check on me. Olivia's house was not that far from me. She frequently dropped in to visit me. My neighbors all thought she was my daughter. Every year, I would join my friends for some travels overseas. I also could travel freely in the US by myself. During those years, I visited many places, including Europe, Australia, and Turkey. I even took Eva with me on a trip to China.

After I returned to State College, I went to a good eye doctor. Soon, he explained to me that my problem with my eyes was because cataracts were forming. I was greatly relieved that I did not have macular degeneration. When I had the cataracts removed in both of my eyes, I was so pleased that I no longer had to wear glasses. The world around again appeared to be so clear and distinct, and I could drive again with confidence. But who would know my good eyesight would only last for two short years, before the doctor detected that I had glaucoma even though I had regular eye pressure. Unfortunately, I had to start to use strong steroid eye drops. But even though I had to adhere to the strict instructions to apply them four times a day, it did not affect my daily life except that my eyes got tired very easily.

Concerned about my future ability to drive, I started to think I should look for a retirement place with transportation facilities offered. I began to pay attention to different retirement residences. I gathered all sorts of information and visited many retirement homes, even in different cities. It was at that juncture, some Penn State professors also had a plan to build one right at the edge of the campus. I checked their blueprint and was pleased with their planned facilities and offerings. So, I made a deposit to reserve a unit.

During these twelve years, I would spend my Christmas in New York with my son and his family. For the Chinese New Year, I would be in Washington, D.C. with my brother and his children. But around Eva's birthday, I would always try to be with her in Atlanta, Georgia, and later, in Oldsmar, Florida. While I was down in Oldsmar, she often took me to visit the area's retirement homes. We were fairly impressed with the beautifully kept, spacious landscape of Regency Oaks in Clearwater, and its friendly people.

In the year 2001, I flew down to Eva's for her birthday, and was scheduled to fly back on the 12th of September. We had a wonderful fiftieth birthday with her friends on September 10. The next morning, before she was leaving for work, she shouted loudly from the living room, where she was in front of the television. I hurried over, just in time to see the horror. A plane was crashing into the World Trade Center. My first reaction was, "What a terrible accident!" but a few minutes later, the news was broadcasting loud and clear. It was the very first terrorist attack on our land.

Because of 9/11, I was delayed in going back to Pennsylvania. Before my plane landed in State College, I had already made up my mind. For two years, I had waited for the Penn State Village to be built. So far, there were no signs of any construction work. I also knew that even though I had been independent for so many years, yet, if I should be in need, Eva certainly would want to be with me. Coming to State College was difficult for both my children, as there were no direct flights, whereas Regency Oaks is located where it is much easier for Leo, and of course Eva.

I soon called the Regency Oaks marketing department, and made a deposit. At the same time, I took back my deposit with the Penn State Village.

Once again, I had to dispose of a household of furniture and pack my important belongings. On August 16, 2002, I moved into my apartment in Regency Oaks in Clearwater, Florida. I was seventy-six years old.

PART II

Stories and Thoughts

Following are some stories written by my mom as part of her writing sessions at Regency Oaks, the retirement community where she now lives. I am grateful that Regency Oaks provided the structured opportunity to write about her life and experiences apart from the original biography which she wrote.

June 15, 2013

My Time with My Father

I was born when my father was almost fifty years old. As I was born to a very extended household, I had to share my father with so many other people, not like some of the other families which basically only consisted of a few core members of parents and children.

When very young, I was not allowed to eat with the adults until I reached ten years old. In the early mornings I was sent to school. In the evenings I was put early to bed. The only times that I could see my father and be with him would be the few hours after school and before bed and only when he was not receiving visitors or in his office.

I was nine years old when my mother died. I was sent away to live with my godparents. During weekends, I would ride the train to come home. It was then that I could have more time to be close to him.

When the Sino-Japanese War started, we were separated again. While he was with the central government at the wartime capital, I was in school in a rural area to escape the Japanese air raids. But when I finished my junior high, I demanded to be with him. He yielded. There, although I was in a boarding school, during weekends, we could always be home together. Thus, only as a teenager, I began to have more intimate time to know my father.

Finally, the war was over. My university unfortunately was far away from home. My father wanted me to transfer to a university so I could be around to keep him company. I tried, but it did not work out. So, I could only be home for my summer vacations.

By the end of 1948, the Communist troops already occupied most areas of China. I had to fly to another city to get married. The night before I left, my father talked to me. He said, "I know you are going to be married. I am very sorry I do not have anything to give you. All I can do is give you an airplane ticket. The political situation is thus, I hope you will understand. But I promise you I will be at your wedding to give you away." A few days later, I received his telegram: "There are no longer any flights between our two cities."

I did not see my father until eight long years afterwards, when I was already the mother of two young children. Only after we went through all kinds of difficulties were we able to make the trip back home. But home at that time was not on mainland China, it was Taiwan, a completely strange place to me.

For the six months that we were in Taiwan, I was very grateful to my mother-in-law. She took care of my two children so I could spend more time in my father's house. That year, my father had his eightieth birthday. He looked almost the same to me as before; but one day he told me that often, he could not sleep. Usually, he would get up at dawn and walk in the yard. I noticed his long full beard had grown thin and had completely turned silvery. We both treasured the brief time together.

In May, due to our US status and also because the children would be starting school, we had to say goodbye to my father. He was doing well except occasionally he would send me letters to say that he missed me.

Then in 1964, different people began to inform me that my father was ill. Then followed the news that he was being hospitalized due to a dental infection. Then my brother who was in the Philippines was asked to go home by the government because my father's condition was very serious. He sent me a telegram from Taipei after he saw my father at the hospital. My husband was in

Taipei at that time, lecturing as a guest professor, and I was in Madison, Wisconsin, with our two children. I have already related my strange experience on the day he passed away so I need not repeat it here.

Father has gone for almost fifty years this year *(2013)*. His love, his concern for others, his love for knowledge will long live in my heart. But the pain, the hurt, and regrets of my not being with him will also dwell in me. Forever, I will miss him.

May 15, 2012

Remembering My Mother

My mother only appears in broken pieces in my memories, but I know she loved me.

I remember every day after school when I came home, she would always have something specially saved for me – certain things might be kept warm, others might be icy cold. Often there would be something exotic like imported mangoes or candies. Of course at that age, I just enjoyed each treat and took it for granted.

Once I remember, she was talking to one of her friends, saying she wanted to have a maroon colored winter coat made for me because she thought the color would look good on me.

Mother did not have the best of health. Often she had to take rest lying down. At those times, I would pull up my little stool and sit by her to keep her company. I often massaged her legs. She seemed to really enjoy those times.

When I was growing up, many a time, people told me that my mother almost died giving birth to me. She had four children: my brother, me, and two younger sisters. I feel I am luckier than my two younger sisters. I knew my mother's love, and later, my godmother's care and love, while my sisters had their nannies and hardly had the opportunity to know anything about our mother, even though one of them bore a strong resemblance to our mother. I do not know why I was sent to live with my mother's best friend, my godmother, a few months before she passed away. Although I was about two hours' train ride away from home, occasionally I would be taken out of school to stay in the hospital where mother was staying. My brother and I had a room together

189

there, so we could be near mother. One morning, mother left us. I was nine years old.

In my memory, mother was pretty with beautiful eyes. She was tall and slim. She has been gone for a long, long time now, but still today, whenever I see or smell the fragrance of tuberoses, it always brings me back to the scene of her funeral. I would see her lying there, in a room fully crowded with all those flowers, with the pungent fragrance of the tuberoses permeating the air.

My grandmother was named Chen Miao Lian. My mom does not recall how she and my grandfather met, but it was probably at one point when my grandfather was in Canton (Guangdong). She had the most children of all my grandfather's wives.

I've been told that my grandmother was so sick after giving birth to my mom that the family was told to prepare a coffin and to make funeral arrangements. In desperation, when a friend suggested that she try opium to ease her sickness, she tried it. The treatment was successful, but she became addicted to opium. She struggled for many years to overcome the addiction, and was eventually successful, but it took many years.

L: Clockwise: Unknown friend, Chen Miao Lian, mom, Yuan Chun Yu, and Mian Mian in the middle. R: Chen Miao Lian

Tracing My Family Tree

Tracing My Family Tree

One summer vacation, when I was still in junior high, my father showed me a thin handwritten book of our family tree. He assigned me the job of making a copy in the traditional way: with Chinese ink and brush. It took me some time to complete the task and hand the original with my copy back to my father. That was the last I saw of the two books.

From that book, today I can only faintly remember that my father's great grandfather had two sons. From that one ancestor, by the time it came down to my father's generation, there were four males, with two sons in each branch, and my father was the oldest among the four. I also was surprised to learn that it was a general practice in most of the Chinese family trees not to include girls. Girls were not included simply because they would be married off to bear other families' last names. They would always be included in their husband's family records as "so and so's wife."

In those years, when I met someone, I was often told to address them as "Uncle" or "Auntie" or as my "Cousin." Back then, families usually were very large, so one was bound to have many relatives, however remotely connected. But the Chinese also have a tradition of addressing close friends of one's parents as "Uncles" or "Aunties," so with my father's wide associations, at times, I was fairly muddled about the real relations between my real blood relatives or distant relatives and friends.

After that summer, as I was growing up, I found my father had written numerous poems, and they were often quoted by people and printed in various papers and magazines. Also, I found a brief autobiography which my father wrote about his youth. Only then, I began to learn a little more about my own family and some of my relatives.

Still, even today, I cannot say I have a good knowledge about my family. In the years past, although there were many chances for me to ask my father about the history of our family, when we were alone, I never thought of the need or had the pressing curiosity to ask. Now I know the chances are lost and it is lost forever. What I know of our past, including my own life, has been learned in broken pieces.

I never knew my grandparents. Only from my father's biography, I read that one year, my maternal great grandfather was fleeing from a province next to ours, due to the Muslim rebellion riots. On their way, he just could not carry two young children anymore, so he dropped his five-year old daughter at the roadside and tearfully only carried his younger son and left with the other refugees. Luckily, not too long afterwards, a camel caravan came by, and someone saw this poor little lost girl who was crying. They kindly picked her up and proceeded forward. Somehow, later, they caught up with my great grandfather, and thus, she was returned to her father. Years later, she was married to my grandfather.

There was no record to tell where the Yu family was originally from. People only knew that my family had been settled at that place in Shaanxi for many generations and had always lived as farmers. They were very poor. My grandfather could only afford to study for two years. When he was twelve years old, he was sent to be an apprentice at a pawn shop in Sichuan province. He walked those hundreds of miles to Sichuan, worked there, and then was able to come home for the first time after nine long years.

My grandfather was married at twenty-five years old, in 1878. It was the fourth year of the Emperor Guang Xu of the Qing Dynasty. The next year, 1879, my father was born. After my father was born, his mother became very weak. There was no extra money for her to be treated. Meanwhile, my grandfather had again left home to work in Sichuan. So, slowly, she died when my father was not quite two years old.

My grandfather had an older brother who was deceased, and left a young widow, Fang. She was very close to my grandmother. My grandmother entrusted Fang to look after her child after she died. It was under Fang's tender loving care and strict discipline that my father grew up.

Since he was far away in Sichuan, my grandfather could not correspond with his home easily. One day, after our house at the west gate area in the town of Sanyuan caught fire, and burned to the ground, grandma Fang could no longer live there. Hence, she took my father with her and returned to her own family in a different village to live. Normally, when a married daughter became a widow, she would not return to her own people, so as not to bring further burdens to them. But now, not only did she herself return home, in addition, she also brought home someone else's little boy with her. In spite of the fact that the Fangs were not that much better off than the Yu family financially, during all those years, while they were with the Fangs, no one ever complained about her or the orphaned boy. On the contrary, they all showed respect to grandma Fang and all loved my father.

When my father was six years old, he begged grandma Fang for a little lamb so he could be just like his older cousins, but she could only afford a lame kid. One day, when the children were herding their lambs in a wide open space, suddenly three wolves appeared, and my father was almost snatched by one. He was barely saved by a farmer who just happened to pass by. In observance of that incident, the villagers began to feel the urgent need for a school in order to offer the children some decent schooling, so as not to waste their precious time in herding sheep.

Thus, the next year, my father was able to attend a newly formed and privately sponsored traditional home school. During this time, most Chinese schools were located in private homes or the memorial halls of family clans. The more well-to-do families were able to sponsor these schools and to hire better-qualified teachers. They would often permit the less fortunate village children to attend these schools. These schools provided instruction on the classical Chinese texts and Chinese history. The primary mode of learning was by memorization and recitation. Science and math were not taught in these traditional curricula.

After four years at the school, grandma Fang took my father back to the Yu family. This time, they stayed at the east gate of Sanyuan, with my father's grand-uncle. He had a good friend who was a well-known teacher, Mr. Mao. Therefore, my father was able to study under Mr. Mao. There, he was initiated in the composition of classical Chinese poetry. At the same time, he also started to learn to write in the cursive style of Chinese calligraphy. That very year, when he was eleven years old, my grandfather had remarried, and came home from Sichuan. They rented a place, also in the east gate area. But my father still lived with grandma Fang. Although my grandfather did not have much formal schooling, he was very diligent in pursuing knowledge. Because there was no money to spend on books, he often would hand copy his borrowed books. While he was home, he would frequently study with my father, often until late at night. My father remembered that he learned a great deal from his father during that period.

In the following year, near where my father was living, there was a firecracker factory. My father went to work there for some odd jobs whenever he had some time. There, he could earn a few coppers each time to help the family. Also, he could earn some money to pay for items that he needed for school.

When he turned twelve years old, his father left for Sichuan again. Later, in Sichuan, his stepmother gave birth to a little girl.

Sad to say, uneventful days did not last long. One day, the firecracker factory had a big accident and my father was almost caught in it. So, the extra income for him was gone for good. Then he heard at that time, the Qing government was sponsoring a special kind of award to encourage outstanding students. After he exhausted himself in preparation, he gathered up his courage and went to take the general test at the county. He was very pleased that he was awarded two ounces of silver which was the currency then. Since each ounce was worth more than 110 or so coppers, compared to the three or four coppers a day he used to earn from the firecracker factory, it was a significant windfall. After this, he would take the tests often, and often was awarded additional prizes. Due to this, his financial situation gradually became less stressed.

1952, 74th Birthday

The Changs

Among the Chinese, we have a saying, "When one drinks water, one should trace back to know about the origin of the water." It is usually used to express our gratitude to our ancestors. It means, "Whatever accomplishment we have attained, it is mostly due to our ancestors' accumulated efforts so we could have that foundation to build on and to succeed."

For me, I never thought I would become a first generation immigrant. Instead of returning to China after our visit to the US, my husband and I stayed in the United States of America and started our own branch of the Chang family here. In the past, when the children were young, our family often was scattered in different places. It was only after I moved to Florida, that my daughter Eva is close by. She began to ask me about our families' stories. She prompted me to write my autobiography. That's what started me to trace the source of our families' origins. I know it will not be complete or perfect, but it will be some reference about our family history.

Because I started too late, some memories have already faded. Many relatives and family friends who could help me with precious materials are no longer with us. Plus the fact that since I spent so many years at boarding schools, away from home, I did not even have the whole knowledge of my own family. Therefore, needless to say, regarding the Changs, my husband's family, I know even less. What I could gather is not much. So I regret to say that the history of the Changs is very limited in this writing.

I met my mother-in-law when my husband was courting me. But I did not meet my father-in-law until my husband and I were soon to be engaged. It was in early May, 1946, after the war had

196

ended. He was the Mayor of Chongqing, the wartime capital, at that time.

My husband did not resemble him at all. He always stood very erect which reflected his military background. In the short time that I was with this family, my impression of him was that he was rather strict with his boys, but was very lenient towards his girls. Before Chongqing, he was a district military representative of the Generalissimo Chiang Kai-Shek, who later became president. He was stationed at Xichang, in Xikang province. That province no longer exists. The Communist government has returned the eastern part to Sichuan province and the western portion was returned back to its original province of Eastern Tibet. Shortly afterwards, he became the governor of Hubei province. By the end of 1948, when mainland China was lost to the Communists, all of Chiang Kai-Shek's government withdrew to Taiwan. My father-in-law left the government and with his wife and part of his family members, went to Hong Kong, and then later settled in Taiwan.

In 1956, for the first time since we were married, when I took my children and went to Taiwan from the States, we stayed with my in-laws. Half of my time, I was at my father's house. Half was with my in-laws. But the children had the whole six months to be with their paternal grandparents. Both of them spoiled the two children. I think the children must have brought them some real happiness. My father-in-law especially seemed to dote on Leo. Fortunately, the children both spoke pure Chinese, so they were able to communicate freely.

It was sad to say that not quite two years after we returned to the US, we learned the bad news that my father-in-law had left us.

My grandfather was named Chang Du Lun (Zhang Dulun). He was the oldest of four sons, and had a distinguished military career. He joined the revolutionary efforts against the Manchu empire, sneaking away from the Manchu Pao-Ding Military Academy with some classmates to do so. He eventually became a Lt. General, acting mayor of Hankou, mayor of Chongqing, and governor of Hubei. During his career, he was dispatched to many different military posts, and was sometimes able to keep his family with him. When the Nationalists lost control to the Communists, he made his way to Hong Kong, then to Taiwan with his family. He passed away in October, 1958.

See page 320 for an abbreviated Chang family tree.

The Changs, 1940s

Grandma Chang (*Shen Shou Jen*)

My mother-in-law was from a very traditional Chinese family. Although the family was not wealthy, they were known locally as a household which had produced good scholars in the past. Her father passed away when she was in her teens. She was a single child, and there were no men in the house to protect her and her mother from the outside world. She learned to face the hardships and unfair treatment from others which she received because she was only a young girl living with a widowed mother in the house. She never retreated from the challenges that she faced in the society which treated women with little respect.

For generations, most Chinese girls were not given the opportunity to study. There were no modern public schools even for boys. However, my mother-in-law's clan had a private school for the boys of the family. So, she would stand outside the school window and listen to the instruction which the boys received and she would try to memorize what the boys were chanting. After a few years, she could recite a great deal of poems and Chinese classics, which enabled her to interpret how to read and write written Chinese characters. She was extremely intelligent. I have seen some of her correspondence, which was very elegantly and superbly composed, often superior to that of many well-educated people.

Unfortunately her parents followed the cruel practice of the time, when they bound her feet at a very young age. Later, after the Republic of China was established, the practice was abolished. But it was already too late for her. The broken bones in her feet could no longer be corrected.

She was married at a tender age into the Chang family. My father-in-law was the oldest son among four brothers. That made my mother-in-law the most important daughter-in-law in the whole large family. All through her life, the responsibility of looking after the whole family was on her shoulders. In this regard, she earned respect from everyone. Her kindness and generosity was not only limited to her own family, but included relatives, friends and servants. All through their married years, my father-in-law could devote all his time to his career and did not have to worry about his household, even when there were some very difficult times. That of course was all due to my mother-in-law's able and clever management.

She was adaptable and learned quickly. For example, she once went to a church and was introduced to some very fine wines which were made from the local grapes by the local French monks at the church. They made very fine brandy and port which my grandmother admired very much. She learned from the monks how to make these special wines, and returned to her own home where she used her own vineyard to create similar brandies and ports. Eventually, her port became quite well known amongst the high-ranking guests at their house, as well as some of the American pilots and officers who frequented their house. The American officers even offered to purchase some of her spirits for their own consumption because it was of such high quality, but of course she could not sell any products commercially.

In 1960, my mother-in-law came to the US to visit my brother-in-law Louie in Connecticut. Then she came to stay with us in New York for a few months. Because she loved flowers, we tried to take her to see spring blossoms. She was so excited to see the large spreads of tulips. In May of 1961, when we moved to Wisconsin, she flew to El Paso, Texas to visit my sister-in-law Yvonne. She did not understand any English, but she made friends with many Americans. Letters from Yvonne also told us that in El Paso, she also managed to communicate with many others.

In the 1970s, we went back to Taiwan during our summer vacation time. In 1983, I went back alone to see her because my husband was not able to travel for a long distance. She already had some slight signs of dementia, but was still healthy. Later, we received a phone call from Taiwan which said that she fell and broke her hip bone. Soon after that, at ninety-three, her condition deteriorated and she passed away.

My husband's parents had nine children, five girls (one adopted) and four boys.

She was born in 1892 in the city of An Lu, Hubei province. Her family was traditionally Buddhist, and her early influence led my father to his eventual path as a Buddhist scholar and educator. She married my grandfather when she was sixteen and he was twenty, the result of an arranged marriage. Her life as a military wife during the tumultuous years following the revolution against the Manchus through the Japanese War and World War II to the civil war and escape to Taiwan had many ups and downs in line with my grandfather's positions in the military and government. She valued education and hired live-in tutors for all the children. In a significant break from cultural traditions and her own life history, she ensured that her daughters had access to schooling and even college educations; she was clearly a progressive woman.

What's in a Name

*I*n *addition to being a famous calligrapher, my grandfather was also a well-known poet. It was customary for people to ask him to name their babies. Therefore, one would think that his children would all have lovely poetic names. To the contrary, his children all had very unorthodox names.*

My grandfather originally named my mother "Hsiang Hsiang." This literally means "thinking thinking." It would be a common expression meaning "I'm thinking about it," as if he were still thinking about what her name should be. When she began the process of applying for college, she adopted the name Nien Tze, which became her legal name. However, she never uses this name with Chinese friends. Her English name is Helena. Her younger sister was named Helen. And my father's eldest sister was also named Helena. I wonder why the name was so popular in China at that time!

Her younger sister was named Mian Mian, meaning flexible, not likely to break. Her youngest sister was named Wu Ming, literally meaning "no name." Needless to say, she hated that name. She later took the name of Yang Tze.

The oldest girl in the family, daughter of the Number One wife, was named Leng, meaning "foolish little girl." This was considered her "milk name," and she eventually took the name Zhi Xiu. A milk name is a name given to a Chinese child at birth, but is later superseded by a more formal name. The milk name may still be used by family members, especially as an endearment.

March 12, 2011

"I Remember Vividly When I Was Young"

As an eighty-some year-old person, writing about my life and the past, I often tried to recollect details about events that I remember. Somehow, I find that I do not remember things in detail, but only the whole experience in general. Of course, many things must have happened when I was young, but only two things stand out in my memory, and even those, I cannot recall the details.

The first one was on the day after we had moved to a new residence. I was taken to a new school for testing. There was not the slightest trace or impression of who took me there. I knew I was to be tested for the first-grade class. In a classroom, a teacher put a book in front of me and asked me to read. I started from the first page and read it all the way through without any problem, except for one character. It appeared in a rhymed couplet in Chinese which meant: Walk a hundred "steps" after a meal; (one) could live up to ninety years old. The character was the word for "step." With that, the teacher said I actually could be admitted to the second grade. As for how I had learned all those other characters in the book, it was all a blank. I must have been about six years old.

The other event left a deep impression in my memory. It happened in 1932. One night, about dinner time, my mother told our maidservant to bring our bedding downstairs and make beds for all of us, my brother, me, and my mother. My Number Three mother, who was on the third floor, also did the same. My father was not in Shanghai at the time. I became very excited because to sleep on the floor was a fresh experience to me. I ran down the stairs and to my big surprise I found that a few of my father's attendants and their families were already gathered there. Their beddings were already spread on the floors of our dining room, whereas my family's bedding was in the waiting room next to it. There were children younger than me too. I thought it was such a happy and lively occasion. Soon, I went to sleep, and the adults gathered in discussions.

I do not remember how we spent the second day. But I do remember we spent the second night still sleeping on the floor. All that time, I could hear sounds like people were celebrating by shooting loud fireworks in the distance.

A couple of days later, things became normal again. By then, I had learned that we went downstairs to avoid the Japanese attack in Shanghai. Our house was located in the British concession, which was in an area protected from the Japanese. But since some of the attendants' families lived in Chinese territory, we welcomed them to stay with us for safety's sake.

First Battle of Shanghai. The 1932 attack was triggered by riots by angry Chinese workers, following years of tension after the first Sino-Japanese War. The incident quickly escalated to full-scale fighting and bombings. The First Shanghai Incident ended with a cease-fire on 5 May 1932, after the Japanese suffered some 3000 casualties (700 killed) and inflicted about 12,000 casualties on the Chinese.

Barbed wire protecting the Shanghai International Settlement during the First Battle of Shanghai, China, 1932

German Federal Archive

Thoughts After the War

Thoughts After the War

I asked my mother to talk about her feelings after the war. She mostly recalls relief that the war and years of conflict with the Japanese were over. She recalls this incident:

She was in a car near a dock. There was a train also stopped nearby. The train was full of Japanese soldiers who had surrendered, and were on their way back to Japan. Chiang Kai-Shek had ordered that the Chinese would not take revenge on the Japanese, only sending them home to Japan. She remembers feeling many conflicting emotions as she watched the train full of soldiers. She felt pity, as they were clearly defeated and disgraced. She felt hatred, for all the evil they had inflicted upon the Chinese. She felt fear, for the unknown futures for the returning soldiers and for herself and the Chinese people.

She also had this story to relate:

In 1992, when I went back to China with some relatives, we visited the memorial in Nanjing commemorating the Nanjing Massacre. The exhibit includes an excavation of bones from a mass grave said to contain tens of thousands of bodies.

I talked to one of the workers there, and asked about the reactions of Japanese visitors to the site. He said that older Japanese visitors were repentant and apologetic about what happened, but younger Japanese visitors do not believe that it happened at all.

From the China Travel Guide:

On Dec 13, 1937, the Japanese army occupied Nanjing and during the following six weeks bore witness to the inhumane disgrace and bloody massacre exerted on the

205

city. No less than 300,000 innocent civilians and unarmed Chinese soldiers were brutally slaughtered in mass and individual beheadings, burying alive, burning, and killing races. More than 20,000 women were raped and many were then killed. A third of the architectures together with their contents were damaged by fire and countless shops, stores and residences were looted and sacked. Corpses were seen floating on rivers and littered the streets and lanes. Whether they were children or the aged, from residents to nuns, few could escape from the savage atrocity...

The remaining bones of victims in the massacre, which were excavated from Jiangdongmen in 1985, are exhibited in a coffin-shaped display hall. There were 208 more bones uncovered from this 'pits of tens of thousands bodies' in 1998. Another tomb-like exhibition hall, which is buried half underground, contains over 1000 items that illustrate the terrible tragedy. Paintings, sculptures and illuminated display cabinets and multi-media screens as well as documentary films all contribute to this reminder of the horrendous crimes perpetrated on the Chinese people.

To this day, many Chinese people refuse to buy Japanese products, just as many Jewish people refuse to buy German products.

July 3, 2011

"The Most Embarrassing Thing in My Life"

When I was nine years old, I lived in Shanghai with my family. But in the fall of that year, my mother passed away. Following my mother's wish, I went with my godparents back to Suzhou. I lived with them and enrolled in a good private school. I was put in the fourth grade. There, in the same class, there was a nice girl, I-Fang Li. We became very good friends. At first, I did not know that I-Fang's father was a retired general and an ex provincial governor who was a mutual friend of both my father and my godfather. They were all involved in the revolutionary movement in overthrowing the Qing dynasty.

One day, I-Fang's mother telephoned my godmother, saying that I-Fang was my classmate and would like to invite me to spend the weekend in their house. Upon that invitation, my godmother packed a little suitcase for me and reminded me how I should behave as a young lady guest for the trip.

The next day, after our Saturday school was over at noon, I followed I-Fang and got onto their private rickshaw and went to their house. They had a big house. The nicest thing was that they also had a very beautiful, large and well-designed garden. Even then, I knew that Suzhou's gardens were famous in China for their styles. So, we had a wonderful time playing there. After dinner, I-Fang took me to her room. We played games until it was about bedtime. Her mother came into the room and saw that we cleaned ourselves and got changed into our pajamas. Then she watched us as we got into bed and left.

It was a very large traditional Chinese bed, with a beautiful embroidered canopy draped over the four posts, which made it feel like we were in a tent. I was sleeping close to the wall on the inside while I-Fang was on the outside. Soon, we both fell asleep.

It must have been close to dawn, in the early morning. I woke up. Immediately, I knew something was wrong, because I felt under me, my bed was wet! Oh! I had wet the bed! How was I going to face anyone in the morning!? I stayed in the bed and did not dare to move. I tried to think of a way to avoid the shame. Finally, I decided I should leave without being seen by anyone in the household. Quietly, I got out of the bed without touching I-Fang. Somehow, I got changed into my clothes and found my way out of the house. In the pre-dawn light, I found the front gate. It was a huge old-fashioned double gate. I struggled and removed the double wooden latch bars and opened a crack in between the two panels. Holding my breath, at last I sneaked out.

I do not have any memory of how I walked back to my godparents' house. I do not remember what happened to my little suitcase. I do not recall what I told my godmother about the incident. I do not even remember how I faced I-Fang in school on the following Monday.

I have been embarrassed by this unfortunate episode until many years later, as I later read and learned about children wetting their beds. Gradually, I began to understand that during those two years when I was nine and going on ten, I often had bedwetting incidents. It was because I lost my dear mother, and on top of that, I had to leave my family and my school at the same time. Having been suddenly put in a completely strange environment had made me insecure. Children under those situations often have the problem of bedwetting. Now, I think I could face the situation, though not without shame. I would not run away and I would definitely apologize to I-Fang's mother. However, at that time, it was too late. All I can say about the incident is that I truly appreciate my godparents' family and I-Fang's family. Even until today, no one has ever confronted me about my shameful behavior.

October 12, 2012

Mr. Wang

By 1939, the Japanese had invaded China. Being a weak nation at that time, soon many schools, universities, and families all had to retreat from the front lines and from some Japanese-occupied areas to the inner land of China. Many students left their homes and followed their teachers and schools to pursue freedom and their studies. I was a lucky one. My family was able to move to where it was safe, and at the same time, to where there were good schools for me.

My school was a school founded by the Oberlin College of Ohio. Most of the funding was from the money paid to the eight western countries which the government of the Qing Dynasty had to pay as the retribution for the Boxer Rebellion. Each year before the war, Oberlin would send two representatives to Beijing to learn the standard Chinese language for six months, and then they would come to our school, the Oberlin Memorial School in Shansi *(Shanxi)*.

I had never been to Shanxi province, the wartime location of the school. Nearly every student and all the faculty members all lived on the campus. Therefore, we truly lived like a large and loving family together. The school was at the wartime location for eight years. I was there only for four years. To this day, I still remember the closeness among all the students and teachers and staff.

During the wartime, it seemed that everyone was poor. In school, I especially remembered our only music teacher. I understood that he had a wife and two young children. It was common knowledge that Mr. Wang Wen Fu, our music teacher, was the hardest working person, and yet he and his family still could not meet their needs. But we students all loved him.

As we had no piano, but an old organ, Mr. Wang encouraged us to sing. When I was at the school, I knew he was the only music teacher for all of us, the junior high and the senior high students. He tirelessly introduced well-known Western composers' works and famous Chinese musicians' songs. We learned church music, spiritual songs of the American South, some of the patriotic Chinese wartime songs, and even excerpts from Western operas. But at the time we did not always know the original lyrics because we had Chinese lyrics written to the melodies. It was many years after having lived in the US that occasionally, I was surprised to find out that I knew these beautiful music pieces from our music teacher, Mr. Wang.

In spite of his heavy load of teaching and administrative work, he organized choruses for each of the junior and senior high students. He often practiced with us patiently and enthusiastically as much as his time allowed, never showing any signs of tiredness, sometimes until dinnertime.

One year, when I was in the eighth grade, a concert was planned to be performed before Christmas. According to the Lunar calendar, 1939 was the Year of the Rabbit. The girls of the choruses thought it would be nice if we could all wear some kind of a badge to identify us. Finally, we decided to make paper cutouts of white rabbit heads with two ears, and we would paint the eyes and mouth red. The project excited many of us, and we quickly finished cutting out all the rabbit heads and waited for the day of the concert.

Mr. Wang had no idea what the girls had done. On the evening of the performance, we distributed the rabbits to all the members of the choruses and pinned them on our uniforms. Girls were in blue Chinese dresses and boys were in their olive green uniforms. We surprised Mr. Wang with a nice rabbit, which he was pleased to wear.

That night, our young voices sang so harmoniously; the songs reached high and far. Everyone enjoyed the beautiful performances. After the concert was over, I saw people congratulating our music teacher.

Later, I left the school and went to a different city. I missed our music classes and the singing. Years after the war was over, I was in Shanghai, and one day, I met a previous schoolmate, and found out about our beloved music teacher. Due to malnutrition, hard work, and lack of money, he died of tuberculosis in his prime. For years, I had wanted to tell him how much I enjoyed his teaching, and how it was because of him that I could appreciate all kinds of wonderful music from around the world. But, I can only keep that wish inside me. Sadly, this unspoken wish will always be one of my regrets, even now.

September 7, 2011

Dreams

Ever since I was young, I have always heard grown-ups talk about their dreams. Most of the time, they would interpret what the dreams meant, and sometimes, people would even consult a dream book. Later, when I could read, I found that dreams played a significant role throughout Chinese history, especially as reflected in its unofficial history books, literature, and vernacular novels. They were full of stories about dreams.

When I was married to my husband, through him, I learned how important dreams were in the Tibetan religions, especially Buddhism. As for myself, for some reason, I rarely had dreams. Or maybe it was just that I did have them, but could not remember them. Yet, on the contrary, my husband seemed always to have dreams, and he often told me he was flying, and most of his dreams were in vivid color.

There were even common symbols in Chinese dreams. Once, the day before my daughter Eva was born, I dreamt that a nice bird with two sparkling shining stars dangling in its beak flew to me. Then I woke up. So, I told some older Chinese friends. They all said that it was a very good omen, and that I would have two bright children. Well, whether it was true or not, it was very pleasant to hear at the time.

Then many years passed. One morning after I took the two children to school, my husband and I sat down to have some freshly brewed tea. I told him not only did I have a very strange dream the previous night, but also, I remembered it so vividly. I told him that somehow, I was in a traditional Chinese house structure. There was a square courtyard. It was not too large. Right in the center, where normally, in the traditional style, there could be a well, instead of a well, there was an earthen stove. When I approached it, suddenly, the whole stove crumbled and sank. I was startled and woke up. Nothing in the dream had any connection with my life at that time. There was no suggestion or association that made any sense to me. My husband felt it was too unusual to ignore, so we took out our dream book which we had acquired a long time ago just for the fun of reading it from time to time. Under the section regarding "the house," surprisingly, we found one entry that said, "When the stove collapses, there will be a death in the household." We did not even have time to make comments to each other. Just then, the phone rang. I picked up the phone. It was my brother-in-law calling from Stamford, Connecticut, informing us that they had just received a telegram that my father-in-law had just passed away in Taipei, Taiwan.

To this day, I still cannot explain the timing of my strange dream and its connection to the actual events of the day as pre-shadowed by the dream book.

Even today, I still wonder.

I remember my parents occasionally consulting Chinese dream interpretation books on some mornings. One or two things made lasting impressions on me. I remember my parents being wary if they dreamed about snakes. It seemed that every time they had a dream about snakes, there was some loss of money or financial setback soon after. In Mandarin, the word for snake is "she," which is the same sound as a word having to do with losing money.

March 6, 2012

Encounters with High Society

Around 1956 or 1957, New York was still a vast strange city to me since I spent most of my time home with my two young children. Only occasionally, because of my husband's classes, sometimes I would be invited together with him by his students to social occasions, and then I would have some outside contact with American society.

As for his students, they were a mixed group. There were actors, authors, professors, and there were also business and industrial professions. The rich ones included millionaires like the owner of the Channel 9 TV station of New York, and the less well-to-do ones were people like ourselves. Often, we would be greeted with surprises.

One day, we received a dinner invitation from Miss Mai-Mai Sze, who was the daughter of the late Chinese Ambassador to the US. She had just published a famous art book on Chinese painting. My husband took me to her apartment. It was either on Fifth Avenue or Park Avenue. I had never met her before. After my husband introduced me to her, she led us into the living room. There was another lady in the room. This lady was very slim and seemed to be in her late 40s or early 50s. She was dressed completely in black. Her hair and her facial makeup left me with a very deep impression. I remembered that she struck me as looking exactly like a top fashion model who had just walked out from a *New York Times* advertisement. Miss Sze introduced us to her saying, "This is my roommate." Unfortunately, I cannot recall her name, but we learned that she was involved with the theater.

As usual, I mostly just listened during these occasions, since my English was not adequate to make the conversation interesting. We had a very pleasant and cozy dinner. I most admired the decorations around us.

Later, when the dinner table was cleared, I asked if I could use their washroom. They showed me the direction and I went.

The door opened to a spacious bathroom. Facing me was a large mirrored wall. The room was also tastefully decorated. As I turned to find the toilet, there it was, right against the wall. And there on top of the water tank stood a pair of golden Oscar statues, glistening in the light! Suddenly, I remembered that Miss Sze had mentioned that her roommate was a costume designer, and these two awards were for her work for movie adaptations of the Broadway shows, "The King and I" and "An American in Paris." That discovery of seeing two popularly coveted statues in a bathroom guarding the top of the toilet was definitely an unexpected encounter for me! It immediately broadened my understanding of how certain sophisticated Americans had clever ways of showing off their achievements.

Irene Sharaff won Oscars in 1951 and 1956, and a Tony Award in 1952. She also won many other awards and was nominated multiple times after this time period. Mai-Mai Sze had her book on Chinese painting published in 1956 by the Bollingen Foundation. See page 299 for more information about these two ladies.

August 3, 2011

"A Most Frightening Experience"

Camping has always been my husband's and my favorite way to spend vacations. We started our family's first camping trip with a Sears Roebuck tent for six when the children were six and seven years old. Through the years, our tents evolved from canvas ones to pop-ups on wheels, to nylon igloos and finally, to a conversion van with beds and cooking facilities. Even up to the present, I still dream that someday, I could go back to camping again.

We had so many beautiful, happy, and funny experiences with and without our children on many trips. However, there was one trip, or more precisely, one night of one trip that still stands out very vividly as one of the most frightening experiences of my life.

It was during one of our trips, while we were returning from the West Coast. The children were long gone. It was just the two of us, my husband and me. We traveled with our nylon igloo tent for two, since it was very light and easy to erect. I could set it up in a few minutes without help. Also, it could be neatly packed into its own slim bag with only a few loose fiberglass pole rods.

Instead of returning on I-90, I-80, I-70, or I-50, we chose to return home by the middle route of I-40 through Tennessee. It would be a new route for us. That day, we drove through the city of Nashville and found a nice state park which had a camping site in a densely wooded area. The woods provided a nice shade in the July sun. It seemed unusually hot for a July day, so we stopped driving early, quickly set up our camp, took a short rest, then went to have lunch. The state park had a large lake. Families with children were noisily and happily splashing around. Dogs were running along the shore. We sat at a picnic table to watch. Then I noticed the water in the lake was not the usual clear color that I

216

generally was accustomed to seeing. It was murky and muddy brown. Yet no one there seemed to mind. After a while, we left and started to drive and have a look around. It was in the late 70s. Gas was still at a reasonable price range. When we traveled, we would always take a large car, since it was equipped with air conditioning and was much roomier. The drive was very pleasant. By dinner time, we went to a restaurant. After our leisurely dinner, we drove back to our camp. It was about eight or nine o'clock in the evening. The day was still bright. But we found out that the mosquitos were not welcoming for sitting outside and reading, so we went into our tent. By then, we began to feel that the heat was stifling and unbearable, so we turned off the light and lay on our mat to rest.

The outside was very quiet. We just noticed that we were the only campers in the entire campsite. After much tossing and turning, we both finally fell asleep.

Suddenly, a crackling lightning bolt woke us both. It was followed by loud roaring thunder. I could tell that the outside was pitch dark. With one of the bolts of bright lightning, I saw that it was 3:30 in the morning. Our nylon tent came with a nice sleeve, so it was rain proof to some extent. Unfortunately, the lightning and thunder were terrifyingly powerful and strong. The rain came down over us as if we were under Niagara Falls. It went on and on for the longest time without ceasing. Both my husband and I were worried and anxious about the incessant lightning. Surely, we could be electrocuted. We had no shelter except two thin layers of nylon over us. The only place we could be a little safer was our car. But then we did not have any umbrellas. In the end, we decided we would have to take a chance and run to the car.

So, with blankets over our heads, we dashed to our car. We were partially drenched by the rain, yet the rain was so heavy we could not open the window in the car or turn on the air conditioning. I looked at the time. It was already close to five o'clock in the morning.

When we finished our trip, safely at home afterwards, one night on the television, we saw a mobile home ad. It showed a poor camper caught in a heavy storm in his tent. Then the ad concluded with an image of a mobile home sitting comfortably dry under a tree canopy. The ad gave us a good laugh as we recalled our own experience.

While we never upgraded to a mobile home or large RV, we eventually bought a conversion van that allowed us to sleep in comfort and security.

The original title of this story/assignment was "The Most Frightening Experience I've Ever Had." I found it ironic that after living through bombings, wars, earthquakes, poverty, medical traumas, and all the other things my mom has experienced, she chose this simple event as the subject of her story.

1986: Dad in the conversion van

April 6, 2011

My Most Memorable Day

Early in the morning on July the 28th, 1988, I drove to the house where two months before, my husband and I had lived. We had moved so many times in our lives, but this had been the last place that we lived together. We had rented this two-storied place for a year. It was a charming and cozy house with a large high deck outside the kitchen overlooking the trees and bushes on the backyard hillside.

I turned the key and slowly walked through the door, walked through the short foyer, and found myself standing alone in the living room, empty and silent. I turned and walked upstairs into our bedroom which was almost the center of our world for the time we were there. The curtains were drawn. The room was vacant without any familiar sights.

Then I walked into my husband's study. There, I could not see his oversized desk, nor was there any trace of all those bookshelves that were once crowded with all his books.

The guestroom was dark and empty too. The whole second floor was so quiet and without life. I went down to the kitchen. When I stood by the window, I could hear my husband saying to me, "Don't rush, finish your lunch. Sorry I am not feeling well. I will go upstairs to lie down." I remembered I dropped my food and ran upstairs after him. As I was calling the doctor and then as I was talking to the 911 operator, before I could even hang up the phone, my husband was gone.

I wanted to go out to the deck to sit down as we used to do after our meals. We sat under the shade and watched the little hummingbirds flapping their tiny wings and hovering around my potted flowers. But then my flower pots and our deck chairs were nowhere to be seen. I stood in the morning sun, feeling so lonesome and alone in the world.

The doorbell rang. The owner of the house came in. Since I had already moved all our belongings to my daughter's house and also had terminated the lease, I had no more right to linger. As soon as the keys were handed over to the rightful owner, I took my last look at our last residence, and walked out to my car. I said to the house, "Farewell! To you, the house, the home of our most peaceful and restful six months of our life together, farewell!"

Oct 5, 2011

My First Regency Oaks Anniversary

It had just turned into October in 2002 after I had moved into Regency Oaks for about two months. I really did not know that many people then, and yet, already people around me were all telling me how wonderful the month of October would be, especially the Regency Oaks anniversary day, with the grand dinner party. It seemed that everyone was anxiously waiting for its arrival.

That year, Regency Oaks' anniversary dinner was held on two separate days for the two buildings. It was chosen for a Wednesday for the North Building and for the following day for the South Building. I vaguely remembered ours, the North Building event, fell on the 15th or 16th. On the day before the event, the dining room staff and Martha *(Activities Director)* had already started to decorate the rooms.

By Wednesday afternoon, the rooms looked so cheerful and pretty, ready for the celebration. The residents happily appeared in their best attire, with most men wearing neat tuxedos and ladies showing off their beautiful evening gowns.

When we entered the dining room we were seated at our reserved tables. On our tables, attractive centerpieces and colorful candies in fancy holders greeted us. Then our hosts, the Regency Oaks owner and members of our management, began the banquet by serving wine to us. They were also formally dressed. Even all the young servers were all in tuxedos.

There was a band playing delightful music while we were eating. The food was excellent and tasty, and the dessert, oh the dessert! It was a frozen chocolate mousse ordered directly from Paris! We all heard that when the dessert was delivered the first time, our dining room manager, Roger, refused it because it was melting. Therefore, a second batch was delivered, and it arrived just barely in time! But we all agreed, it tasted heavenly, and we all enjoyed it.

This October, it will be my ninth Regency Oaks anniversary. I am definitely ready to celebrate the wonderful occasion again, with or without the dessert from Paris!

2003: Fun at Regency Oaks, red fright wig and mask

August 15, 2012

Another Anniversary

Tomorrow, August 16, means that I will be living at Regency Oaks for exactly ten years. Ten years? It's not a short time, and yet somehow, it seems that I just arrived a short while ago. Well, it must have been a very pleasant ten years, otherwise, why did I not feel the days and hours dragging by?

So, there must be things that made me happy here, and I just took them for granted. I think it is about time I should take a good look!

First of all, there is the beautiful landscape. I used to be a habitual morning walker, but not anymore. It was so wonderful to walk in the early morning on our beautifully maintained open ground. Recently, I had to give up the walking because of a worn hip joint. But I have hope that once it's repaired, I could resume the pleasant walk.

When I came, I was the only Chinese resident. Unlike many of our other residents who knew something about Florida, I had flown down straight from Pennsylvania. But things soon changed. I made new friends and some of these friends have become very special. Friendships have given me much newfound happiness.

Then there are the numerous activities catering to our minds, our general health, and our entertainment. Best of all, everything is so conveniently provided. I have been able to widen my life experiences, much more than if I had been living by myself.

Even before I moved here, I knew that one day, I would have to give up driving. Here, I feel so confident that our wonderful transportation services will take care of me. I no longer have to be concerned about going places.

Our dining time is a relaxing, sociable occasion. Although often, I do miss the far better prepared Chinese vegetable dishes, I can easily cook some for myself if I feel like it.

One more important undertaking I picked up after I moved in, is painting. I am not a serious painter. I like to do it to amuse myself. Not that I would not do it if I lived alone. However, here, with the comradeship, after ten years of retirement, I finally started to learn. I truly treasure this experience.

Of course there must be other things not to my liking, but nothing significant.

Looking back, I think the past ten years slipped by so fast and so pleasantly due to my wise move and my nice living environment!

Some of this autobiography and all of the essays were completed as part of a Regency Oaks program, "The Write Stuff," which encouraged residents to write about their lives.

From Regency Oaks Marketing Brochure!

Jan 1, 2013

My History Classes

Back when I was a student in China, we had Chinese history classes in fifth and sixth grades in elementary schools. We learned our early history which mixed facts and legends. In those two years, we learned about five thousand years of history, so of course we studied only the most basic important events and people.

Then in junior high, we learned more about the different dynasties. We also learned more detailed stories and facts about certain heroic deeds and great achievements accomplished by famous emperors, officials, and generals. We also learned the main schools of philosophic thought about loyalty, propriety, justice, benevolence, and so forth. Besides these topics, we also touched upon a little of world history, which mainly covered the few powerful nations of Europe.

Then in senior high school, history classes were not taught like introductory classes any more. We needed to think and compare the different regimes of the various dynasties, and what impact those government structures had on the later generations and the nation as a whole. Another important topic was the relations between the later dynasties and foreign powers. We were made to be aware of the causes which led us to be such a weak and backward nation.

For the last two years in senior high, world history was taught in a more mature manner too. Unfortunately, five thousand years is a long period. Every year when we came to the last part of our modern or recent period, we often ran out of time. Summer vacation always cut the classes short. For me, I regret to say I never had a good grasp about the details of our warlords' civil wars or the end of the Qing Dynasty and the beginning of the revolution and the founding of the Republic of China.

In college, history courses were no longer required for everyone unless it was one's major subject. Since I majored in Chinese literature, I usually selected courses which helped me in my major studies.

By the time I was preparing to go back to school again, I had already left college for almost thirteen years and was a mother of two children. But my biggest problem was that immediately after my husband and I got married, we left China in a hurry, not knowing that we would never be able to go back. That created a serious problem: I did not have any documents to show my college work. Then I found out that if I could pass two graduate classes with good enough grades, I could be admitted to start my advanced studies. So, after deliberation, I selected an American history class and another class. Thinking perhaps that decades of watching the Hollywood version of the history of America, plus ten or so years of living in this country, I should at least have some basic background, I enrolled in this course. Another worry was that I knew that my English was definitely inadequate compared to the other students. How would I know that besides these two concerns, the subject itself would present much greater difficulties for me?

First of all, the way I used to study Chinese history was not suitable for the study of American history. For one thing, we had five thousand years of history, and one cannot know the exact details of every event. On the other hand, the US was not even two hundred years old. Therefore, you can learn almost everything almost as if it just happened yesterday. Another problem for me was to remember all the strange foreign names, especially the names of all the legislators and the laws they helped to pass. I found myself spending countless hours looking up new vocabulary which was rarely used by a housewife!

After one semester's struggle, I managed to turn in papers and passed the course exams. Finally, I was admitted and registered under the Chinese Department at the University of Wisconsin as a graduate student. At present, all I can remember from that course was President Roosevelt's plan to change the Supreme Court!

So many years have passed again. I have been retired and living here at Regency Oaks. Lately, I've been attending Professor Farrar's American History course. *(He was a Regency Oaks resident and former professor who volunteered to give lectures.)* It is wonderful for me to sit in the class, no textbooks to bring, no notes to take, and no exams to take. The professor actually does not mind that we, the audience, do not always remember what he talked about previously, and he himself sometimes repeats what he has already said. He brings a lot of related interesting books and old papers for us to see. The knowledge I have accumulated through these three or four years gave me a much deeper understanding of the nation, the people, and its culture. I am grateful for this opportunity.

Recently, I went to see the movie, *"Lincoln."* I felt I could truly empathize with the president. I know now I can admire and appreciate all our founding fathers and their struggles, passions, and concerns for the nation. I am pleased to say that I am no longer an ignorant U. S. citizen!

September 19, 2011

Autumn

Spring and autumn are my two favorite seasons. Yet, they always bring me entirely different emotions.

Spring brings with it a world full of new life and growth -- the tender green buds, and later, the rosy world of flowers. But autumn, though it comes with the beautiful colors of gold, rust, and red, often makes me feel that it is the prelude to the melancholy symphony of winter. But it does not mean that I do not appreciate the fall season. I think I was very lucky that I had the fortune to live in a small hilly town for a long period of my life. Every year in the fall, I could spend lovely time in the woods. Our town was situated among many mountain ranges. While in the street of the town, one could see the silver maple trees changing color with the weather from luxurious green to gold and then bright red. Outside of the town, one did not have to drive far before all the gorgeous colors would appear before one's eyes.

There were so many forests and valleys and they all seemed to be coming out of some artist's brushes. The colored pictures were so dazzlingly brilliant. I especially liked to be in some of the forests before sunset. Often, you would see the small leaves flickering against the sun's rays. They looked like hundreds of golden raindrops falling from heaven. Or maybe they are little golden butterflies happily dancing in the cool air.

I have learned that autumn foliage would always present a more splendid view if viewed from a hillside, instead of at the same level. One year, the *New York Times* had an article on autumn leaves. I do not remember what the story was about, only that I was so impressed with the detailed description of the different colors of the various trees. The writer used many words for colors that I did not even recognize.

However, the splendid foliage color show inevitably is short-lasting, the last glow before the lifeless winter. Now that I am living in a warm part of the country, winter is no longer a threat to me, but I do miss the resplendent colorful autumn.

"Winter is no longer a threat." Mom enjoying the snow, 1984.

October 15, 2013

Autumn Revisited

My friend came back from the north, and brought back a bright red maple leaf for me. Holding it in my hand, the beautiful color tells me that the fall season has come and we are already in October now! September, October, and November, the three autumn months, are often referred to as "the eventful autumn period" in Chinese history books. Many unusual events in Chinese history happened during these months, especially the month of October.

In the modern period, it is interesting to note that two entirely different political regimes both were established in October in China. The first one was the Republic of China, which overthrew the Qing Dynasty and became an independent nation on October 10, 1912. The National Day is also known as the Double 10th. Then on October the 1st, 1948, the Chinese Communist government claimed their new victory and established the People's Republic of China.

Unfortunately, in recent days, it seems as if the US Congress is following the Chinese tradition of "the eventful autumn" as fights over the government budget drag on.

Autumn is such a colorful and romantic season. Sadly, this year, autumn will probably just slip away. Instead of leaving the usual brilliant and pleasant memory in people's minds, there will only be worry, anxiety, and sighs!

October 18, 2011

Halloween

It was a strange sight to me. I saw children dressed in all kinds of costumes, some even wearing masks on their faces. All carried all sorts of bags or fancy containers. They were all roaming the busy streets, with younger ones holding onto their older sisters and brothers. Talking and laughing, they either walked in small groups or just in twos or threes. I was greatly puzzled: it was very late in the afternoon, and it was getting dark. Why were they still in the streets? How come some of the children even stopped strangers and asked for money and candy? I was also stopped a couple of times by children asking for candy too. But I was walking home in the middle of Manhattan. Where were their parents? Well, that was way back in 1951, my first year in the United States, and I had never heard of the word "Halloween."

A few years later, when my own children started school, I also began to get bags and costumes for my children, and yes, candies for the trick or treaters too. Since then, from here and there, I learned that Halloween probably could be traced to the observance of "All Souls' Day" in Europe.

In China, we do not have Halloween, but it reminded me that many hundreds of years ago, the Buddhists observed a day similar to All Souls' Day. This day always falls on the 15th of the seventh month in the lunar calendar. The legend says that one of the enlightened Bodhisattvas *(Buddhist practitioner)* had dreamed that his deceased mother was suffering in hell due to the sins she had accumulated in her lifetime. She begged her son to help her so she could be relieved of her suffering. After he woke up, the Bodhisattva was sad, so he tried to help. He diligently went through a great deal of hardship, and was finally able to save his mother from remaining in hell on *(lunar)* July 15. So many centuries ago, Buddhists observed that day as a special day for praying and offerings for the dead so as to help them lighten their pains and sufferings in hell.

However, I do not know when the custom started of having lit lotus shaped lanterns floating on flowing waters at night. Lanterns were originally used for light and peace to guide all souls, living or dead. Since the lotus grows in the mud, and yet the flowers grow above the water, and are never touched by the mud, the lotus flower has been used in India, China, and Japan as a symbol of purity and divinity. Therefore, the floating lotus lantern event has become a part of the ceremony of that special day. In our Western calendar, during August, occasionally, you might see a celebration on the television. China, Japan, and Korea, all traditionally Buddhist countries, all observe this occasion. When one has the chance to watch the flower lanterns serenely floating on the water at night, one will feel peace, love, and tranquility in one's heart.

Now, as for my children, they only know the American Halloween. My son has been going with his children to "trick or treat" for many years. But I wonder whether the children in Manhattan can still freely go trick or treating in the street, and not have any fears? And will their candies be safe to eat?

September 30, 2012

Mid-Autumn Festival

In the earliest days, there lived a queen in her beautiful heavenly palace. She had a white rabbit in charge of making a longevity elixir, especially prepared for her. One day, a young palace girl stole the elixir. The queen ordered her people to catch the girl. The girl ran for her life and finally ran to the moon. So, through the centuries and the generations, on the 15th day of the eighth month in the lunar calendar, when the moon is at its fullest and brightest, we can still see the running girl's shadow in the moon. There are many variations on the story, but the main story remains about the same.

In later years, we named that day the Mid-Autumn Festival. It is a very popular holiday. I remember that when I was a little girl, on that day, most families would have a table set outdoors fully piled with all sorts of food. They were the offerings for the Goddess of the Moon. Our lunar calendar differs from the Western calendar by a month or month and a half. So, the Mid-Autumn Moon Festival would usually fall around September of the Western calendar. This is always in the midst of the season of abundance. Of course, years ago, most of the Chinese were farmers. By this time, the harvest was mostly over and done, so people could relax and have the leisure to enjoy some of the rewards from their yearly hard work in the fields. There would be pears, persimmons, dates, pomegranates, and various seasonal fruits.

Most importantly, among the different tasty pastries, there would also be the Moon Cakes. No one has been able to tell me when this tradition started. There are different kinds of cakes, depending on which region the cake is made. But all have sweet or salty fillings and they are all made in the shape of a round moon. On the 15th, after supper, weather permitting, families would gather outside to appreciate the full moon. When the formal offerings were made to the Moon Goddess, and after the Goddess had tasted the food, of course the offerings should not be wasted, so the children and the seniors would be served first, then the adults and the servants would also get their share. Usually, this would be the time for someone to tell the ancient elixir story, which we children would never grow tired of hearing.

There is another story concerning the Moon Cake. Legend goes that shortly after the end of the Ming Dynasty, the Han people, the most populous ethnic group of the Ming Dynasty, were planning to rebel against the rule of the northern Tartar invaders. They wrote their attack plans on pieces of paper hidden in the Moon Cakes, and passed the cakes as gifts among the Han people just before the Mid-Autumn Festival. The rebellion was supposed to be on the 15th. But alas, the rebellion failed. We are only left with the heroic story.

This year, the lunar August 15th fell on our September 29. In the evening, I went to participate in the party sponsored by the Overseas Chinese of Tampa Association. I was surprised to see so many Chinese people there. But the gathering was so noisy that I could not enjoy the interesting program. I stayed a short while and soon just came back home.

At midnight, I got up from the bed and peeked up at the sky. There, way up in the dark sky, there was the round full moon. A thin veil was floating in front of it. Sad to say, the happy romantic memory of my Moon Goddess was lost to the cloudy night.

March 20, 2012

"A Letter to a Friend"

Dear Tien Hua,

Can you believe it? Our first and only independent trip! I mean just you and me, planned by ourselves without any help from the travel agents, was taken some ten years ago already! Today is the first day of spring. I took my album out and looked at the pages. The brilliant colors of those flowers still glisten in my eyes. I want to thank you for asking me to make that trip. It was my only trip that was devoted especially to see flowers.

We were very lucky that year. The spring was late in Europe. We thought we'd be missing the peak of the tulips but it turned out we arrived just in time for the best blooming! The delicate pink, the bright red, the yellow, the gold, the mixed, the purple, the white – when I close my eyes, I can still see them so vividly showing off their beauty in front of me. Looking at the pictures, it seemed that I was back at that fairy paradise again.

I could not forget how lucky we were for our second destination. Because I had seen some film about the Belgian Royal Greenhouse Garden, I persuaded you to go there. After numerous inquiries, we finally found one lady who not only knew where the Royal Greenhouse Garden was, she was also on her way there. So eventually we reached the legendary two-mile long greenhouse. Do you remember that she told us that each year, the garden only opens to the public for two days in May, and we had gotten there on the last day for the year!

The garden is open for three weeks a year, in late April and early May.

"A Letter to a Friend"

After tulips in the Keukenhof in Holland and the Royal Greenhouse Garden of Brussels in Belgium, we went on to England. There we visited most of the famous palace gardens. Then we went on to Ireland and Scotland. We saw the huge beautiful flower clock in Edinburgh and then went back to London. We had a wonderful high tea at the Kew Gardens amongst all those blooming flowers. In the end, it was time for the famous big May London flower show. Before this trip, I only knew the western poets always sang and rejoiced about the month of May. It was on this trip that I began to deeply appreciate why all these praises and songs about May have been written. Indeed, it is such a happy and merry time!

Tien Hua, I would like to thank you again for asking me to take this trip with you. It is my most memorable spring flower trip. Someday, I wish maybe I could do it again.

My warmest regards,

Helena

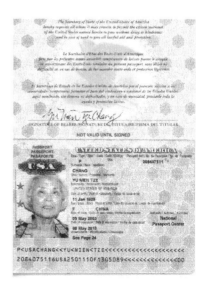

April 3, 2012

Bok Tower

Bok Tower

Shortly after I moved to Florida, I frequently heard the name of "Bok Tower," and I have been waiting for the chance to go and visit it. It has almost been ten years until this last Monday, my daughter and my son-in-law suggested the trip. Monday morning, we had breakfast at my daughter's house. Then we started the drive towards the famous destination.

It took us about two hours. I was a little disappointed on our way over. There was no attractive scenery to be seen. But when we approached the entrance, the view started to be more interesting. There were numerous orange trees growing all over the place with ripe oranges brightly hanging on them. We drove a few minutes among the oranges before we saw the parking lots. Already there were lots of cars there.

We walked a very short distance and there we saw the beautiful Mediterranean styled visitors' center. Colorful flowers in pots and in the ground welcomed us along the way. The center is a spacious building. In one area, there was a small exhibition of watercolor paintings. Most of the paintings were all scenes from different points in the garden itself. They were all for sale with prices marked on them.

In another area, there were pictures and a history of the original owner's family. It showed how Mr. Bok left his native Den Helder, Netherlands, with his parents when he was young, and how he made his fortune and became the owner of the magazine, *"The Ladies' Home Journal."* The Bok Tower was founded in 1929. It covers fifty acres of land. Mr. Bok remembered what his grandmother had always told him: a person should try to think of others by making the world a little more beautiful. Thus, Bok

Tower, this garden, later became the most generous gift to the city after he passed away.

We followed the paths and strolled to various areas in the park. There was the famous carillon tower standing so tall by itself. It was built with pink marble and some other greyish stones. The sculptures were exquisitely carved and placed on all four sides. The bells would play beautiful music for different occasions. Then there was a memorial site built on one of the highest spots of the whole peninsula, which was close to three hundred feet above sea level. Standing at this place, one can see miles away on account of the height. There were also ponds and so many kinds of trees, and more flowers. The birds were hidden among the trees, singing away. It is truly a peaceful and beautiful paradise!

Finally, we sat down at their cafeteria, relaxed, and had a leisurely lunch before we started home.

While in the car, I started to think, in the US, through the years, I have traveled to many national and state parks. I've learned that so many of them were all given to the public as gifts by private persons. To be sure, many of the donors were well-to-do people. But nowadays, China is full of rich people. Can I dare to hope that someday, they will do the same, to make the world a little more beautiful?

Bok Tower was constructed on Iron Mountain in Florida's Lake Wales Ridge, at 298 feet above sea level. Frederick Law Olmsted Jr. was commissioned to design the project.

June 6, 2012

Thirteen Days and Five States

Although I have never been a long-distance hiker, I do enjoy walking. All through my life, walking between two and five miles a day had been my daily routine until about three years ago. Then continually, for three nights, I could not sleep well due to a light pain in the right side of my hip joint.

The orthopedic specialist pronounced, "You have some arthritis there, and you have lost some bone too." I asked, "Do you mean I have to have a bone replacement operation?" The doctor paused, then said, "How old are you? It is just beginning to erode. You take care of it and you may get away without the operation. Go home now, and when the pain is severe and unbearable, come back and I will operate on it then."

From then on, I learned to pamper myself. I gave up my daily walking exercise. Three years passed. Life was peaceful, until…Three weeks ago, my oldest grand-daughter's graduation invitation arrived.

My dear daughter made all the travel plans for us. I just followed. She had taken many trips with me, so she knows that her mother is a good traveler. For some two hundred dollars of savings, we did not take a direct flight. Unfortunately, the first leg of our trip to New York was a little late. Therefore, we had to run to catch our next connection. As soon as I sat down in our plane, my hip joint started to complain.

When we arrived at my son's house, I was surprised to see all my three younger teenaged grandchildren were so much taller than when I saw them the previous year. The two boys, ages fifteen and sixteen, were both 6' 4 ½" tall! And the younger granddaughter was 5' 9". They wanted to take a walk. I did not join them as I usually do.

The next day I rested, while the whole family went to a track meet for all the private high schools in the area. The following morning, we left really early and drove to New Haven. The parking spaces were very scarce. We quickly squeezed into a spot and emptied all the quarters we prepared for the event, then hurriedly walked to the first ceremony site, which was at an open space without reserved seating. My protesting joint had to keep up with all the long legs of my son's family by half running and half walking. That was not a friendly movement for my painful joint. The ceremony lasted about three hours. Sitting on the folding chairs wasn't a pleasant experience. Once that was over, there was another march to have lunch. The food was excellent, which made me feel better. Then there was another march to another ceremony. Then we walked back to our car and drove to a relative's house for a Mexican BBQ dinner. Late that night, we finally drove to our hotel.

The next morning, after breakfast at the hotel, we got into the car and drove to Yale again. There was another long walk to an open space. We found some seats, but in the middle of the ceremony, a heavy rain came down. Luckily, it was soon over. The handing out of the diplomas was moved to a church -- another walk. By noon, the whole ceremony came to a close. We were treated to a nice buffet at the dean's house. Of course, that also required walking.

After I had fulfilled my duties as a grandma, I had to fulfill my other duty as a younger sister. That took my daughter and me to Washington, D.C. We stayed with my nephew and visited my brother for a couple of days. Then, my nephew and his wife offered to drive us to New Jersey to see my younger sister Natalia.

It was a nice one night visit, and after another four hours sitting in the car, we returned to D.C. again. The next day, our last day in D.C., after a tour of three memorials in the city, we finally got on our homeward bound plane. And now, I hope that I will have a chance to recuperate…

Unfortunately, my mom needed surgery a few months later. Her first hip replacement was uneventful and she recovered very quickly. She scheduled the second hip replacement in the following year, but this surgery was problematic. She had some nerve injury and developed foot-drop, the inability to flex and lift her foot, causing her to walk like a marionette. I treated her with acupuncture and massage for many months, and she regained much functionality. However, it seems that the new joint made the leg on that side a little longer, so she still has some problems with balance and walking.

July 26, 2013

The Rain

This morning, unexpectedly, just as I sat down in a shelter to wait for my transportation to take me home, a powerful rain came. It came with such strength, within a few minutes, the parking lot quickly changed into a shallow pool. I watched the raindrops splashing, bouncing, and making circles and waves on the surface of the puddles. Then all of a sudden, I became aware that this was the first time in many years that I actually was sitting quietly and peacefully watching the rain fall.

My memory went back to the year I was in a new school, writing my first composition. I was very proud that I made the observation that like rain, everything in the world all has both good and bad sides. I only remember that I wrote it, but I have forgotten my grade and everything else about it.

Years later, I learned more of Chinese poetry. There were so many sentimental lines expressing the emotions moved by rain, especially the spring rains. So, when I grew into a teenager, I loved to walk alone in the drizzling rain, and thought it was very romantic. I wanted people to think that I was a sophisticated young lady!

After I got married, we lived for a while in Darjeeling, India. Darjeeling was a famous summer resort place for the British people. It was about nine thousand feet high in the Himalaya mountains. I did learn from school that the area has the highest yearly precipitation in the world. But I could never have imagined that the downpour would start in late April and last until almost September without stopping! I definitely remember that our laundry had to be sent to the local laundries and when they

242

were delivered back, they were always still damp. Worst of all, we had to sleep under the damp curry-scented sheets!

Then we came to the US. Only occasionally, I would pay some attention to rain because it was causing droughts or floods, but other than that, rain only created some slight inconveniences for my life.

When it was time for my husband and I to choose a place to retire, we had to forgo quite a number of beautiful places due to friends' warnings about their prolonged rainy seasons.

At last, I have settled in Florida. Although Florida does have summer thunderstorms, in between the storms, the clear blue sky will quickly appear. However, now that I do have the time and a beautiful view from my window, somehow, I no longer seem to have the urge to sit by the window, quietly listening and watching the rain.

November 23, 2013

Chestnuts

In the back part of my junior high school there was a swing log set at the edge of the playground under a large stout tree. The students all liked to stand on the round log and balance themselves while the thick round log swung from side to side. One late autumn afternoon when I was happily swinging on it, something fell from the tree and hit my head. It pricked me. Then I saw a dark brown oval-shaped ball rolling in front of me on the ground. I jumped off the log and picked the ball up. Its outside shell was full of prickly spines and further pricked my fingers. Cautiously, I held it and looked at it. There was a big crack in the shell, and through the crack I could see there were three smooth shelled chestnuts snuggled neatly inside. Someone came up to me and saw it and said, "Oh, it's chestnuts!" Then we found there were a few more scattered around on the ground. My friend suggested we should eat it. So that was how I was introduced to the taste of fresh chestnuts for the first time.

But I had known how roasted chestnuts tasted since I was six or seven years old. Before my mother passed away in Shanghai, every year in the late fall, when the famous small, sweet, and moist Liangxiang chestnuts became available, every day after school, my mother would have a small bag of those roasted chestnuts kept warm under a blanket, waiting for me. And that little bag was for me only. Thus, chestnuts have long been one of my favorite snack foods. Then mother was gone, followed by the Sino-Japanese War, which changed everything. Only many years later, I remembered that day in Sichuan, when the raw chestnuts hit me. But there were no more roasted Liangxiang chestnuts for me.

Some decades ago, in New York City, I was happy to find a street vendor peddling roasted chestnuts. He was holding a small barrel-shaped thing on his shoulder with one hand and with the other hand, showing me a very small bag while calling out, "Roasted chestnuts for sale!" I was so happy to have this encounter, so I bought a little bag and hurried home. I showed it to my husband, but he surprised me by saying, "You'll be disappointed!" I could not wait and quickly cracked one. That chestnut was so big and the color was almost black. Inside the shell, not only did the nut not have any taste, it was also dry. The little bag contained five or six chestnuts. I peeled all of them, and indeed I was deeply disappointed. I asked how my husband knew about them. He told me that the first time when he was studying in the US, he had exactly the same experience as I did. Also, he told me, these were Italian chestnuts. They were shipped from Italy via sea. Perhaps that was the cause for the flavorless and dry nuts.

During the early 1950s, when we were living on Staten Island, New York, my Italian landlord had a small chestnut tree in his front yard. He told me that a few years ago, most of the American chestnut trees died in some kind of blight, so later they all planted the Chinese chestnut trees which were more resistant. That was why his tree was still young and not bearing fruit.

One year, I was visiting Japan. In Kyoto, on our way to the Clearwater Monastery, our tour group passed a small store. They had many small paper bags mounted on a board. We all looked but did not know what the bags were. Then I saw a small sign in Japanese characters. Immediately, I knew they were Liangxiang chestnuts from China, because even though I do not know Japanese, the characters for the chestnuts remained the same as the original Chinese characters. Indeed, they were the famous Chinese Liangxiang chestnuts, and my favorite! I quickly bought a small bag and caught up with my group.

Many years later, we moved to Pennsylvania. One year, the local farmers' market had a large supply of chestnuts. They were small. I bought some and was told that this was their first harvest from their recently planted Chinese chestnut trees. I was so pleased with my new discovery. My family all enjoyed them that night. I went back the next day and bought a lot of them and shared them with my friends. From that year on, my friends and I would always look forward to the chestnut season. That market would even save a certain amount for us. We could freeze some and save them for winter and Christmas! Gathered around the hearth, roasting chestnuts and telling stories – what warm and sweet memories!

Florida is too warm for chestnut trees. Since I left the north, one of my good friends *(Olivia)* would faithfully send me some chestnuts every year from Pennsylvania when they become available. This year, the other day, she called me from California where she was visiting one of our good mutual friends. She told me to watch out for the package which she had just sent by overnight mail. It contained the roasted Liangxiang chestnuts that our mutual friend brought home directly from China. It was not much. But it was truly fresh! I was so moved by their friendship for me. This time, when I enjoyed the moist and sweet chestnuts, it was not just because I like the nuts so much, it was definitely because of the care and love that these chestnuts brought to me!

April 15, 2013

StoryCorps

It has been my habit for a long time now to turn on the radio the first thing in the morning after I open my eyes. Then I would let myself drift off in a light sleep as the radio news goes on. The National Public Radio news always starts at 5:00 and ends at 9:00 on week days. On Fridays, they have a special short program, the "StoryCorps," which consists of a recorded dialogue between two people. They could be good friends, a couple, a teacher and student, or a parent and a child. These conversations are recorded and stored in the Library of Congress archives. Most of the time, I would still be half dreaming. However, many a time, the few short minutes of story told by the participants would fully wake me up. The heartfelt emotions and strong love expressed in those short moments between the two speakers always touch me deeply.

This last Friday, as usual, I was half asleep but slowly I became aware that it was the StoryCorps recording that I was hearing. It was between an adult son and his mother. It seemed that the son was calmly explaining why he gave up his career as a concert pianist and went back to the service. Then his mother was telling him that he need not ask for her understanding. She was very proud of his choice. By then I was fully awake, and I was in time to listen to the son's reason. Somehow, I was able to figure out, even though I had not clearly heard the beginning, the son was an officer in the Marine Corps. One day before he was to be deployed, a heavy door closed on his hand. At the emergency room, the doctor told him he could save his three injured fingers through a long procedure and rehabilitation. But his mind was on his orders and that he had a few hundred Marines to lead; there definitely was no time to wait for him to undergo the long and slow treatment. He thought about the war. He debated his responsibility to his country and his men. Finally, he chose to sacrifice his hand, his career as a concert pianist, and at the same time disappointing his mother's life-long wish for him to become a concert pianist. In order to shorten the days needed before the deployment, he decided to accept the doctor's other treatment and to have the three injured fingers amputated.

I could not help my tears running onto my pillows. I thought about his long years spent on practicing, the years of the mother's care and hope for the son, and his effort made to become a concert piano player. Then I thought of the war and his patriotism. I felt so sorry that I did not even catch his name. I just felt that it was such a waste! What sacrifices! What loyalty!

Now after listening to this story, I became even more deeply appreciative of the fact that there is such a wonderful program of keeping these precious stories for us. And I also appreciate that the NPR Broadcasting stations have offered such a program. In a mere five minutes, it can record and save some of our pure and beautiful love, selflessness, and honor that exists in humanity in this world.

"Taps"

"Taps"

In China, during the Sino-Japanese War and WWII, all students had to receive some military training. I spent more than three years of my junior to senior high years at a school mainly funded by the Oberlin College. Although our school was mostly run like American schools, we also followed the Chinese government's requirement to have some military training. The uniforms and drills did not make much difference for our schooling schedules. The only thing that left a deep memory on me was that we did not proceed with our daily life with bells, but with bugles. Our buglers were volunteers from upper classes trained by our military instructor. When I was awakened by the morning bugle for the first time, I was really surprised. Then followed the bugle songs for the flag raising ceremony, classes, meals, drills, meetings, evening study hours, and finally, the "Lights Out" bugle song.

Later, I found out that by being our buglers, these schoolmates of ours could get some financial subsidies for their tuition. I still admire them to this day. They were always the first up and last to rest no matter what kind of weather it would be, and they also had to sacrifice class hours to be punctual for their duties.

Soon after my first exposure to the bugle signals, I learned a song composed by some smart schoolmates. The words, in Chinese, went with the tune of the morning wakeup call, and can be translated as:

> The day is light
> Urging the pig to get out of bed
> I've come to check on the pig
> The pig is still in his bed

249

Out of the different bugle calls, I just remember the gathering call and the lights out "Taps." When you heard the first one, you automatically knew there was something happening. You must hurry to attend. But the second one, lights out "Taps" always brings a peaceful and restful feeling for me. However, when it was deepest winter, the lonely sound came in the darkness. A melancholy sadness would always accompany the silent peacefulness.

I did not know that the "Taps" I heard in China were the same as the American bugle call. Years later, as I watched war movies, I found that the lights out "Taps" were played at soldiers' funerals to honor them.

In a recent lecture, I learned the story about the origin of "Taps." The story went back to the Civil War in the US. One day, a northern Union officer asked a good shooter to shoot a hidden sniper from the South who was hidden in a tree and who was giving the Union soldiers a lot of problems. The man tried and raised his rifle, aimed, and fired. He was so accurate that immediately, the Southern sniper fell off the tree and died. The shooter went over to check. As he turned the body, he saw it was his son. When he tried to search the son's pockets for something to remember him by, he found a piece of paper, and upon it was a poem written by his son. The sad shooter went back and asked his superior to grant a formal military funeral service for his son. His officer said he could not do it for a Confederate, but he could give him one bugler. The poem was later seen by a musician who arranged the lyrics and music which became the song now known as "Taps."

There are several legends concerning the origin of "Taps." The most widely circulated one states that a Union Army infantry officer, whose name often is given as Captain Robert Ellicombe, first ordered "Taps" performed at the funeral of his son, a

"Taps"

Confederate soldier killed during the Peninsula Campaign. This apocryphal story claims that Ellicombe found the tune in the pocket of his son's clothing and performed it to honor his memory, but there is no record of any man named Robert Ellicombe holding a commission as captain in the Army of the Potomac during the Peninsula Campaign.

"Taps"

Day is done, gone the sun,
 From the lake, from the hills, from the sky;
 All is well, safely rest, God is nigh.

Fading light, dims the sight,
 And a star gems the sky, gleaming bright.
 From afar, drawing nigh, falls the night.

Thanks and praise, for our days,
 'Neath the sun, 'neath the stars, neath the sky;
 As we go, this we know, God is nigh.

Sun has set, shadows come,
 Time has fled, Scouts must go to their beds
 Always true to the promise that they made.

While the light fades from sight,
 And the stars gleaming rays softly send,
 To thy hands we our souls, Lord, commend.

And now I know why I always feel sad whenever I hear "Taps" and why I will always love this song.

There are many versions of verses for "Taps."

251

April 27, 2012

The Month of May

Before 1948, in my memory, the month of May was a month full of national insults and many protest memorial days. Starting from the very beginning, May 1st was our Labor Day. That basically was because of the Russian influence at the time. Soon after, it was the May 4th movement. It began with the university students protesting against the warlords, the government, the Germans and the twenty-one concessions demanded by the Japanese. The memorial days continued through the end of May, to May 30th. The last date honored a Chinese diplomat who was brutally killed by the Japanese in 1915. Those were the years China was under all kinds of foreign oppression. We were poor, we were weak, and we were looked down upon by the Western countries, the Russians, and especially by the Japanese. We as students frequently attended meetings to be reminded of these shameful events. Therefore, May was not a happy or merry month. Besides, we did not have the tradition to celebrate the month of May as Westerners do. As for Mother's Day, we did not observe it until very recent years after we had more close contact with the US.

Nowadays, of course everything has changed. China is no longer under the shackles of all those unequal treaties with so many foreign countries. For the past few decades, it has become more open to the modern world. Its people could raise their heads and live with our newly earned dignities.

As for me, since I came to the States, I have gradually managed to leave those unpleasant memories behind. Every year, I would welcome the spring and celebrate May – the beautiful flowers, the gentle breezes, and best of all, my children and my husband all celebrated Mother's Day with me.

Unfortunately, many years ago, it was in May that my husband passed away. However, the month of May does not depress me anymore. I feel secure, I feel free. So I can often sing the song which we both liked to welcome May:

One day when we were young
One wonderful morning in May
You told me you loved me
When we were young one day…

February 12, 2012

Reflections

W hen I was twenty years old, I was a full-blooded Chinese, and never in my wildest dreams did I imagine that I would die as an American citizen!

I met my husband when I was twenty years old. He often asked me, "What is your view about a human's life?" He would always laugh because my answer would always be, "Life is full of happiness."

I lived through several wars. First, the Japanese attacked us, then there was World War II, and then there was the civil war between the Communists and the Nationalists in China. In the end, my husband and I were forced to arrive in New York in America as refugees. At first, we were referred to as "displaced people." During those few years, life was truly difficult for us, but we believed that by working hard, tomorrow would be a better day, so somehow, we remained fairly happy through our struggles.

After long hard work and numerous sacrifices, we were finally able to settle down and began to have a comparatively worry-free life. By then, my husband had become a successful lecturer, writer, and a well-known Buddhist scholar among European and Oriental Buddhists. For me, I was pleased that I could help my husband in most of this work, supporting his parents, raising two good children, and also having my own teaching job. I am only sorry that my husband did not really enjoy the fruit of his own success for long, but died still in his prime years.

Looking back on those long years since I was twenty, I found that our life was not all that easy. Often it was full of worries. My husband and I had never even argued once over money matters.

We both were the products of the traditional Chinese teachings and culture. Respect filial responsibilities to our parents, do not covet other people's wealth, always be humble and respect others. These ideas had always unconsciously guided and supported us.

However, I am also deeply aware that later, we were definitely influenced by the American spirit and culture. We recognized that in general, in American society, everyone is equal. People are more adventurous and more full of initiative in all kinds of their own undertakings. I like the straight-forward relationships between people, although I think in recent years, people are becoming too self-centered and rude, almost to the point of disregarding the welfare of others. I especially appreciate that I have learned to be more independent than I used to be. I too, have become more daring in expressing myself without too much hesitation, compared to how I would have been in Chinese society.

At present, I have lived in America much longer than I lived in China. I have been leading a happy life, even though I am alone. I attribute this all to the fact that both my husband and I could have a successful happy life. While we were transplanted from a Far Eastern country thousands of miles away to this Western land of America, I can say our lives are a happy "East Meets West" story.

255

October 1, 2013

Fifty Years

I was a first-generation foreign immigrant when I came to the United States. And this year marks the fiftieth anniversary of my US citizenship. I am proud to be a US citizen. But beginning in the past few years, I often become frustrated and disappointed, and sometimes even feel very depressed by the directions our government and our people are heading.

When I arrived in the US, it was in the early 1950s. Everywhere I went, I saw people working hard. I admired the people who were all so respectful and courteous to others. Children from families whether poor or well-to-do, mostly seemed to live with their parents. The parents were not hard pressed making a living to the point that the children were left to look after themselves. Teachers enjoyed a certain amount of respect in the society. It seemed the government officials had much greater concern for the people's welfare and they also regarded the nation's well-being as the highest priority during their tenure.

Somehow in the past ten years or so, I noticed that our richest country in the world has more people depending on food stamps, and children going to bed hungry. People have lost their civility and have become impatient and rude. National honor slipped down from a high priority of government officials to a distant concern behind personal gains. We promote democracy to the world, yet we are no longer the model of a true democratic nation. Other countries laugh behind our back and we fail to pay attention.

I don't have a sharp pen, nor do I have a loud voice to wake up people. I can only hope that our nation can soon change for the better.

July 18, 2012

Thoughts of Home

All day long, I was tangled under clusters of grey clouds. Later in the evening, I sat down in my usual chair, listless. I sat in the room without turning on the light. Then when I looked under my feet, it was silvery bright. It was lit by the moon. I stood up and walked to the window, raised my head, and looked up. There, a bright full moon proudly was shining way up in the clear sky. Suddenly, a strong emotion engulfed me. A very simple poem repeatedly appeared in my mind:

(The original poem in Chinese is translated here)

> Bright light in front of my bed
> Shined like fresh frost on the ground
> I raise my head to look upward
> There is the bright full moon
> Then, lowering my head, I long for my old home

I have been away from my old home for more than sixty years; and never had I had such strong longings for that far away town over the ocean. I sat down again, as scenes from my childhood kept coming to my mind. I thought of how in summertime, people would gather in the courtyard or in the garden after their baths, all ready to listen to someone's story; how in severe cold winter, the family would gather around an open fire with snacks and chat. And when festivals came, the new clothes and lanterns, especially during the August Harvest Moon festival, when all the work in the fields was done, and it was time for a happy family reunion, because the moon is extra bright and round and perfect in shape, just like a family should be, everyone around together. Maybe that's why I was moved that night. I missed the old traditions and the togetherness. Instead of being a grandmother lovingly doted upon by everyone in the family, I am now all alone, all by myself.

But strangely, I thought, I had never felt like this before. Why? Why? I asked myself.

Recently, I heard that Ghana's Vice President had written a biography, in which he reminisced that years ago, in Ghana, they had a Moon Dance. Whenever there was a bright moon, people would gather under the swaying trees, play their music, and dance in the moonlight. However, when the electricity came, soon, the dancing gatherings disappeared with a switch. As for the moon, hardly anyone would pay attention to it anymore.

I have an old record of Paul Robeson's singing "Going home, going home, I am going home." I stood up and put it on, and let my tears flow.

2016 Passport: Where is home now?

August 21, 2013

Embroidered Satin Pillow

I went to see a friend who just returned from the hospital after having an operation for a serious condition. As I was invited to sit and chat, I saw a familiar sight on the sofa. It was a light aqua colored satin cushion with gathers and a beautifully embroidered pine tree and two dancing cranes, made in the typical traditional Chinese style. I burst out, "This must be from China!"

My friend's response was, "Yes, but how did you know?"

After I came home, the image of that pillow brought me back to another time and another world. I was very young then, perhaps about ten or eleven. I was in my godparents' house in Suzhou. Suzhou was an old, small industrial town. My godfather had a daughter who was older than me. The two of us were my godfather's favorite children. That day the three of us were on our way home from downtown. A wedding party happened to be in progress. Crowds were standing by the sidewalk and watching the long trail of fancifully decorated cars carrying gifts from the bride's family. It was a popular practice then for some well-to-do families to show off their wealth when they were marrying off their daughters. Usually the bride was carried in a fancy enclosed sedan chair leading the way to her in-laws' house. Following her in a long line would be people carrying loads of household items, big and small. The gifts were not covered so people could see and admire them. Bedding would be one of the most important items. We were in a narrow alley, so we had a good observation point for viewing everything. Among the gifts we saw a stack of shining embroidered satin pillows.

As soon as we entered the living room at home, my godfather said, "You two girls come here. I want to ask you something.

Did you enjoy watching the wedding parade? Did you see those beautiful embroidered pillows?" We both answered, "Yes."

He continued, "Do you like those pillows?" We did not know why he was asking that question. We did not answer. So he asked again, "Do you know what is inside those beautiful looking pillows?" Again, we did not know. He answered for us. "The inside is stuffed with dried rice straw. You know straw is very cheap, often discarded by people. That is why I want to talk to you. You are two beautiful girls. I do not wish you to grow up to be like those straw filled pillows – pretty and shining outside, and yet the inside is nothing to be valued and treasured. Remember this. You should fill your inside with solid knowledge so you will be respected by people."

For more than half of a century, that talk was unintentionally pushed to some hidden corner of my mind. Only now, when I saw my friend's embroidered cushion, my godfather's voice rang in my ears again. I ask myself at this last stage of life, "How did I live my life? Did I live as a straw filled embroidered satin pillow?" The answer? I cannot honestly say.

September 27, 2017

Last Thoughts

Y esterday, Eva showed me the stack of manuscript pages of our family history which I had given to her a few years ago. Then she told me that she had included some of my writing which I did through the years, when I joined "The Write Stuff" group after I moved here to Regency Oaks. What surprised me was she had spent a good amount of time and collected much material about some of the people that my husband and I had come to be associated with, especially the few key people who had greatly affected our lives.

I have lived here in Florida for about fifteen years. I started this project about ten years ago, writing my story for Eva. My original biography ended with my arrival here, but the pieces which I intermittently wrote for the writing group roughly covers the most recent years.

Now that my loosely traced memories have been retyped, edited, and enhanced with Eva's new material, it is ready to be put into a book. It was not my original idea, which was just to write a brief history in response to Eva's request for a family history. But then we thought about Leo's children—my grandchildren. They never even had the opportunity to meet their grandfather, and they know very little about our family story, so I agreed with Eva to have this manuscript printed. A book will serve as a lasting resource for my grandchildren to understand more about their roots from the other side of the world.

Last Words from Eva

All through our lives, the role of Buddhism was never far from our minds and hearts. Although my mother does not emphasize the role of Buddhism in this history, my father's dedication and unwavering efforts to promote the understanding of this religion in the West guided our paths through life. His faith guided him in all his choices in major life decisions and paths.

My mother was dedicated to him and his efforts, typing and re-typing all his manuscripts in the days before word processing and computers. When asked about her thoughts on Buddhism, she demurs, saying, "My thoughts are only a housewife's understandings."

Yet after my father passed, and she had moved back to State College, she and some friends started a Buddhist study group, which is going strong even to this day.

My father's intellectual accomplishments and daily meditation practice, and my mother's steadfast practice of metta (compassion, loving kindness) are equally inspiring. According to some Buddhist belief systems, I must have lived an exemplary life in the past to have been born into such a special family.

There are more stories that remain untold – what happened to some of their friends and family during the Cultural Revolution, tales of espionage, assassinations, how my father learned the art of "corpse-walking," fortunetellers, face-readers, eerily accurate horoscopes, my father's years in Tibet, experiments with psycho-active drugs, and much more. But this book is already much longer than we ever planned...

PART III

References

Most of the information in this section has been gleaned from other sources. I thought it would be interesting to share some stories about the fascinating people that my parents encountered in their lives. I took advantage of the treasure trove of information available on the internet to learn more about some of the cast of characters that graced my family's life.

I have begun this section with a summary about the Sino-Japanese War which served as a backdrop for the happenings in my mother's early years.

My apologies for failing to follow formal citation styles; however, I have done my best to provide information about source materials. I encourage interested readers to explore some of these sources themselves.

The Second Sino-Japanese War

Conflicts between the Chinese and Japanese marked the end of the nineteenth and beginning of the twentieth centuries. Even though the Chinese outnumbered the Japanese, the latter had embraced Western advances in military technology, and thus were victorious over the Chinese.

The Second Sino-Japanese War ran its course during my mother's childhood, and led to her many moves. She was in fact a refugee within China even before she became a refugee in the US.

Permission has been granted by Alpha History for use of this material for limited distribution as part of this family history. From Alpha History, "a free online textbook and resource centre for history students:"

The Second Sino-Japanese War (1937-45) had a significant impact on the course of the Chinese Revolution. Known in China as the 'War of Chinese People's Resistance Against Japanese Aggression', it was a catastrophic conflict for the Chinese people, causing up to 20 million casualties. It also had serious political repercussions for the nationalist Guomindang and the Chinese Communist Party (CCP). Japan's invasion of China in the early 1930s and the war that followed capped off decades of antagonism between the two nations. The political and economic development of Japan stood in stark contrast to that of China. The Meiji Restoration of the late 19th century had propelled Japan into the modern world. The Japanese had tapped into Western knowledge to develop an industrialised economy. Japan's military, once a barefoot army of *samurai*, was now a well trained Westernised armed force, equipped with modern weapons. Its government was dominated by militarists and expansionists who hoped to make Japan an Asian imperial power.

264

The First Sino-Japanese War erupted in August 1894 over control of the Korean peninsula. This war ended with a Japanese victory in a little over eight months, despite Japanese forces being greatly outnumbered by the Qing armies. The Treaty of Shimonoseki, signed in April 1895, saw China surrender control of the Liaodong peninsula, west of Korea, and the island of Taiwan. Six years later, following the disastrous Boxer Rebellion, Japan won the right to station troops in eastern Manchuria, giving them a military stronghold on the Chinese mainland. The collapse of the Qing dynasty in 1911 allowed Japan to further expand its sphere of influence in China. In 1915 the Japanese government issued Chinese president Yuan Shikai with a set of 21 territorial and concessional demands, which Shikai had no choice but to accept. An incident in Mukden, Manchuria in September 1931 provided the Japanese with the pretext for a full military invasion of Manchuria. Once established there, the Japanese set up the puppet state of Manchukuo and installed the last Qing emperor, Puyi, as its ineffectual head of state. In May 1933 the Nationalist president Jiang Jieshi *(Chiang Kai-Shek)*, who was more concerned with fighting the communists than Japanese imperialists, signed the Tanggu Truce, effectively recognising the legitimacy of the Manchukuo puppet state.

Full scale war between China and Japan began in July 1937, following an incident near the Marco Polo Bridge in Wanping, near Beijing. After Japanese troops opened fire on local soldiers a brief ceasefire was negotiated, however both sides increased military numbers in the region. When the Japanese launched an invasion in late July, the Nationalists and CCP were seven months into a shaky alliance, dubbed the Second United Front. The Nationalist armies attempted to resist the invasion but were quickly overcome by the technological supremacy and preparedness of the Japanese. China's underdeveloped industries were incapable of supplying munitions or engineering quickly or in sufficient quantities. Unlike the Japanese, the Chinese military had no tanks and only a few aircraft. The first phase of the war was a blitzkrieg of Japanese victories as their forces moved swiftly along China's east coast. Almost a half million Japanese troops moved against Shanghai, Nanjing and other locations in mainland China, while Japanese military planes bombarded regions where their foot soldiers could not penetrate. In late 1937 the Nationalist government was forced to retreat from its capital, Nanjing, to Chongqing in western China.

Japanese troops were notorious for their brutal treatment of civilians and military prisoners. The Japanese occupation of Nanjing from December 1937, often referred to as the 'Rape of Nanjing', is the most infamous example of Japanese brutality in China. Estimates suggest that the Japanese massacred 300,000 people in and around the city, many of them civilians. Historian Jonathan Fenby describes the Rape of Nanjing as a uniquely "urban atrocity" because of "the way the Japanese went about their killing, the wanton individual cruelty, the reduction of the city's inhabitants to the status of sub-humans who could be murdered, tortured and raped at will". Thousands of civilians were buried alive, machine gunned or used for bayonet practice. Females were taken and forced into labour as "comfort women" (sex slaves for Japanese officers and soldiers). The Japanese also conducted human experimentation in secret bases in China. Unit 731 in the country's northeast was the largest biological and chemical warfare testing facility. Prisoners there were injected with diseases like anthrax, smallpox, cholera, dysentery and typhoid. Other experiments studied the effects of food deprivation and extreme cold; amputation without anaesthesia; and the effects of chemical weapons and flamethrowers. The Japanese also air-bombed cities like Ningbo and Changde with fleas carrying bubonic plague. Vast swathes of China were decimated by Japan's 'scorched earth' warfare, epitomised by the slogan "kill all, loot all, destroy all".

While Jiang Jieshi had some early assistance from Soviet Russian leader Joseph Stalin, the Nationalists had little support from foreign powers. In June 1938 Jiang ordered the dikes of the Yellow River dam to be blown, a desperate attempt to slow the advance of the Japanese invasion. While this ploy worked, it also caused a devastating flood that killed between 500,000 to one million Chinese civilians, rendered up to ten million homeless and ruined millions of acres of important farmland. The resulting food shortages, famine and human suffering only contributed to rising peasant hatred of Jiang Jieshi and the Nationalist regime. Other problems confronting Jiang and the Guomindang government were widespread corruption, rising inflation and high desertion rates caused by poor treatment of Nationalist soldiers, most of whom were unwilling conscripts.

Beyond 1938 the Sino-Japanese war reached a virtual stalemate. China's geographical size, her lack of infrastructure and scattered pockets of resistance all helped to slow the Japanese advance. By 1940 the Japanese controlled the entire north-eastern coast and areas up to 400 miles inland. They installed a puppet government in Nanjing under Wang Jingwei, a former Guomindang leader and political rival to Jiang Jieshi. Foreign assistance for the Chinese finally came after the Japanese bombing of Pearl Harbour in December 1941. As the United States was drawn into World War II, China became an important theatre in the war against the

Japanese. In 1942 US general Joseph Stillwell was sent to China to assist with training, reorganisation and equipment. Jiang's authoritarianism, however, hampered their collaboration. Jiang's wife Soong Meiling, dubbed "Madame Chiang" by the Western press, proved a more skilled diplomat than her husband; she was instrumental in securing some foreign assistance.

"The Nationalist government, which bore the major brunt of the fighting, was so depleted physically and spiritually that it was manifestly incapable of coping with the new challenges of the postwar era." -- Immanuel Hsu, historian

During its war with the Japanese the CCP continued to consolidate its base in Yan'an, while the Red Army – later reorganised into the Eight Route Army and the New Fourth Army – defended the inland areas of the northwest. The Japanese had no desire to occupy rural areas in the interior, which created a misleading perception that the communists were successful defenders. Favourable reports from foreign visitors also came out of the Yan'an Soviet during the war period, such as praise from the American Dixie Mission of 1944 and from US president Franklin Roosevelt's special emissary, Patrick Hurley. Zhou Enlai also became well respected among diplomats and foreign journalists. These factors were exploited by CCP propaganda, which helped generate support for the party and allowed it to present as an alternative national government to the Guomindang. By 1942 CCP membership had grown to 800,000, a twentyfold growth from the beginning of the war five years earlier. Scholars like David Goodman suggest the CCP's tactics during this period were an essential element of the party's eventual rise to power.

The Second Sino-Japanese War came to an end in August 1945, after the United States detonated nuclear weapons over Hiroshima and Nagasaki. Russian troops invaded from the north and suppressed Japanese forces in Manchuria, while Japanese forces in China were ordered to surrender to Jiang Jieshi and the Nationalists. In assessing the impact of the war, historian Jonathan Fenby describes it as "an extended body blow for a regime already shot through with weaknesses. The length, scale and nature of the conflict had debilitated China and the Nationalists". China emerged from the war politically unsettled, economically exhausted and scarred by an enormous amount of human suffering. With the CCP growing in size, popularity and prestige, and the Guomindang government grossly unpopular, the Chinese stage was now cleared for a civil war between the Nationalists and the communists.

Grandfather Yu You Ren

My maternal grandfather cast a large shadow. His role in modern Chinese history set the course for my mother's life. One could write an entire book about my grandfather, but that endeavor will be left to someone else. There are in fact at least three books written in Chinese about his life. I have excerpted some information from Wikipedia, which will give a brief overview of his life. His name is spelled several different ways in this article, a holdover from the various Romanization systems in use over the last century:

Yu Yu-jen (Chinese: 于右任; pinyin: *Yú Yòurèn*); (April 11, 1879 – November 10, 1964) was an educator, scholar, calligrapher, and politician in the Republic of China.

Early Life

He was born on April 11, 1879 in the town of Hedaogang in Sanyuan County, Shaanxi Province north of Xi'an, China. His father was Xin Sangong and his mother surnamed Zhao. In 1880, while his father was on business in Sichuan, his mother died and so his aunt brought him to live with her in the village of Yangfu where they lived together for 9 years. After a short stint as a goat herder, he went to a private school at the Mawang Temple in Yangfu and studied under Mr. Diwu. In 1889, he returned with his aunt to Sanyuan and entered the school of Mao Banxiang, under whom he began to study archaic and modern forms of poetry. On occasion, he also had the chance to read a few poems by such Southern Song patriots as Wen Tianxing and Xie Fangde. At the age of 17, he came in

270

first place on entrance examinations and went on to study at the schools like the Dao Academy in Sanyuan, Weijing Academy in Jingyang, and Guanzhong Academy. In 1898, he married Miss Gao Zhonglin.

Revolutionary Beginnings

In 1900, at the age of 22, Yu Yu-jen wrote a letter for the Pacification Commissioner of Shaanxi, Cen Chunxuan, imploring him to take the opportunity of assassinating the Empress Dowager Cixi who was fleeing to Xi'an during the Boxer Rebellion, which would provide the impetus for true reform of the government, but Yu was stopped from sending it by his classmate Wang Linsheng. Yu wrote many poems venting anger and frustration with the government. These were collected into a book entitled *Poetry Drafts from the Hall of Tears and Mockery*. His friend Meng Yimin helped Yu to have it published.

In 1903, he passed the civil service examinations to become a Provincial Graduate (juren), but due to the satiric contents of *Poetry Drafts from the Hall of Tears and Mockery*, the government branded him a revolutionary. Wanted by the Qing government, Yu fled and sought refuge in Shanghai. With help from Ma Xiangbo, he was able to enter the Aurora Academy (later Aurora University (Shanghai)) under the assumed named of Liu Xueyu. Along with Ye Zhongyu and others, Yu established the Fudan College (later Fudan University) in memory of his days at Aurora (using the same character *dan* in *Zhendan*, the Chinese name of Aurora, and adding the character *fu*, for "reviving" China). Ma Xiangbo was elected as school president.

In 1906, Yu fled to Japan and while there was able to meet Dr. Sun Yat-sen and the Tongmenghui through the introduction of Kang Xinfu and he thereafter officially joined the Tongmenghui. After returning to China in 1907, Yu started a newspaper called *The National Herald* (also known as the Shenzhou Daily), but its facilities were destroyed in a fire less than a year later. In the following year, Yu's father died. In March 1909, Yu established another newspaper called *The People's Voice* (Minzhu Bao) in Shanghai, strongly condemning the culture of corruption in government. Attracting the attention of officials, he was arrested and sent to jail, and the newspaper was closed in June 1909. Released from jail and still undaunted, he established another newspaper called *The People's Sigh* (Minxu Bao) but less than two months later it was shut down and he was thrown in jail again. In 1910, he established yet another newspaper called the *Min Li Pai*, the offices of which virtually served as the contact headquarters for the Chinese Revolutionary Alliance.

Post Xinhai Revolution

In 1912, Yu Yu-jen is nominated to and accepts the post of Deputy Minister of Transportation and Communication, but less than three months later is forced to resign along with Dr. Sun Yatsen's government. After Yuan Shikai took control of the government and the Min Li Bao is shut down, Yu was placed on the wanted list by Yuan Shikai's government. In 1918, Yu returns to his native Shaanxi Province, where he becomes commander of forces responsible for revolutionary activities in the northwest. In 1922, his post as commander is disbanded and he returns to Shanghai where he established Shanghai University along with Ye Chucang and assumes the post as president of the school. In 1925, he is ordered to organize along with Wu Zhihui, Wang Jingwei, and others the political affairs committee to handle party affairs. In 1927, Yu becomes a standing member of the Nationalist government committee. In the following year, he is also appointed as the Director of Audit. In 1932, Yu assumed the post of Director of the Control Yuan.

In 1936, Yu collects examples of Chinese characters and compiles them into the *"Thousand character essay in Standard Cursive Script"* as the book Standard Cursive Script, the first edition of which is published. Yu also donated his entire collection of more than three hundred rubbings from Stele to the Xi'an Forest of Stele Museum.

In 1941, along with other members of the art and cultural world, Yu takes the initiative to name the fifth day of the fifth lunar month every year as Poets' Day. Yu also meets the modern painting master Zhang Daqian at Dunhuang in Northwest China and comes to realize the amount of destruction that has occurred to the art and cultural heritage at Dunhuang. After returning to the government headquarters in Chongqing, he immediately proposes that a Dunhuang Art Academy be established.

Following the loss of Mainland China to Communist forces, Yu follows the Chinese Nationalist government to Taiwan in 1949 at the age of 71.

In Taiwan

In 1950, after the establishment of the Kuomintang (Chinese Nationalist Party) committee, Yu became a member of its review committee. In 1956, Yu received the first National Literary Award presented by the Ministry of Education. In arranging his diaries in 1962, Yu wrote poetry revealing pain at not being able to return to his hometown in China. Yu died from pneumonia in 1964 at Taipei Veteran's Hospital and in 1967 his remains were interred at Datun Mountain in Taipei's Yangmingshan National Park. In 1966 a large bronze statue of Yu Yu-jen was placed at the summit of Yushan. The statue remained there until 1996 when it was cut down and thrown into a ravine by Taiwan independence activists.

Calligraphy

Yu was a scholar of calligraphy and is regarded as one China's modern masters. His works in cursive and semi-cursive manner are intensely animated. He is perhaps best known for his calligraphy and published related works on the topic. Because his later years were spent in Taiwan, his writing style is very popular and his works are considered very desirable by collectors. Yu completed numerous inkworks, stone carvings, and title plaques while living in Taipei including works for the National Museum of History, Din Tai Fung, Xingtiang Temple, and the Shilin Official Residence.

The Pamir Snow Gnawing Association (帕米爾齧雪同志會) established a cultural park known as the Pamir Cultural Park in a quiet and secluded mountainous area of Taipei City called Wuzhishan. The park commemorates about 300 KMT soldiers who hid out in the Pamir Mountains after the Chinese Civil War and were able to eventually escape to Taiwan. It had engraved at the site examples of the titles and poetry of Yu Yu-jen into stones and rocky outcroppings, forming a beautiful outdoor garden of his calligraphy. Among the hills of the area is an open space where the association erected a monument. Each of the characters for the title calligraphed by Yu Yu-jen was engraved into individual slabs of marble and then inlaid into a concrete pillar.

My grandfather wrote a poem describing his feelings of longing for his homeland as he looks across the sea from a mountainside in Taiwan. It has become a famous poem and is much admired by Chinese people on the mainland as well as those in Taiwan.

Following is a translation of the poem; it was written near the time of the Chinese New Year in 1962:

"Getting A Sight of the Mainland,"
written on January 24, 1962.

Bury me on the highest mountaintop
So that I can get a sight of the Mainland.
Mainland I see none, tears of sorrow cascade.
Bury me on the highest mountaintop
So that I can get a glimpse of my hometown.
Hometown I see none, but lives forever in my mind.
The lofty sky is deeply blue, the vast wildness not seen through.
Oh, boundless universe, would you hear me and this elegy of the nation.

Statue of Yu Youren at the Sun Yat-sen Memorial Hall in Taipei

Garma C. C. Chang

My father Chang Chen Chi (张澄基, Zhang Cheng Ji) was born on August 28, 1920 in the lunar calendar. This translates to October 9, 1920 in the Gregorian calendar. My mom is not sure exactly where he was born. It was probably Canton (Guangdong), although it may have been Shanghai or even somewhere in Hubei. I have his old Chinese passport which states that he was from "Hupeh." His "FORM OF AFFIDAVIT TO BE USED IN LIEU OF A PASSPORT" in India states that he was born in Canton, China, as do several other documents.

I'm sure it seems strange that I have referenced someone else's biography of my father, but Pastor David Lai has done a fine job of summarizing the highlights of my father's accomplishments. I have excerpted some text from a post online by Pastor David Lai. I have not attempted to fact-check his narrative with regard to references to Tibetan masters. Although there are a few minor factual errors which I have learned about in the course of this project, it is a respectful summary of his accomplishments. I am very appreciative of this effort to document my father's role in introducing Buddhism to the West:

Professor Garma C.C. Chang -The Illustrious Pioneer
By Pastor David Lai | Jul 30, 2017
From Tsemrinpoche.com

The Chinese Buddhist scholar Professor Garma C. C. Chang (1920-1988) was one of the few pioneering scholars who introduced Buddhism to the West primarily through the publication of books and his illustrious teaching career as a professor. He was an authority on Buddhist philosophy and was best known as an editor and translator of the teachings and practice of Tibetan tantra along with Zen Buddhism. Chang's aim was to introduce people to vital books on achieving Buddhahood through strict Zen meditation or via esoteric tantric meditative techniques.

His name Garma is a derivative of the word Dharma and C.C. Chang literally stands for Chen-Chi Chang, or in the Chinese order of placing the surname first, Chang Chen-Chi. In Pinyin, his name is spelt Zhang Chengji. He was born in Hubei, China in 1920. His father, Zhang Dulun was initially a senior army officer and was later promoted to be the provincial governor of Hubei. His mother was a devout Buddhist and was influential in shaping his childhood. Consequently, Chang's childhood was filled with frequent visits to Buddhist temples and the recitation of many Buddhist sutras.

While studying, Chang found school to be meaningless and boring, and he instead filled his time by reading voraciously on philosophy and books on spirituality. He developed a keen interest towards philosophies that made him ponder the meaning of life and the uncovering of life's great mysteries. After much effort at grappling with the archaic language used in such works, he was able to read a few volumes of sutras. He felt at peace reading the Buddhist teachings because they were deep and gave him an overwhelming sense of compassion. Therefore in 1935, at the age of 15 he left school, setting aside the ridicule and objection of friends and relatives in order to engage in Dharma study and practice as a lifetime pursuit.

At 16, he followed an old lay master up into the Lushan Mountains in order to engage in a 100-day retreat and during this period, he was said to have been able to discern both true and false Dharmas. After the retreat, he came to the conclusion that nothing is more meaningful than the study and practice of Dharma. The following year, Chang wanted to travel to Tibet in order to deepen his realisation of the Dharma but his father objected. His father felt that Tibet was too remote and transportation in the region was undeveloped and unreliable.

In the end, his father made arrangements for Chang to visit Gangkar Monastery on Mount Gangkar, or Minya Konka Riwo in Tibetan, located in Kham, which is now part of Szechuan province. Gangkar Rinpoche was Chang's mother's teacher and the patriarch of the monastery. He remained in the monastery for eight years studying at the feet of this great master. Aside from studying the Buddhist teachings and practices, he also studied the Tibetan and English languages at this time.

Chang's Tibetan master was the 9th Gangkar Rinpoche Karma Chokyi Senge. This master was born in Minya in 1893. On the day of his birth, it was said that the entire region witnessed two suns in the sky, which was considered to be auspicious. A few days later, was recognized as the incarnation of the 7th Gangkar Rinpoche. At the age of three, he was enthroned in the monastery as the tulku incarnation of Gangkar. He grew up to be a very famous scholar, master, lineage holder, and was followed by many disciples. He taught both sutra and tantra, and bestowed important empowerments unto many high lamas and ordained the famous disciples.

In 1948, Chang married Yu Nien Tze (Helena) in Hankou and in 1949 he immigrated to the United States where he arrived in the 1950s with his wife via India, Taiwan, and Hong Kong. In the United States, Chang became research fellow at the Bollingen Foundation in New York from 1955 onwards. During this time, he wrote many books, beginning with The Practice of Zen published in 1959, The Hundred Thousand Songs of Milarepa published in 1962, and Teachings and Practice of Tibetan

Tantra published in 2004. The book on Tibetan tantra was based on an earlier publication in 1993, which was itself based on the original version published in 1962.

In his book Teachings and Practice of Tibetan Tantra, Chang wrote about the generation of yogic heat in the body (Tibetan: tummo). In addition, he also taught tantric teachings on how sexual bliss can be transformed onto the path of awakening. John C. Wilson writes in the 1962 book's introduction that Chang's work on Tibetan tantra is hard to grasp with just a few readings. Therefore Chang advises that a serious practitioner should first be initiated and well guided in the basics before starting any actual tantric practices. As such, Chang's book is only intended to be a source of reference for would-be tantric practitioners.

Chang's extensive efforts in receiving teachings during his life and his written works regarding the Mahayana tradition has blazed a trail for others to follow. His first published Buddhist text in English was the Practice of Zen, which draws on the rich Chinese Mahayana tradition. Even earlier than that, he had translated The Hundred Thousand Songs of Milarepa into English in the 1950s, a large collection of verses by Milarepa, all of which cemented Chang as a foremost Tibetan translator of his time.

Ernst Schönwiese a Austrian writer, lyricist and program director became a student of Professor Chang in 1971, who at that time was teaching Buddhist Philosophy at Pennsylvania State University. During the ensuing years, Schönwiese translated and published several important works by Professor Chang like The Mahamudra Handbook (1979), The Practice of Zen (1982), and The Buddhist Doctrine of Totality of Being (1989).

Aside from Schönwiese, C.T. Shen was another important student of Chang whom he met in India in 1950 and later became a very successful entrepreneur in the United States. Over the years, Shen contributed financially to Buddhist teachers, Buddhist meditation centres, and the development of Buddhism in America. So he was a co-founder of the Buddhist Association of the United States (BAUS). In a 1996 speech that he gave on his life in Buddhism, C.T. Shen spoke glowingly of his mentor and friend, Garma C.C. Chang. In his talk, C.T. Shen, a great Buddhist philanthropist, whose contribution to the Buddhist cause is legendary, attributed Garma C.C. Chang as the second most influential person in his life after his mother and that they shared a similar spiritual journey.

Kenneth Chen gave an excellent review of Practice of Zen back in 1961 and the review was published in Philosophy East and West, Vol. 11, No. 3 (Oct., 1961), pp. 174-176 (University of Hawaii Press).

"To the growing list of books on Zen Buddhism in English, Mr. Chang Chen-Chi has made a significant contribution. However, the author differs from many of the contemporary writers on the subject in that he has not been influenced by Japanese writers on Zen Buddhism. Again, he is not writing his account from secondary sources, but has gone back to the primary materials in Chinese. Finally, through his years of residence and study in Tibetan and Chinese monasteries, he has acquired a profound knowledge of the wider aspects of Buddhist philosophy that is fundamental to the proper understanding of Zen theory and practice... The author aims to show from these selections how Zen masters lived and worked – in other words, how they practiced Zen – in the hope that these might serve as examples for beginners at the present time. In addition to these translations, there are also discussions on the nature and problems of Zen. In the latter category, he seeks to throw some lights on such questions as, Is Zen completely unintelligible for the intellect? as Suzuki insists, and, What is Zen enlightenment? In answer to the first question, the author makes this sensible distinction between understanding Zen and realizing Zen, and that "to understand Zen through an intellectual approach is not reprehensible, but is the only way for the beginner, for who can get into Zen without having first some understanding or conceptual knowledge about it?" (p. 117)…"

Books in English by Garma C. C. Chang *(books in Chinese not listed)*

The Practice of Zen. 1959

The Hundred Thousand Songs of Milarepa – the life-story and teaching of the greatest poet-saint ever to appear in the history of Buddhism. University Books, New York, 1962.

Teachings of Tibetan Yoga. 1963

The Buddhist Teaching of Totality: The Philosophy of Hwa Yen Buddhism. 1971

Treasury of Mahayana Sutras: Selections from the Maharatnakuta Sutra. 1983

The Six Yogas of Naropa & Teachings on Mahamudra. 1986

Teachings and Practice of Tibetan Tantra. 2004

From a book review of <u>The Hundred Thousand Songs of Milarepa</u> on Amazon, by "Average Jeff," who is actually Jeff Shear, author and long-time friend of our family:

Garma C.C. Chang, the translator of these songs, single-handedly preserved this book for the West, for it surely would have disappeared, overlooked by religious popularizers. The degree, Cha Gyur Khan-po, 'professor of translation,' was conferred upon the late Professor Chen-Chi Chang by his guru, a living Buddha, Kong Ka Lama, at the Kong Ka Monestary at Meia Nya, Tibet. The monastery is of the Kargyutpa School, which descended directly from Milarepa's line of gurus. C.C. Chang was more than a translator, however. He was among the greatest Buddhist scholars and teachers of the twentieth century. His studies of both exoteric and esoteric Buddhism are powerful because they are unvarnished. Unfortunately, not all his works are still in print. As he brought Milarepa to the West, he also brought what is perhaps China's greatest contribution to Buddhism (and recall, it was China that gave us Zen), the teachings of the 8th century Hwa Yen school, which is contained in C.C. Chang's book, still in print: The Teaching of Totality. I was deeply fortunate to have known Professor Chang, and I remember his reverence for Milarepa, his delight at the songs. I remember him imploring his students to delve deep into these teachings, from one of Tibet's greatest masters. Now there is this new edition. By itself, the story of Milarepa is magnificent, a tale of naive cruelty, healing, heroic effort and finally mercy and enlightenment. Milarepa is the psalmist of the Himalayas, and the late Professor's translation is a triumph of the heart. The book is a monument and a refuge.

I regret that we have not provided more information and insights into my father's life and personality, but that will have to be another project!

Peter Gruber

My family owes an immense debt to my "Uncle Peter" for all his support over the years. His financial support, wise counsel, and deep personal commitment to Buddhism made many things possible for my father and my family.

The following is taken from the website of the Gruber Foundation:

Peter Gruber, Co-founder and Chairman Emeritus

Born in Budapest, Hungary, in 1929, Peter Gruber escaped to India with his parents in 1939, three months before the Second World War engulfed Europe. During the Japanese bombing of Calcutta, his parents sent him to a boarding school in the Himalayas, where he was educated by Irish Christian Brothers and Jesuits. These early experiences sparked what has become a lifelong questioning of the meaning and purpose of life, and a far-ranging search for knowledge and understanding.

After the war, Gruber nurtured his growing interest in science, religion and philosophy as a student in Australia. He also studied Buddhism for a number of years and eventually moved to New York City where he founded the Oriental Studies foundation, which sponsored the translation and publication in English of Tibetan texts. He served briefly in the U.S. Army Finance Corps and later went to work on Wall Street.

In the span of his career, Gruber has built a successful asset management business as a legendary pioneer in emerging markets, making possible the support of areas of special interest to him, from educational programs to the recognition of excellence in the most worthy human achievement.

As for his philosophy of philanthropy: Once, when being asked to fund a health program for the needy, a worthy undertaking, he realized that no amount of money would adequately address this ongoing need. Instead, he chooses to invest in individuals. He has leveraged his ability to effect change by focusing on outstanding individuals most able to contribute to improving our lives. Someone like Sir Alexander Fleming, who played a major role in developing penicillin, presents an ideal example of why supporting the advance of research can be more effective than contributing the same money to alleviate immediate needs. Funds put toward an unending problem would be used up without the problem being solved; conversely strategic funds given to medical research require less investment, but can contribute more to the public good for generations to come.

It is Peter Gruber's vision, along with that of his wife, Patricia, which established the Gruber Foundation and continued to guide it until the transition to Yale University. Mr. Gruber was an emeritus member of the Board of Directors until his death in 2014.

Dr. Chia Theng Shen (C. T. Shen)

Dr. Chia Theng Shen (C.T. Shen)

Dr. Shen was the other pivotal friend of the family, enabling my father to pursue his work at many critical junctures. The following is abridged from the website of the Buddhist Association of the United States, an organization founded by Dr. Shen:

Dr. Shen, Chia Theng (1913-2007), co-founder of the Buddhist Association of the United States (abbreviated hereafter as BAUS), was born on Dec. 15, 1913 in Chekiang, China. [He obtained] his B.S. in Electrical Engineering [in 1937][and then] served for the next ten years in Central Elec. Mfg. Works and then in the National Resources Commission in the Chinese government. In 1947, Shen had his own international trading company opened in Shanghai and then moved his business to Hong Kong in 1949. In 1952, he and his family came to the United States and, along with some business partners, established a shipping company and thereafter had held various shipping executive positions until his retirement in 1980. In 1973, Shen was conferred with an honorary Litt. D. by St. John's University in New York.

Ever since his youth, Shen had always felt spiritually drawn to the Buddhist teachings of personal cultivation toward enlightenment and compassion for all sentient beings. But it was not until he came to the United States that he started to study Buddhism seriously. Guided by some learned Buddhist friends in the States, Shen has attained a deep understanding of the profound and subtle principles of the religion. He has the vision that the ever-new wisdom embodied in the Buddhist teaching, along

285

with other world religions, will help bring about world peace and alleviate the suffering of mankind. He has therefore dedicated himself to the cause of promoting friendship and mutual communication among all religions, and to introducing the Buddha Dharma into the Western world, in particular America...

Over the years, Shen's efforts and financial support has led to the formation of the BAUS in 1964, and in 1971 the Institute for Advanced Studies of World Religions in New York. Since accurate translation and publication of the Buddhist scriptures into western languages are essential if Buddhism is to be appreciated beneficially by the Western world, Shen donated in 1968 a property in San Francisco to Rev. Hsuan Hua to establish the Buddhist Text Translation Society for just that purpose. In 1971, he furthermore helped found the Institute for the Translation of the Chinese Tripitaka (ITCT) in Taipei, Taiwan. The most important publication of the latter is a 496-page book entitled *A Treasury of Mahayana Sutras*, which was published in 1984 by Penn State University.

To allow North American Buddhists to have a place for regular Dharma Assembly and to attend lectures given by renowned Dharma masters and learned Buddhists from all over the world, Shen and his wife, Upasika Woo Ju Shen, donated in 1969 a property in Bronx, N.Y. to BAUS to establish the Temple of Enlightenment. In 1970, Shen started the Bodhi House in Long Island, N.Y., which has been used as headquarters of the 16th Karmapa of Tibetan Buddhism and conference places for various Buddhist gathering. Shen later supported the 16th Karmapa again financially to establish the Karma Triyana Dharma Monastery in Woodstock, N.Y.

Dr. Chia Theng Shen (C. T. Shen)

In 1980, a 125-acre parcel of land, located in Putnam County, N.Y., was donated by Shen to the BAUS to build the Chuang Yen Monastery which, with its Great Buddha Hall which houses a 37-foot statue of Buddha Vairocana – the largest Buddha statue in the Western hemisphere, Kuan-Yin Hall, Thousand Lotus Memorial Terrace, library, statues of Kuan-Yin and Amitabha, and beautiful landscape designed with the theme "Pure Land" in mind, has become an attraction for Buddhists as well as tourists.

Dr. Charles Muses

*T*he following is taken from the Wikipedia entry on Dr. Charles Muses. He led quite a colorful life, a real-life Indiana Jones:

Charles Arthur Muses (/ˈmʌsɪs/; 28 April 1919 – 26 August 2000), was an esoteric philosopher who wrote articles and books under various pseudonyms (including *Musès, Musaios, Kyril Demys, Arthur Fontaine, Kenneth Demarest* and *Carl von Balmadis*). He founded the Lion Path, a shamanistic movement. He held unusual and controversial views relating to mathematics, physics, philosophy, and many other fields.

Muses was born in Jersey City, New Jersey, and grew up in Long Island, New York. His father abandoned the family when Muses was a young boy forcing his mother to support Muses and a large, extended family on a school teacher's salary. Years later he would remark in lectures that if his mother had not had an overarching faith in "young Charlie" he might never have been able to escape the confines of his impoverished youth.

In 1947 Muses received his Master's Degree in philosophy from Columbia University, New York. In 1951 he received his PH.D in philosophy from Columbia University. Muses' doctoral thesis focused on the famous seer, Jacob Boehme, and one of his followers Dionysius Freher. It was entitled, *Illumination on Jacob Boehme, The Work of Dionysius Andreas Freher*, and was published by King's Crown Press in 1951...

In 1991, *In All Her Names: Explorations of the Feminine in Divinity*, was published by Harper San Francisco. The book was edited by Joseph Campbell and Charles Muses. Each contributed a chapter to the book along with Riane

Eiser and Marija Gimmutas. The title of Muses chapter is, The Ageless Way of Goddess: Divine Pregnancy and Higher Birth in Ancient Egypt and China...

Charles Muses edited, *Esoteric Teachings of the Tibetan Tantra*, which was translated into English by Chang Chen Chi. The book was first published in 1961, by The Falcon's Wing Press. Muses states on page ix, of the introduction, "In these considerations also lies the true meaning of the most secret tantric path, in Tibet called the Vajrayana or Thunderbolt Vehicle. It is secret only because most do not have enough of the intelligent love-will to find and pursue it. For those who place such a level of high desire first, however, the precious means (upaya) will mysteriously arise in their lifetimes, and they will be able to tread this path of Love-Will-Wisdom, of Heart, Hand and Head harmoniously joined. But heart or love must rule the other two or wisdom will become unwise and the love-will will deteriorate again into self-will."

Muses had no success in attaining a tenured position as a faculty member at an institution of higher education. Forced to give lectures to earn a living, he wrote books and began traveling the world. He continued these pursuits for the remainder of his life.

In 1985, Kluewr-Nijhoff first published Muses book entitled, *Destiny and Control in Human Systems*. In it he proposes a method called 'chronotopology,' which he claims can measure the qualitative multidimensional structure of time...

Muses also envisioned a mathematical number concept, Musean hypernumbers, that includes hypercomplex number algebras ... Some of these are based on properties of magic squares, and even related to religious belief. He believed that these hypernumbers were central to issues of consciousness.

Muses was arrested in March, 1957 in Egypt when he tried to remove a number of very valuable artifacts from Egypt on the argument that he did not realize that a license was required. He was finally convicted in August, 1957, but later allowed to return to the United States.

From findagrave.com:

...In 1952 his fiance, Charlotte (Barth) Howell, purchased 640 acres in Indian Hills, Colorado, where she built Falcon Wing Ranch, an Egyptian Mystery learning school. It was completed in 1954, to Charlie's carefully planned specifications. This is where he taught Astrology, Numerology and Egyptology. Charlotte (Barth) Howell, founded the publishing house, The Falcon's Wing Press. She was the publisher, and Charles was the senior editor ... His true passion being Archeological discoveries and Egyptology, which took them on expeditions around the world. In 1957 he discovered the Pyramid of Ameny Qemau, in southern Dahshur, Cairo, Egypt. On 20 June 1957, he was arrested in Cairo, Egypt, charged with attempting to smuggle Egyptian antiquities abroad. A marriage record for Charles Arthur Muses and Charlotte (Barth) Howell, was recorded 4 June 1954, in Fairfax County, Virginia. He was 35 years old, and she was 59 years of age, 24 years his senior. They later divorced. He traveled and moved from place to place. It has been stated, that he was located in Canada the last year of his life. At the time of his death, there is evidence that he was remarried, although her name is unknown. He died 26 August 2000. The place of his death and burial are unknown.

Dr. Max Jacobson

When I first started working on this story with my mom, I was not able to find much information about Dr. Jacobson. Recently, as we resumed work on our project, I returned to the internet, and much to my surprise, I found a wealth of information about Dr. Max Jacobson.

The doctor had a high-profile practice on Fifth Avenue in New York, treating many famous people from all walks of life. He was dubbed "Miracle Max" and "Dr. Feelgood," and was for a time an indispensable part of President Kennedy's entourage. Here is the Amazon review of a recent book published about the doctor:

> An exposé of the mysterious doctor who changed the course of history
>
> Doctor Max Jacobson, whom the Secret Service under President John F. Kennedy code named "Dr. Feelgood," developed a unique "energy formula" that altered the paths of some of the twentieth century's most iconic figures, including the President and Jackie Kennedy, Marilyn Monroe, Frank Sinatra, and Elvis. JFK received his first injection (a special mix of "vitamins and hormones," according to Jacobson) just before his first debate with Vice President Richard Nixon. The shot into JFK's throat not only cured his laryngitis, but diminished the pain in his back, allowed him to stand up straighter, and invigorated the tired candidate. Kennedy demolished Nixon in that first debate and turned a tide of skepticism about Kennedy into an audience that appreciated his energy and crispness. What JFK didn't know then was that the injections were actually powerful doses of a combination of highly addictive liquid methamphetamine and steroids.

Author and researcher Rick Lertzman and *New York Times* bestselling author Bill Birnes reveal heretofore unpublished material about the mysterious Dr. Feelgood. Through well-researched prose and interviews with celebrities including George Clooney, Jerry Lewis, Yogi Berra, and Sid Caesar, the authors reveal Jacobson's vast influence on events such as the assassination of JFK, the Cuban Missile Crisis, the Kennedy-Krushchev Vienna Summit, the murder of Marilyn Monroe, the filming of the C. B. Demille classic *The Ten Commandments*, and the work of many of the great artists of that era. Jacobson destroyed the lives of several famous patients in the entertainment industry and accidentally killed his own wife, Nina, with an overdose of his formula.

The book is entitled, "Dr. Feelgood: The Shocking Story of the Doctor Who May Have Changed History by Treating and Drugging JFK, Marilyn, Elvis, and Other Prominent Figures" by Richard A. Lertzman, William J. Birnes

Interviews with the authors hint at assassinations and dark deeds carried out to silence people who had come into sensitive information from JFK during his drug-induced forays resulting from his injections from Dr. Jacobson.

I was shocked at the extent of Dr. Jacobson's influence over political figures and celebrities, and I found it difficult to reconcile the image of a renegade doctor who caused rampant methamphetamine addiction in his clientele with the caring and thoughtful doctor who returned the gift of sight to my parents. However, the one incident where my father had heart palpitations and had to be sedated after an injection might indicate that perhaps he may have received an accidental amphetamine overdose.

Prince Peter

*P*rince Peter of Greece was part of the expatriate circle of friends of my parents in India. He lived a fascinating life, complete with political intrigues regarding his lineage and succession rights as royalty of Greece and Denmark. Excerpted from a long and fascinating article in Wikipedia:

Prince Peter of Greece and Denmark (Greek: Πρίγκιψ Πέτρος της Ελλάδος; 3 December 1908 – 15 October 1980) was a Greek prince, soldier and anthropologist specialising in Tibetan culture and polyandry. Born in Paris and high in the line of succession to the Greek throne, Prince Peter was deemed to have forfeited his succession rights by marrying a twice-divorced Russian commoner, Irina Aleksandrovna Ovtchinnikova. Following his first scientific voyage to Asia, Peter served as an officer of the Greek army during the Second World War. The Prince returned to Asia several more times for his research of Tibetan culture. He strongly protested against the royal family's treatment of his wife. After King Paul's death, he declared himself heir presumptive to the Greek throne, on the pretext that female dynasts had been unlawfully granted succession rights in 1952. Peter eventually separated from his wife and died childless in London.

Chang Dai-Chien

*C*hang Dai-chien *(also Chang Da Chien, Zhang Daqian), world famous artist, as recounted from Asianart.com:*

Chang Dai-chien was born on May 10, 1899 in Nei-chiang, Szechwan as Chuan Chi, the ninth child of a wealthy family who had converted to Roman Catholicism. Resisting his family's efforts to push him into a business career, Chang briefly entered a Buddhist monastery before beginning serious study of Chinese calligraphy and painting at the age of 19. After an extended visit to Kyoto, Japan, Chang settled in Shanghai in 1919 to study with prominent artists Tseng Hsi (c.1861-1930) and Li Jui-ching (1867- 1920). In a training method typical among art students in China, Chang made many arduous copies of artistic masterworks, beginning to develop his legendary (and notorious) ability to recreate works from diverse periods.

Because of his family wealth, Chang first entered the Chinese artistic community as an amateur painter and connoisseur. The collapse of several family businesses in 1925 deprived Chang of his income and compelled him to begin selling his art work. His first exhibition of 100 paintings in 1926 was a great success and launched his career. The start of the Sino-Japanese War in 1937 began a period of war and revolution that repeatedly disrupted Chang's artistic efforts, forcing him into flight several times. In 1939 he found refuge in the remote desert outpost of Tun-huang, where he spent more than two years copying the legendary murals in the Caves of the Thousand Buddhas.

Leaving China in the wake of the Civil War of 1949, Chang sojourned in Hong Kong, Taiwan, India and

Argentina before settling in 1954 into a 30-acre compound outside Sao Paolo, Brazil that he named the "Garden of Eight Virtues." Chang continued to exhibit his art in the US and Europe, traveling to Paris in 1956 for a breakthrough show of his paintings at the Musee d'Art Moderne. Chang's meeting with Pablo Picasso during this trip was given considerable attention in the press as a meeting of the masters of Western and Eastern art. A dam construction project in the mid-1960s that would flood his home caused Chang to leave Brazil. California had impressed Chang during his numerous trips to the state, the first of which was in 1954. Chang moved to the Monterey Peninsula in 1967, eventually a home in Carmel and another on the scenic 17-mile drive. Chang relocated to Taiwan in 1976, spending the last seven years of his life painting and creating his garden home known as the "Abode of Illusions." He never returned to California after 1979.

In addition to his prized original works, Chang has become equally infamous for his recreations of Chinese masterpieces. His copies span 1,000 years of Chinese art and demonstrate a virtuoso talent for emulating, and even improving upon, the work of painters before him. Today many of these forgeries, still attributed to others, hang alongside Chang originals in museums worldwide. An article in the Washington Post Sunday Magazine on January 19, 1999 examined the controversy surrounding the reputed 10-th century Chinese painting The Riverbank owned by the Metropolitan Museum of New York, believed by some to be Chang forgery.

Chang's artistic legacy is immense, controversial and complicated. Beyond the difficulty posed by a 'life spent in nearly perpetual exile and travel, Chang was a highly social personality who enjoyed his fame and actively contributed to the creation of an heroic persona. As a young artist he adopted the posture of bearded sage, reveling in unconventionality and romanticism, the beginning of a life-long process to create a unique aura that often overshadowed his artistic efforts. The exhibition Chang Dai-chien in California will present an often overlooked element of Chang's legacy, demonstrating his status as a truly global artist.

There is a story in Wikipedia that is interesting, although it differs from the previous account:

Chang was born in 1899 in Sichuan Province to a financially struggling but artistic family. His first commission came at age 12, when a traveling fortune-teller requested he paint her a new set of divining cards. At age 17 he was captured by bandits while returning home from boarding school in Chongqing. When the bandit chief ordered him to write a letter home demanding a ransom, he was so impressed by the boy's brushmanship that he made the boy his personal secretary. During the more than three months that he was held captive, he read books of poetry which the bandits had looted from raided homes.

My mother says that it was my grandfather who encouraged the government to set up an art institute to preserve the great treasure of the Dun Huang Cave paintings. Chang Dai-Chien was able to work there with the institute to study and paint in the cave painting style.

Natacha Rambova

We have her to thank for recommending that my father pursue obtaining a grant from the Bollingen Foundation. The Wikipedia article about this woman describes her as:

> … an American film costume and set designer, best known for her marriage to Rudolph Valentino. Although they shared many interests such as art, poetry and spiritualism, his colleagues felt that she exercised too much control over his work and blamed her for several expensive flops. In later life, she continued her spiritualist activities, as well as studying Egyptology."

She was born Winifred Shaughnessy in Salt Lake City and was a talented ballerina. She took a Russian stage name when performing with the Imperial Russian Ballet Company. She later became a costume designer, meeting and marrying Rudolph Valentino in the course of her work.

Both Rambova and Valentino were Spiritualists, and they visited psychics and took part in séances and automatic writing. Valentino wrote a book of poetry *Daydreams* with many poems about Rambova. She too wrote a book about the time she spent with him, claiming to be in contact with him in the afterlife via psychics. She married Rudolph Valentino in 1923 and divorced him in 1926. She worked at many jobs in Hollywood and then in the New York art world and finally married a Spanish nobleman.

Eventually she became an authority on Egyptian antiquities and was one of the editors of the *"Egyptian Religious Texts and Representations," No. XL* in the Bollingen Series.

Natacha Rambova

There is an entry in the IMDb website that has more details on her life. She was shot in the leg when she left her first husband, a controlling Russian dance impresario; was rumored to have had an affair with Alla Nazimova, an exotic actress who engaged Rambova as a costume and set designer; and much more.

Mai-Mai Sze And Irene Sharoff

*T*hese are the ladies featured in the story about the Oscars on the toilet tank. Again, we have Wikipedia to thank for the following information. Excerpts follow:

Yuen Tsung Sze (December 2, 1909 – July 16, 1992) — known as **Mai-mai Sze** — was a Chinese-American painter and writer. The Bollingen Foundation first published her translation of the *Jieziyuan Huazhuan* or *The Mustard Seed Garden Manual of Painting* with her commentary in 1956.

Mai-mai Sze was born Yuen Tsung Sze in Tianjin on December 2, 1909. Mai-mai is a nickname meaning "little sister," and this was the name under which she published all of her books. In 1915 she moved to London with her father Alfred Sao-ke Sze, then the Chinese Ambassador to the Court of St. James. The family lived there until 1921, when Alfred Sao-ke Sze was appointed Chinese Ambassador to the United States and settled in Washington D.C. Mai-mai Sze moved there with him and attended the National Cathedral School until 1927, when she enrolled at Wellesley College...

Following her graduation from Wellesley, Mai-mai Sze's primary activity appears to have been painting. She exhibited a landscape in the 1933 Salon d'Automne, and also with Marie Sterner Galleries...

Sze was notably photographed by several important artists, including Carl Van Vechten, George Platt Lynes, and Dorothy Norman. Some of these photographs were published in fashion magazines including *Vogue*...

Sze also engaged in political affairs as an active advocate for war relief in China, and as writer and speaker on foreign relations with the Far East...

There is little documentation of Sze's relationship with the costume designer Irene Sharaff. The two women were living together at the time of Sze's death in 1992, and they coordinated the donation of their personal collections of books to the New York Society Library together, in 1989. In his history of the Bollingen Foundation, William McGuire wrote that Sze and Sharaff were both students of Natacha Rambova, who held private classes in comparative religion, symbolism, and Theosophy in her New York apartment in the 1930s.

Mai-mai Sze died in New York Hospital on July 16, 1992, at age 82.

Irene Sharaff (January 23, 1910 – August 10, 1993) was an American costume designer for stage and screen. Her work earned her five Academy Awards and a Tony Award.

After working as a fashion illustrator in her youth, Sharaff turned to set and costume design. Her debut production was the 1931 Broadway production of *Alice in Wonderland*, starring Eva Le Gallienne. Her use of silks from Thailand for *The King and I* (1951) created a trend in fashion and interior decoration.[1]

Sharaff's work was featured in the movies *West Side Story* (Academy Award, 1961), *Cleopatra* (Academy Award, 1963), *Meet Me in St. Louis, Hello, Dolly!, Mommie Dearest, The Other Side of Midnight, Who's Afraid of Virginia Woolf?* (Academy Award, 1966), *Guys and Dolls, The Best Years of Our Lives, The King and I* (Academy Award, 1956), *An American in Paris* (Academy Award, 1951), *Funny Girl* and *Porgy and Bess*.

She also designed sets and costumes for American Ballet Theatre, the New York City Ballet, and the Ballet Russe de Monte Carlo, and contributed illustrations to fashion magazine's such as Vogue and Harper's Bazaar. Among her Broadway design credits are *Idiot's Delight*, *Lady in the Dark*, *As Thousands Cheer*, *A Tree Grows in Brooklyn*, *Flower Drum Song*, and *Jerome Robbins' Broadway*.

The TDF/Irene Sharaff Lifetime Achievement Award was named for Sharaff. She was its first recipient in 1993. The award is now bestowed annually to a costume designer who, over the course of his or her career, has achieved great distinction and mastery of the art in theatre, film, opera or dance.

Irene Sharaff died in New York City of congestive heart failure, complicated by emphysema, at the age of 83. Sharaff bequeathed her collection of books, along with that of her partner, Mai-Mai Sze, to the New York Society Library.

Dorothy C. Donath

Dorothy C. Donath

*O*ver *the years, my father had a number of unpaid volunteers who helped to edit his manuscripts. They included Miss Gwendolyn Winser, Mr. Gerald Yorke (see page 303), Mr. George Currier, and Mrs. Dorothy C. Donath.*

Mrs. Donath came to our house in Staten Island every weekend to edit my father's work. I remember her mostly because she was a smoker...My mom tells us that until Mrs. Donath started coming to our house, we did not speak English at home. After she became a regular visitor, we spoke English more and more, accelerating the decline in my and my brother's Chinese language skills.

She was a diligent and dedicated editor who gave generously of her time and energy for over four years in order to help my father with the publication of The Practice of Zen.

She later wrote a book entitled, Buddhism for the West, published by McGraw-Hill in 1974.

Gerald Yorke

Another fascinating individual who was involved in mystical practices of the time, he also provided editorial input for my father's books. My father sent manuscripts to England and received edited drafts back from Mr. Yorke for many years. I remember collecting many British stamps from the envelopes of these drafts.

According to on-line sources, he was a student/associate of Aleister Crowley, an English occultist, ceremonial magician, poet, painter, novelist, and mountaineer. Crowley gained widespread notoriety during his lifetime, being a recreational drug experimenter, bisexual and an individualist social critic. He was denounced in the popular press as "the wickedest man in the world" and a Satanist.

It was also stated that Yorke was also the personal representative to the West of the Thirteenth Dalai Lama (died 1933) and the author of an original foreword to a secret book on the Kalachakra initiation. Yorke was also a member of the A∴A∴, the magical order established by Aleister Crowley (died 1947), and towards the end of Crowley's life was known as his chief disciple.

From a book review of <u>Aleister Crowley, The Golden Dawn and Buddhism</u>, a collection of essays by Gerald Yorke:

> …For four years, from 1928 onwards, Gerald Yorke was one of Aleister Crowley's closest associates, studying with him, acting as his agent, working on his publications, and participating in his magical ceremonies. During that time he also investigated the path of the mystic through a series of "magical retirements" in the course of which he invoked his "Holy Guardian Angel" whilst tramping alone across the deserts of North Africa, and practiced yoga and meditation in the solitude of a cave on the Welsh coast.

When he and Crowley fell out in 1932, Yorke set out for China, where he travelled, studied Buddhism, and worked as a Reuter's correspondent for some three years. On his return to England he resumed contact with Crowley, but as a friend rather than a follower, and after Crowley's death in 1947 Yorke was one of the handful of people who laboured to preserve the legacy of "The Beast." In the process he assembled one of the most significant collections of Crowleyana and occult-related books and documents in the world and remained fascinated by the subject, even though on a personal level he had rejected the occult in favour of Buddhism. Immensely knowledgeable, he gave freely of his time and thought, and was instrumental in the publication of many of the most important works of his times on the occult, yoga and Buddhism.

Above all, Yorke's essays offer a rare blend of straightforward scholarship and genuine first-hand experience. He had known Crowley as few others, and had learned directly from him the principals and practice of magic. Gerald Yorke sifted through a vast archive of then-unpublished Golden Dawn material, and was acquainted with a number of former associates of the Order; he had also studied and practiced yoga, meditation, and aspects of the tantras at a level unimaginable to most Western practitioners of his time. And he wrote on all of these topics with his characteristic wit and good humour.

Diluwa Khutugtu Jamsrangjab

Diluwa Khutugtu Jamsrangjab

In Chinese, the name or title of this personage is "Hutuketu," but other Romanizations of his name use other variants, such as Khutugtu. In any case, this is the man who visited us in 1957.

From Wikipedia, the free encyclopedia:

Diluwa Khutugtu Jamsrangjab (Mongolian: Дилав Хутагт Жамсанжав, 1883 – 7 April 1965) was Mongolian Khutugtu, a Tibetan Buddhist tulku, politician and Mongolian-American scholar. Jamsrangjab was a Durved-Mongolian. His autobiography was published in English.

When Jamsrangjab was born to commoners, Bashlu and Gimbeles, in Zagdsambar of Zasagt Khan (in modern Zavkhan Province), there spread mysterious but amazing tales about his birth. At his age of 5, Bogd Khan declared Jamsrangjab to be the after-life of the late Diluwa. Jamsrangjab with his parents moved to the capital city Niislel Khuree. He studied the philosophy of Buddhism so hard that he was awarded religious dignities at the age of 7 and 21.

In 1916 the Diluwa Khutugtu was sent to the south-eastern frontier of Bogd Khaanate Mongolia with the Mongolian general, Khatanbaatar Magsarjav to ease the conflict between the Mongols and the Republic of China.

Diluwa Khutugtu Jamsrangjab was arrested in 1930 due to the accusation that he was linked with the so-called anti-communist leader, Eregdendagva. He was freed later after he didn't accept the trial. On 26 February 1931, the Diluwa Khutugtu was fled to China. After he had gone, false rumours about him spread among people. At the time, he didn't know he would never come back to his homeland again.

After he came to the United States in 1949 with the assistance of Owen Lattimore and fellow professors, Jamsranjab worked at the Johns Hopkins University. There he joined American-British professor Owen Lattimore's the Mongolia Project. In New Jersey, he founded a Monastery with Kalmyk American lamas in 1950-1952. He was elected the chief lama of the Monastery there. When he was in the USA, he still worked for the international recognization of Mongolian independence.

He influenced Chan Kai-Shek to declare "Mongolia can be a member of the United Nations like other independent nations" in 1960. On 7 April 1965, the last Mongolian Khutugtu, Jamsrangjab, died at the age of 82 in New York City. In 1990, the supreme court of Mongolia proved his innocence and abolished all decrees that accused him of false political crimes.

Gongga Monastery

I have quoted from Wikipedia once more to provide some information about the monastery where my father spent time in his youth:

> Gongga monastery is located at the west side of Minya Konka. It is perched on a small bench on an otherwise steep hillside with altitude of 3030 m overlooking the terminus of a large glacier that descends off the west side of Mt Minya Gongga 7556 m, the highest peak in the east Tibet. Gongga monastery is the sealed shrine of the Kagyu sect's succession living Buddha, who is known as Tulku Rinpoche. The reincarnation was formally started here by the Kagyu sect. From this origin, systems of reincarnation — including the Dalai Lama and the Panchen Lama–were adopted by all major sects of Tibetan religion.

I only know of my father's lama as Gongga Lama. The numerous names given for this personage are confusing. Kong Ka Lama, Bho Gangkar Rinpoche, Bogangkar, and so on are honorifics Romanized from Chinese and Tibetan, so they can be difficult to sort out.

The Bollingen Foundation

The grant from this foundation supported our family in the early years after our arrival in America. The following is taken from Wikipedia:

The Bollingen Foundation was an educational foundation set up along the lines of a university press in 1945. It was named for Bollingen Tower, Carl Jung's country home in Bollingen, Switzerland. Funding was provided by Paul Mellon and his wife Mary Conover Mellon. The Foundation became inactive in 1968.

Initially the foundation was dedicated to the dissemination of Jung's work, which was a particular interest of Mary Conover Mellon. The Bollingen Series of books that it sponsored now includes more than 250 related volumes. The Bollingen Foundation also awarded more than 300 fellowships. These fellowships were an important, continuing source of funding for poets like Alexis Leger and Marianne Moore, scientists like Károly Kerényi and artists like Isamu Noguchi, among many others. The Foundation also sponsored the A. W. Mellon lectures at the National Gallery of Art.

In 1948, the foundation donated $10,000 to the Library of Congress to be used toward a $1,000 Bollingen Prize for the best poetry each year. The Library of Congress fellows, who in that year included T. S. Eliot, W. H. Auden and Conrad Aiken, gave the 1949 prize to Ezra Pound for his 1948 *Pisan Cantos*. Their choice was highly controversial, in particular because of Pound's fascist and anti-Semitic politics. Following the publication of two highly negative articles by Robert Hillyer in the *Saturday Review of Literature*, the United States Congress passed a resolution

308

that effectively discontinued the involvement of the Library of Congress with the prize. The remaining funds were returned to the Foundation. In 1950, the Bollingen Prize was continued under the auspices of the Yale University Library, which awarded the 1950 prize to Wallace Stevens.

In 1968, the Foundation became inactive. It was largely subsumed into the Andrew W. Mellon Foundation, which continued funding of the Bollingen Prize. The Bollingen Series was given to Princeton University Press to carry on and complete. Over its lifetime, the Bollingen Foundation had expended about $20 million.

When Paul Mellon decided in 1963 to dissolve the Bollingen Foundation, he said that the founding generation was reaching the age of retirement, and it would be hard for others to maintain the original mission and standards. What he might have said was that the Bollingen Foundation was the work of a single generation. For two decades its concerns had been at the center of Western intellectual life, but the 1960's saw a shift in the cultural preoccupations and critical concerns of intellect in the United States and Europe.

From the website of the Princeton University Press:

"Never before in the history of publishing has there been an author list as distinguished as that of Bollingen, nor has a publishing program had a more telling impact on the thought of its time. . . . It is safe to say that any of the titles . . . is a book of lasting value by a top scholar in his or her field, and any library . . . should acquire as many of the Bollingen books as possible."--Jean Martin, *Wilson Library Bulletin.*

The Bollingen Foundation

The New School

My father lectured at this institution for many years, and met many interesting people through this venue. Here's the summary from Wikipedia:

> The New School is a private research university in Lower Manhattan, New York City, located mostly in Greenwich Village. From its founding in 1919 by progressive New York educators, and for most of its history, the university was known as The New School for Social Research. Between 1997 and 2005 it was known as New School University. The university and each of its colleges were renamed in 2005.

> The New School established the University in Exile and the École libre des hautes études in 1933 as a graduate division to serve as an academic haven for scholars escaping from Nazi Germany among other adversarial regimes in Europe. In 1934, the University in Exile was chartered by New York State and its name was changed to the Graduate Faculty of Political and Social Science. In 2005, it adopted what had initially been the name of the whole institution, the New School for Social Research, while the larger institution was renamed The New School.

> The New School has launched or housed a range of institutions such as the international research institute World Policy Institute, the Vera List Center for Art and Politics, the India China Institute, the Observatory on Latin America, and the Center for New York City Affairs.

The MacDowell Colony

I knew my father spent time at this institution, but I had no idea what a prestigious institution it has been. The list of artists and creative people who have spent time there is most impressive. From the website of the MacDowell Colony:

The MacDowell Colony is an artists' colony in Peterborough, New Hampshire, United States, founded in 1907 by Marian MacDowell, pianist and wife of composer Edward MacDowell. She established the institution and its endowment chiefly with donated funds. She led the colony for almost 25 years, against a background of two world wars, the Great Depression, and other challenges.

The mission of The MacDowell Colony is to nurture the arts by offering creative individuals of the highest talent an inspiring environment in which they can produce enduring works of the imagination.

Over the years, an estimated 7,700 artists have been supported in residence, including the winners of at least 79 Pulitzer Prizes, 781 Guggenheim Fellowships, 100 Rome Prizes, 30 National Book Awards, 26 Tony Awards, 24 MacArthur Fellowships, 9 Grammys, 8 Oscars, and 8 National Medals for the Arts. The colony has accepted visual and interdisciplinary artists, architects, filmmakers, composers, playwrights, poets, and writers, both well-known and unknown.

In 1896, Edward MacDowell, a composer, and Marian MacDowell, a pianist, bought a farm in Peterborough, New Hampshire, where they spent summers working in peaceful surroundings. It was in Peterborough that Edward, arguably America's first great composer, said he produced more and better music. Not long after — falling

311

prematurely and gravely ill — Edward conveyed to his wife that he wished to give other artists the same creative experience under which he had thrived.

Before his death in 1908, Marian set about fulfilling his wish of making a community on their New Hampshire property where artists could work in an ideal place in the stimulating company of peers. Their vision became nationally known as the "Peterborough Idea," and in 1906, prominent citizens of the time — among them Grover Cleveland, Andrew Carnegie, and J. Pierpont Morgan — created a fund in Edward's honor to make the idea a reality. Although Edward lived to see the first Fellows arrive, it was under Marian's leadership that support for the Colony increased, most of the 32 studios were built, and the artistic program grew and flourished. Until her death in 1956, she traveled across the country to further public awareness about the Colony's mission, giving lecture-recitals to raise funds for its preservation.

At its founding, the Colony was an experiment with no precedent. It stands now having provided crucial time and space to more than 7,900 artists, including such notable names as Leonard Bernstein, Thornton Wilder, Aaron Copland, Milton Avery, James Baldwin, Spalding Gray, and more recently Alice Walker, Alice Sebold, Jonathan Franzen, Michael Chabon, Suzan-Lori Parks, Meredith Monk, and many more.

In 1997, The MacDowell Colony was honored with the National Medal of Arts — the highest award given by the United States to artists or arts patrons — for "nurturing and inspiring many of this century's finest artists" and offering them "the opportunity to work within a dynamic community of their peers, where creative excellence is the standard."

Chinese-American Assimilation

The following is taken from a segment about Chinese Americans on the Hoover Library website, and highlights how difficult it was for Chinese people to gain residency and citizenship status:

The first Chinese to reach America were lured by opportunities for wealth, but legislation soon restricted them to the menial labor market. The Chinese endured extremely hard work, hatred from "European Americans," and prejudicial laws passed exclusively to limit their rights. Yet the United States remained a beacon of hope to the poor.

Chinese sailors and merchants arrived in New York City in the early 1800s, but the first Chinese to stay were lured to "Gum San" (Gold Mountain) after gold was discovered in California. In the 1850s, new California laws banned all Chinese from the gold fields, yet they stayed on to develop coastal fisheries and reclaim swamp land for farming.

During the Civil War in the 1860s, records list many Chinese immigrants who joined the Northern armies. During the war and after, the Chinese were welcomed as inexpensive laborers to finish the transcontinental railroad. Those of European descent grumbled about "cheap labor" but there was plenty of menial work that only the Chinese agreed to do.

Then a nationwide depression in the 1870s made jobs hard to find for all. Special taxes and restrictive laws began to target only the Chinese. In 1882 Congress passed the Chinese Exclusion Acts, legally suspending further immigration and denying them the basic rights of citizenship that were granted to other races.

313

Individual cruelties and mob massacres in "Chinatowns" across the United States illustrated the hatred that had infiltrated "European America." It was not until 1898 that a U.S. Supreme Court decision established the legal right of citizenship by birth for all Americans, regardless of ethnic background. So as the century drew to a close, the children of Chinese immigrants born in the U.S.A. were legally American citizens.

The U.S. government continued to clamp down on the rights of the Chinese living in America. Angel Island in San Francisco Bay became the main "processing center" for incoming Asians, but it was a Chinese immigrant's worst nightmare. To ferret out illegal entries, Chinese citizens were detained for long periods of time under degrading conditions.

Chinese immigration was declared permanently illegal in 1902, although loopholes were found and family members of Chinese already living in the U.S. were allowed entry. And even though the federal government still denied citizenship to Chinese immigrants, opportunities for employment were abundant and more money could be made here than in China.

Early in the 20th century, the Chinese population in America was made up mostly of men living in "bachelor communities." Illegal smuggling of Chinese women and girls was a booming business. Many had been promised the riches and freedoms of this western world, then swindled on their arrival and forced into houses of prostitution.

A new immigration station opened on Angel Island. In 1910, this scenic island in view of the glimmering San Francisco coastline, became both the point of entry and a nightmare for Chinese immigrants.

314

Hundreds if not thousands of "paper sons" arrived - non-relatives who had begged, borrowed or purchased their way into a family of Chinese Americans, carrying false papers for proof. Highly suspicious officials had to separate the legal from the illegal entries, and Chinese citizens were detained in prison-like barracks for weeks. Sometimes the weeks turned into months, even years, before final decisions were made. Many "sons" were deported back to China.

The Chinese Exclusion Acts were repealed during World War II, granting citizenship to hundreds of thousands of Chinese in America. This repeal also introduced thousands of young men to the military draft. Japanese Americans became the enemy, replacing Chinese Americans as the hated peoples of Asian origin.

President Roosevelt repealed the Chinese Exclusion Acts that had placed severe restrictions on Chinese immigration and rights to citizenship in the late 19th and early 20th centuries. Further immigration law changes allowed families to be reunited by allowing wife and family to join the father in the United States. However, a quota system was set in place to allow only 105 new Chinese immigrants per year. Soon after the 1943 repeal, 14,000 Chinese Americans were drafted into the armed forces during World War II.

The Angel Island immigration station had been closed in 1940 after fire destroyed several buildings, so now it was reverted into a processing center for Japanese prisoners of war. Hatred of Japanese Americans replaced the prejudice against Chinese Americans during WWII, although many Americans did not bother to distinguish between any of the peoples of Asian origin.

The Chinese had faced hostility in America for several generations. For the most part, these immigrants were prisoners of low-paying jobs in Chinatowns across the country. But beginning in the 1950s, educated Chinese nationals were able to break out of the ghettos and make major contributions to the American economy.

During the 1950s, thousands of Chinese citizens from Taiwan came to the United States to study at American universities. Studying in America was one thing, staying here was another. Chinese nationals could stay in America only if they were employed after graduation - if they failed to find work, they had to remain in school. Many Chinese nationals found the resources to become professional students in the States.

Finally in 1965, Chinese immigration was changed to be on an equal basis with all other countries of the world. The American government established an annual quota that enabled 20,000 Chinese to receive U.S. citizenship. Thousands who had been in the U.S. for ten or more years applied for permanent residency. The Chinese who were granted permanent residency applied for nationality.

At first the increase in these Chinese immigrants added to the old unsolved problems of overcrowding, poor health care, and lack of job opportunities in the Chinese communities. But by the 1970s, a new generation of Chinese Americans was able to find employment. Their skills and education, acquired from years of study in the U.S., freed them from the low-paying labor jobs that had imprisoned earlier generations of Chinese immigrants.

The number of Asians in the U.S. increased substantially in the 1970s, in particular the thousands of Vietnamese who escaped the new Communist government. But Chinese immigrants arrived as well, due to the expanded relationship between the U.S. and Red China, plus America's continued protection of Taiwan. By the end of the decade there were over 400,000 Chinese immigrants (both mainland Chinese and Chinese from Taiwan) living in the United States.

Chinese immigrants continue to arrive in America where they often face further struggles to escape poverty. Yet they are willing to work hard so they can fulfill their dreams of a better life. For Chinese Americans born here in the States, America is home where they have filtered into nearly every region of the country, as well as into job markets, schools, the arts, and government. But prejudice is still experienced - from the bias some hold against all minorities to an ethnic superiority from those born in China.

According to a 1990 census, 529,837 Chinese-born people were living in America. Searching for work and a fresh start, a new wave of Chinese immigrants is pouring into the West Coast and especially New York. About 12,000 arrive in Manhattan's Chinatown legally each year. Just as many come in illegally...

In 1997, Angel Island in San Francisco Bay was designated a National Historic Landmark. Several of the buildings on the island are being restored and - similar to Ellis Island in New York Harbor - may become the site of a West Coast immigration museum. "The incarceration experience was right in the Bay ... questioning their citizenship, loyalty, allegiance. It's all about exclusionary laws."

Yu Family Tree

Yu Family Tree (Pinyin)

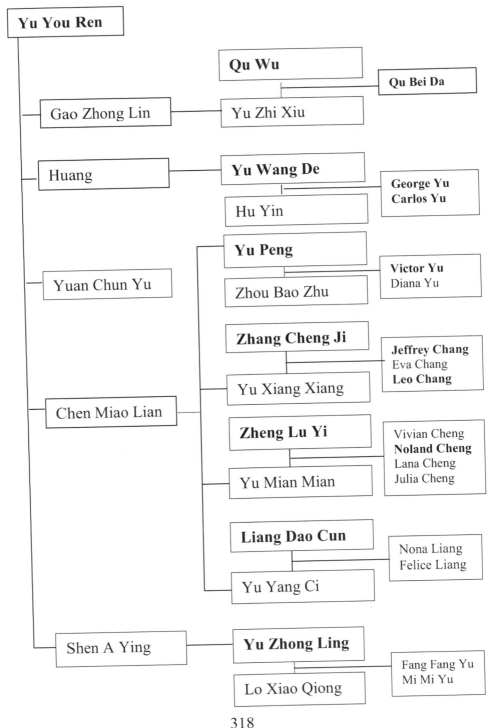

318

Nanjing after the war. Qu Mei Jun (wife of Bei Da), Mian Mian, Grandfather, Qu Bei Da, Zhou Bao Zhu, Yu Peng, and cousin. Victor and Diana in front.

Yu Peng, Yu Yang Tze, Yu Mian Mian, mom, Zhou Bao Zhu (Peng's wife), around 1983. Rare picture of siblings together, as for the most part they lived scattered around the world.

Chang Family Tree

Zhang Family Tree (Pinyin)

Zhang Du Lun	Shen Shou Zhen
Zhang Kai Ji (Louie)	Lin Chong Zheng (Jean)
Zhang Rui Ji (Helena)	**Xu Bao Ding (Paul)**
Zhang Cheng Ji (Garma)	Yu Hsiang Hsiang (Helena)
Zhang Hong Ji	Deng De Fang
Zhang Rong Ji (Lynette)	**Qian Shu Shi**
Zhang Qiong Ji (Yvonne)	**Zhao Zi Fan (George)**
Zhang Zai Ji (Edward)	Chen Yu Chen
Zhang Heng Ji	**Zhou Zhong Ying**
Zhang Xiang Ji	**Deng Yao Ji**

Back: Louie, Edward, Helena, Lynette, Hong Ji, Garma
Front: Jean, Grandma, Heng Ji, Grandpa, Yvonne

Made in the USA
Columbia, SC
27 May 2018